Ius Gentium: Comparative Perspectives on Law and Justice

Volume 121

Ius Gentium is a book series which discusses the central questions of law and justice from a comparative perspective. The books in this series collect the contrasting and overlapping perspectives of lawyers, judges, philosophers and scholars of law from the world's many different jurisdictions for the purposes of comparison, harmonisation, and the progressive development of law and legal institutions. Each volume makes a new comparative study of an important area of law. This book series continues the work of the well-known journal of the same name and provides the basis for a better understanding of all areas of legal science.

The *Ius Gentium* series provides a valuable resource for lawyers, judges, legislators, scholars, and both graduate students and researchers in globalisation, comparative law, legal theory and legal practice. The series has a special focus on the development of international legal standards and transnational legal cooperation.

Sonja C. Grover

Litigating the Politics of Human Rights

Contemporary U.S. Culture Wars on Trial

Springer

Sonja C. Grover
Faculty of Education
Lakehead University
Thunder Bay, ON, Canada

ISSN 1534-6781 ISSN 2214-9902 (electronic)
Ius Gentium: Comparative Perspectives on Law and Justice
ISBN 978-3-031-82462-3 ISBN 978-3-031-82463-0 (eBook)
https://doi.org/10.1007/978-3-031-82463-0

This Springer imprint is published by the registered company Springer Nature Switzerland AG
The registered company address is: Gewerbestrasse 11, 6330 Cham, Switzerland

This book is dedicated to human rights defenders everywhere.

Foreword

In recent decades, the intersection of politics and human rights has been at the forefront of some of the most crucial debates in human rights literature and jurisprudence. Similarly, human rights are often the focal point of intense cultural and political battles. At the core of these struggles lies a fundamental question: what does it mean to have fundamental rights, and who gets to decide on the scope of those rights? As communities grow increasingly interconnected, affirming human rights, countering violations, and responding to the so-called "culture wars" have never been more urgent. In this context, an important shift in the United States Supreme Court jurisprudence has taken course, to the detriment of established fundamental rights, and in stark contrast with international and comparative case law on similar legal issues. What are the impacts of such a drastic jurisprudential turn, and what are the forces behind this seemingly erosion of democratic values?

This book, *Litigating the Politics of Human Rights: Contemporary U.S. Culture Wars on Trial*, offers a meaningful exploration of how the United States Supreme Court jurisprudence navigates the tumultuous waters where legal principles and politics collide, demonstrably at the cost of the protection of fundamental human rights. The book deeply engages with the United States Supreme Court's contemporary politicization of fundamental human rights issues and at the center of its inquiry lies the link between the so-called "culture wars," the protection of human rights, and the politicization of litigation.

Turning to courts offers a unique form of protecting and advancing human rights—one that is not confined solely to the courtroom but resonates across public opinion and political discourse. Litigating requires a meaningful balancing act: leveraging legal tools to uphold fundamental norms and the rule of law while recognizing that the outcome of these battles often reflects deeper, underlying power dynamics. The underlying theme of the book reveals the inconvenient truth that permeates recent U.S. Supreme Court jurisprudence: that every decision is more than a mere interpretation of the law; it reflects society's broader struggles over the recognition and protection of fundamental human rights.

Litigating the Politics of Human Rights engages with the U.S. Supreme Court's recent jurisprudence through the prism of its conservative majority efforts to reframe fundamental human rights matters as alleged political questions. Throughout its six chapters, which dwell upon a range of human rights, from women's to education rights and freedom of expression, the book dives into the myriad challenges and consequences that arise when politics and human rights collide under the guise of "culture wars."

The book weaves a rich tapestry of landmark U.S. Supreme Court cases as well as international and comparative human rights jurisprudence. While the main focus is on the Supreme Court of the United States case law, it brings together perspectives from diverse international and comparative jurisdictions to shed light on "whether a consensus international human rights law perspective on the various so-called 'culture war' issues exists or is likely to emerge."

From the significant rulings in international tribunals to the comparative law perspectives, the cases featured within these pages reveal the detrimental consequences of reframing fundamental human rights as purely political questions. By focusing on the "politicization" of human rights and the notion of "culture wars," the book offers a fresh narrative that goes beyond the legal concepts and procedural intricacies. It provides a critical lens through which we can understand how human rights are not just defined but also contested, reshaped, and often undermined.

Litigating the Politics of Human Rights explores how human rights litigation can serve as the battleground for those who seek to disturb gained progress, resist social change, or enforce new forms of exclusion. In doing so, it does not shy away from the complexities and contradictions inherent in these struggles. It illuminates how the language of rights can be both empowering and divisive, used to advocate for both inclusion and exclusion. From the discussion of US "education culture wars" to the clash between freedom of expression and freedom of religion, the book mobilizes concepts such as "revisionist history," privatization of abortion restriction enforcement, the value of plurality, and de-democratization as ways in which the Court impedes on recognized rights and freedoms, diminishing them to purely policy matters.

Human rights litigation is, at its core, a fight for human dignity and justice. It is a testament that seeks to affirm what is right, even in the face of overwhelming odds. This book unequivocally demonstrates "through an examination of relevant case law [… that] 'culture war' litigation most often undemocratically attempts to use the courts to legitimize the erosion of basic human rights." As you embark on this critical path, you will find a compelling call to action—not just for human rights scholars and practitioners, but for anyone who believes in the power of the law to transform society. The book is an act of resistance to the erosion of democratic principles and a contribution to reclaiming the role of courts as a cornerstone of democratic societies governed by the rule of law.

For anyone seeking to understand the present—and perhaps the future—of human rights in the United States, this book is an essential guide. It offers not just an in-depth analysis of recent controversial Supreme Court decisions that touch on crucial human rights, but also a window into contemporary "culture wars" and the politicization of litigation. As you engage with the debates and cases presented in the manuscript, you will be challenged to think deeply about the role of Courts in upholding the rule of law in a democratic society, and specifically how the Supreme Court of the United States is shaping the future of fundamental rights.

For those who litigate human rights cases, this book will serve as both a guide to understanding the politicization of human rights litigation in the United States and a challenge to push the boundaries within this critical field. For scholars and jurists, it will provide a rich tapestry of ideas, strategies, and stories that illustrate how human rights can—and must—be protected in the courts.

In a global order where human rights are far too easily compromised, this book reminds us that courts have a crucial role to play in a democratic society, one that should not be lightly delegated to political actors. Through detailed discussions of a myriad of cases, *Litigating the Politics of Human Rights* is an invitation to reflect deeply on how human rights are not merely protected or denied in the courts, but rather actively constructed and contested in ways that have far-reaching implications for society at large.

Université de Montréal
Montreal, QC, Canada

Miriam Cohen

Canada Research Chair on Human
Rights and International Justice
Montreal, QC, Canada

Acknowledgment

I wish to acknowledge my husband Roshan for his love and unwavering enthusiasm for my academic endeavors which is a great encouragement to me. I sincerely thank Dr Anja Trautmann, Editor for Law at Springer and Dr. Brigitte Reschke, Executive Editor for Springer Law for their support of this academic work. I also express my gratitude to Dr Miriam Cohen, Professor of International Law at the University of Montreal and Canada Research Chair on Human Rights and International Justice for allowing me the honor of having her write the foreword to the book.

Contents

Chapter 1
Introduction: The Role of the Courts in Affirming Fundamental Human Rights as Essential to Democracy

Abstract This chapter sets out the theme of this work as illustrated by the US and comparative law cases analysed in this monograph. That theme concerns the proper role of the courts in safeguarding and perpetuating substantive human rights consistent with democratic principle. In so doing the courts must resist those voices both from within and outside of the judiciary that attempt to reframe core fundamental democratic rights matters as essentially socio-cultural and political 'culture wars.' The latter reframing, as we will discover through the cases here discussed, too often leads to judgements that are not well grounded legally, that undercut bedrock democratic ideals and that weaken constitutional protections for the vulnerable.

1.1 Introduction: Overview of the Monograph Objectives

The objective of this monograph is to examine, through selected contemporary landmark case examples of the United States Supreme Court jurisprudence, the tendency of the Court's current conservative majority to evade, by various tactics, ruling on the fundamental human rights issues actually presented to the Court. The respectful view here is that in doing so the Court's conservative majority has, in effect, too often politicized its analysis of human rights issues rather than proffered objective legal analysis of the substantive issues. The United States Supreme Court cases analyzed in this work[1] thus are held to be representative selected examples of those that, on the view here, have been reduced to litigation on the politics of human rights. The latter being the improper focus rather than the nature, and scope of fundamental human rights and their constitutional underpinnings in a democratic society. The destructive implications for society of such a judicial approach are addressed in the case commentaries and the monograph's conclusion.

[1] The US cases discussed include also some US federal cases which may or may not ultimately be taken up by the United States Supreme Court.

S. C. Grover, *Litigating the Politics of Human Rights*, Ius Gentium: Comparative Perspectives on Law and Justice 121, https://doi.org/10.1007/978-3-031-82463-0_1

To gain a broader perspective on the universal fundamental human rights issues at the core of the selected United States Supreme Court cases discussed here the author presents also key comparative law cases and explores the contrasting or comparative legal approach taken in those cases. The purpose of including here a comparative law approach is then to better inform the understanding of the issues overall. However, please note that the comparative case law selected may not be in all aspects identical to the US cases discussed and analyzed. Furthermore, the various larger contextual legal environment specifics may impact the particular court's perspective. Yet the comparative law cases discussed address something of the fundamental human rights issues also under consideration in the US selected cases here analyzed. Hence the judicial approach in those comparative law cases (particularly that adopted by international human rights courts and other international courts) is instructive on whether a consensus international human rights law perspective on the various so-called 'culture war' issues exists or is likely to emerge.

We begin our case analysis and discussions with consideration of (on the view here) a stark example of the United States Supreme Court's contemporary politicization of a fundamental human rights issue. The United States Supreme Court case to be discussed in this introduction (to be examined in more depth in Chap. 4) is the case that overturned a 50 year super precedent legalizing abortion in the United States. I refer to *Thomas E. Dobbs, State Health Officer of the Mississippi Department of Health et al. v Jackson Women's Health Organization et al.* (hereafter also referred to as *Dobbs*)[2] We will focus in this introductory chapter on Justice Thomas' concurrence in *Dobbs.* That concurrence reflects, it is here contended, a certain dominant view of the conservatives on the Court that liberal politics is driving the posing of *purported* constitutional questions to the Court which are in fact allegedly political policy questions masquerading as constitutional issues. The contrary respectful view of the current author is set out that in fact Justice Thomas' perspective in *Dobbs* amounts to a relinquishing of the Court's jurisdiction to establish the contours of constitutionally protected fundamental human rights in various contexts such that the vulnerable can realistically turn to an independent judiciary for protection of those rights.

[2]Thomas E. Dobbs, State Health Officer of the Mississippi Department of Health et al. v Jackson Women's Health Organization et al (hereafter also referred as Dobbs) United States Supreme Court No. 19-1392 October term 2021 Decided June 24, 2022.

1.2 Thomas E. Dobbs, State Health Officer of the Mississippi Department of Health et al. v Jackson Women's Health Organization et al. (United States Supreme Court) No. 19-1392 October Term 2021, Decided June 24, 2022

For the purposes of this introduction, we will consider only Justice Thomas' concurring opinion in *Dobbs*. In that opinion the Justice (on the analysis here) lays out clearly and unapologetically his strategy to sidestep the fundamental human rights issue at the core of the case. Rather than addressing whether women and girls (who together are not a minority of the US population) should have, as a matter of a fundamental right, the opportunity to access a legal abortion if certain criteria are met, Thomas instead reframes the issue ostensibly as a largely abstract political question about State rights.

In *Dobbs*, the United States Supreme Court conservative majority ruled that access to a legal abortion with certain conditions met is *not* a fundamental constitutional right. Therefore, the majority reasoned further, States are immune from judicial interference in their regulation of abortion where there is a constitutional challenge. The latter provided that the State regulations imposed serve a legitimate governmental interest and are proportionate and hence meet the judicial test of rational basis review.[3] Let us turn then to Justice Thomas' concurring opinion[4] and why it is here argued that Justice Thomas' concurring opinion politicizes a fundamental human rights issue and ultimately then also the Court.

Justice Thomas holds that the US Constitution's Fourteenth Amendment Due Process Clause does *not* provide for an implied fundamental constitutional right to obtain an abortion. The Due Process Clause guarantees due process as a necessary antecedent of any deprivation of life, liberty or property. Justice Thomas maintains that the purported right to an abortion is not encompassed within the US constitutional guarantee of liberty and to hold that the drafters would have contemplated the converse is "farcical".[5] In addition, Justice Thomas rejects the very notion of *substantive due process* in the first instance. The Justice maintains that substantive due process is in fact an oxymoron with no constitutional basis. Justice Thomas argues further that the US Constitution guarantees due process as a matter only of procedural safeguards (process) detached from any fundamental rights the deprivation of which are at issue in the particular case.[6] That is; Justice Thomas holds that the due process afforded by way of the Fourteenth Amendment does not and was not intended to guarantee the absence of any and all infringements on fundamental liberty or other basic rights under any and all circumstances or process

[3] *Dobbs* Syllabus Alito Majority Opinion Reliance Interests p. 7 item 5(d).

[4] *Dobbs*, Justice Thomas Concurring Opinion pp. 1–7.

[5] *Dobbs*, Justice Thomas Concurring Opinion p. 1.

[6] *Dobbs*, Justice Thomas Concurring Opinion p. 2.

arrangements.[7] Put differently, Thomas argues that the Fourteenth Amendment guarantees no substantive rights and this includes any alleged right to abortion.[8] The current author holds the converse view; namely that the Fourteenth Amendment does guarantee fundamental rights. This being the case in that the US Constitution is grounded on democratic principles. Those democratic principles do *not* contemplate arbitrary infringement of basic human rights where there is no compelling governmental purpose consistent with democratic values, but where perhaps *pro forma* low level process protections were yet afforded to the complainant.[9] Where such a compelling governmental purpose/reason *consistent with democratic values* exists for the infringement of a basic right, and the infringement is proportionate, only then has substantive due process been afforded.[10]

Process guarantees incorporated through the Fourteenth Amendment, Thomas argues, cannot define the fundamental rights to life, liberty and property subject to those procedural safeguards when their deprivation is contemplated.[11] While the latter is perhaps a matter for debate, this author would highlight the necessity of recognizing that *fundamental human rights in part shape what is fair process in the specific case* i.e., what level of judicial scrutiny is applicable. The more severe the nature and category of basic rights deprivation contemplated, the higher the level of judicial scrutiny is needed to test whether the government can justify the fundamental rights violation at issue. Thomas' view (as this author understands it), however, is that the Fourteenth Amendment represents process requirements in a vacuum insofar as those requirements are unguided by the underlying fundamental human rights at issue in a case. Respectfully, the current author views Thomas' interpretation of the Fourteenth Amendment as providing an unintentional potential opening for unchecked authoritarian infringements of fundamental human rights by government. The latter being a foreseeable outcome of a judicial approach with but the window dressing of certain of the process trappings of democratically inspired judicial decision-making; a necessary but insufficient mechanism to ensure justice. That is, 'rule of law' in the form of 'due process' without 'substantive due process', on the view argued by the current author, is but a *pro forma* empty exercise. It is procedure untethered to the fundamental human rights that due process is designed to protect and hence the values upon which the judiciary in a democracy is grounded. *Without regard to the fundamental human rights delineating to a large degree what constitutes due process procedurally in any instant case; questions of fundamental human rights can easily be reframed as but political questions to be subjected to legislative discretionary decision-making*. As a case in point then consider that in *Dobbs* Justice

[7] *Dobbs*, Justice Thomas Concurring Opinion p. 2.

[8] *Dobbs*, Justice Thomas Concurring Opinion p. 2.

[9] "…substantive due process has its most profound impact in instances where the claim is a fundamental right, because then in order to show an adequate justification [for deprivation], the government must meet strict scrutiny." Chemerinsky (1999), p. 1534.

[10] Compare Chemerinsky (1999), pp. 1501–1502.

[11] *Dobbs*, Justice Thomas Concurring Opinion p. 2.

Thomas in fact frames the complex abortion rights question thus: "The right to abortion is ultimately a *policy goal* in desperate search of a constitutional justification (emphasis added)."[12] The case examples to be discussed in the chapters that follow are also illustrative of just such a result; namely the judiciary erroneously framing fundamental human rights issues as politically based policy matters which, on the view here, undermines not just the judiciary but the democracy itself.

The United States Supreme Court cases to be discussed in this work, it is here argued, often involve the Court's conservative majority, in the first instance, erroneously reframing fundamental human rights matters as supposed political questions. This then results in the Court adopting *rational basis judicial review* rather than the *strict scrutiny review* (the latter is to be applied when considering government infringement of a fundamental human right (a constitutional right) or violation of the rights of a protected class). Adoption of rational basis judicial review greatly stacks the deck in favor of the government. It will be argued here further, contrary to Justice Thomas's view in *Dobbs*, that in such instances where fundamental human rights are, from the outset, *incorrectly re-framed* as political matters (often mischaracterized as policy 'culture wars'), the procedure selected (rational basis judicial review) *does*, by implication, define the right at issue as non-fundamental and not constitutionally based (if that right is even held by the conservative justices to exist).[13]

Not surprisingly (but arguably, on the view here, at worst somewhat disingenuously, and at best unconvincingly), Justice Thomas, as with the Majority in *Dobbs*, contends that nothing in the Dobbs decision (regarding the overturning of *Roe v Wade*[14]) puts in jeopardy the accepted constitutional grounding of other United States Supreme Court majority previously presumed implicit fundamental rights. This despite the fact that *Dobbs* marks the end in practice of the constitutional protection of a previously judicially inferred right to abortion of the *previable* fetus.[15] In particular the additional concerns raised by *Dobbs* involve those inferred fundamental rights relating to or encompassed by the liberty guarantee or any derived privacy right therefrom. The *Dobbs* United States Supreme Court majority suggested that the latter rights were not at legal peril of being declared by the conservative court majority to be constitutionally infirm (e.g. the right of married couples to obtain contraceptives, the right of those of age of consent to engage in private consensual sex acts, the right to same-sex marriage etc.)[16] At the same time, Justice Thomas held in *Dobbs* that the United States Supreme Court's substantive

---

[12] *Dobbs*, Justice Thomas Concurring Opinion p. 5.

[13] See Legal Information Institute, Cornell Law School, Rational Basis Test https://www.law.cornell.edu/wex/rational_basis_test (Accessed August 15, 2024).

[14] *Roe v Wade* 410 U.S. 113 (1973) Decided January 22, 1973.

[15] The Supreme Court of the United States in *Roe v Wade* had "...expressly declared that the right to privacy is safeguarded through the due process clause of the Fourteenth and Ninth Amendments. *Roe was unquestioningly a substantive due process case* (emphasis added)." Chemerinsky (1999), p. 1508.

[16] *Dobbs*, Justice Thomas Concurring Opinion pp. 2–3.

due process landmark cases should be reconsidered in future cases.[17] According to Justice Thomas in his Dobbs concurrence, all rights held to be fundamental and constitutionally-based substantive due process rights were so declared by the United States Supreme Court *in error.*[18] On that basis, Justice Thomas argues, that these likely should, after a case-by-case consideration be struck from the list of fundamental rights judicially recognized by the Court as protected by the Constitution.[19]

Thomas further suggests that in *future privacy cases*, after allegedly properly negating as constitutionally based the right to contraception, same sex marriage and the right to same sex consensual intimacy between adults, the Court should turn its attention to other 'constitutional' rights purported to flow from the liberty right and derivative privacy rights articulated in the Fourteenth Amendment. He suggests that in those cases the Court could consider whether any of the contested substantive due process rights (rights explicitly enumerated and/or those unenumerated but allegedly implied) are protected by the 'privileges or immunities of citizens' of the United States (those born or naturalized citizens) articulated in the Fourteenth Amendment.[20] These rights include, according to United States Supreme Court case law, for instance, the right to vote, to petition congress, to peaceably assemble and to move freely between US States and the privilege of habeas corpus.[21] Justice Thomas thus puts on the potential chopping block certain contested fundamental civil and political rights that establish and undergird democracy; many of which rights are not explicitly enumerated in the US Constitution. Indeed, subsequent to the United States Supreme Court ruling in *Dobbs*, the legitimate fear among many legal experts and large segments of the general population is that some US States will enact blanket abortion bans that prohibit US citizens travelling to another US State to obtain an abortion even if abortion is lawful in the travel destination State. This type of legislation, if enacted, would thus interfere with a previously taken-for-granted right to inter-state travel for lawful purposes by US citizens. This extension of the abortion ban would pose a litigation challenge in that the right of US citizens to interstate travel within the US is a non-enumerated implied constitutional right. It is thus an open question whether the current conservative majority on the United States Supreme Court would uphold such a bar to interstate travel where the purpose of the travel is to obtain an abortion lawful in the particular destination State.

The proposed Thomas judicial strategy (articulated by the Justice in *Dobbs*) regarding discarding various enumerated and non-enumerated fundamental rights

---

[17] *Dobbs*, Justice Thomas Concurring Opinion p. 3.

[18] See *Dobbs* Justice Thomas Concurring Opinion p. 3, Justice Thomas agreeing with the view that "…any substantive due process decision is "demonstrably erroneous" … "we have a duty to "correct the error" established in those precedents" (internal citations in the quotes omitted).

[19] *Dobbs*, Justice Thomas Concurring Opinion p. 3.

[20] *Dobbs*, Justice Thomas Concurring Opinion p. 3.

[21] For discussion of case law relevant to the privileges and immunities stipulated in the Fourteenth Amendment see US Congress: Modern Doctrine on Privileges or Immunities Clause, Constitution Annotated https://constitution.congress.gov/browse/essay/amdt14-S1-2-2/ALDE_00000815/#essay-1 Accessed August 16, 2024.

(through declaring them not to be constitutionally based) threatens, on the view here, democratic values and institutions grounded on fundamental human rights. This is the risk then that eliminating, by judicial fiat, the notion of substantive due process rights poses. Justice Thomas in contrast, considers the failure to jettison the notion of substantive due process rights (a notion he considers a "legal fiction") as in fact what creates particular societal dangers.[22] Justice Thomas argues that substantive due process rights as articulated by judges puts judges in an "exalted position" above the People.[23] To this one can raise the point that it is for the Court *in service to the People* to declare what is the law and, in so doing, guide the People on what constitutes the contours of democratic interpretations of the Constitution. The latter includes then also delineating categories of fundamental constitutionally based explicitly enumerated and non-enumerated implied derivative fundamental rights and their scope. Justice Thomas contends, however, that in declaring what are the substantive due process rights enumerated and implied in the Fourteenth Amendment and set out in the related United States Supreme Court case law, the Court is engaged in "policy-making rather than neutral legal analysis."[24] Indeed Justice Thomas laments what he views as the proliferation of due process substantive rights and holds them to be based on the Court's "extraconstitutional value preferences."[25] On the view here, in contrast, due process substantive rights concern constitutionally based fundamental rights essential especially to protection of the vulnerable and to democratic values.

One counterargument to the Justice Thomas perspective is that there is nothing inherent about affirming (as constitutionally based) an enumerated or implied substantive due process right that would morph the exercise into one of so-called 'judicial policymaking'. No such hypothetical enhanced risk of 'judicial policymaking' exists then when affirming substantive due process rights compared to that which exists in judicial nullification, in essence, of previously declared and affirmed fundamental constitutionally protected rights (as occurred in *Dobbs*). What constitutes *ipso facto* 'judicial policymaking' as opposed to objective judicial decision-making is a core issue. It is one *not* resolved/decided by Justice Thomas' call in *Dobbs* to discard all substantive due process fundamental rights.

It is noteworthy, this author contends, that some if not all of the current United States Supreme Court conservative justices appear to have a consistent pattern of *in effect* holding selected liberty rights affirmation to be mere 'judicial policymaking' while not so with (on the view here) improper extension of the protection afforded by other fundamental rights. The latter in such a manner as is consistent with their conservative worldview (i.e., as with the First Amendment right to religious free expression used (improperly on the view here) to, for instance, legitimize and render lawful the discriminatory exclusion of certain protected groups in the marketplace

---

[22] *Dobbs*, Justice Thomas Concurring Opinion p. 4.

[23] *Dobbs*, Justice Thomas Concurring Opinion p. 4.

[24] *Dobbs*, Justice Thomas Concurring Opinion p. 4.

[25] *Dobbs*, Justice Thomas Concurring Opinion p. 4.

(i.e., in regard to access to certain public accommodation services as will be discussed in the context of case examples in a later chapter). The conservative United States Supreme Court majority then delegates back to the States to legislate the very negation of the fundamental substantive due process rights that the Justices have cleared for the same. This all emanates then from the purported disentangling of the plaintiff asserted fundamental rights matter from its *previously acknowledged* constitutional moorings (we will consider *Dobbs* and the contested issue of an alleged constitutionally based right to abortion in detail in Chap. 4). Yet it is here contended that the United States Supreme Court conservative majority's policy and value preferences can be no more insulated from its judicial decision-making/ constitutional interpretation negating a substantive due process right than they can be in affirming one. 'The People' can but hope that in a sincere and thoughtful exchange amongst all the Justices on the Court as to the law as it is best understood *most consistent with democratic values* the Court is led to issue a just ruling that serves the general good and protects the most vulnerable.[26]

Justice Thomas further contends that while the Court recognizes the need for equal protection for all classes in regard to fundamental rights "divined"[27] from the due process clause; the same strict scrutiny standard is not applied by the Court in regard to non-fundamental rights and inequities therefore persist that the Court tolerates. It hardly seems reasonable, however, on the view here, to argue that the creation of further inequities by eliminating judicial recognition of previously acknowledged constitutionally protected fundamental rights (that many highly vulnerable persons especially rely on) is the solution. Finally, Justice Thomas argues that reliance on substantive due process rationales have, at times, been wielded to judicially create or abet great harms.[28] Justice Thomas cites *Dred Scott v. Sandford*[29] as, in his view, a case in point in which the Court's alleged reliance on a certain category of substantive due process rights has been responsible for indubitable great harms.[30] Let us take a closer look then at the Dred Scott case, and in what ways, if any, the outrageous ruling in *Dred* may be instructive on the need for the courts to affirm rather than discard substantive due process rights.

[26] "If the plaintiff can show a deprivation of life, liberty or property without adequate justification, the plaintiff has then set out a substantive due process claim." Chemerinsky (1999), p. 1527.

[27] Justice Thomas' terminology *Dobbs*, Justice Thomas Concurring Opinion p. 4.

[28] *Dobbs*, Justice Thomas Concurring Opinion p. 4.

[29] *Dred Scott v. Sandford*, 19 How. 393 (1857).

[30] *Dobbs*, Justice Thomas Concurring Opinion p. 6.

1.2.1 Substantive Due Process Rights: Historic Lessons from Dred Scott on the Risks of Their Disavowal

The current author argues that the United States Supreme Court majority in *Dred Scott* disregarded the due process of law guarantee of the Fifth Amendment. That guarantee, among other things, does not permit the deprivation of liberty of a citizen of the US without due process of law. This the majority accomplished by simply ignoring substantive due process rights under the Fifth Amendment (foundational human rights matters that must be considered to achieve justice). Hence the Dred majority simply assumed that a person may be considered property, a slave, based on their African ancestry and the fact that their forebearers had been forcibly transferred to the US as alleged slaves. On that basis the 1857 Dred United States Supreme Court majority held that Dred Scott was a slave notwithstanding that he had been born in the United States.

Thus, the United States Supreme Court Dred majority declined to, in the first instance, recognize the full personhood, in the natural rights sense, of all persons. This, of course, would include also then those who were at the time of the Dred case or prior considered by statutory municipal US law to be slaves and who were living in the United States. Rather the notion of the right to property in the Fifth Amendment was considered by the *Dred* United States Supreme Court majority *apart* from the foundational question of whether *any* human being-*US citizen or not*-can constitutionally properly be considered as 'property'. Hence an illegitimate undemocratic restriction[31] on the substantive due process liberty right of the Fifth Amendment was held by the Dred United States Supreme Court majority to be constitutional. The latter was accomplished by way of a *racist interpretation* applied by the majority United States Supreme Court in the Dred Scott case. The restriction on substantive due process rights in *Dred* served *in effect* to exclude those of African descent from Fifth Amendment 'rule of law' procedural safeguards. The latter including but not limited to the application of the judicial test of strict scrutiny to be met in regard to assessing the legitimacy of the governmental purpose in deprivation of Dred Scott's liberty. Note then that substantive due process considerations (a search for justice and respect for human dignity) dictate in part the nature and quality of the procedural safeguards likely to be honored in practice.

It is noteworthy in regard to substantive due process considerations that in the Dred Scott case one of the two dissenting Justices, Justice Benjamin Curtis, makes note of the key foundational fact (then known also to the United States Supreme Court) that "*Slavery, being contrary to natural right*, is created only by municipal law (emphasis added)."[32] Thus, Justice Curtis held in *Dred* that Wisconsin's

---

[31] The denial of liberty rights to persons of African descent born in the United States but alleged to be 'slaves' by those who held them in bondage.

[32] Bill of Rights Institute *Dred Scott v Sanford* (1857) Excerpts from the Majority and Dissenting Opinions https://billofrightsinstitute.org/e-lessons/dred-scott-v-sanford-1857-excerpts-from-majority-and-dissenting-opinions (Accessed August 16, 2024).

prohibition on slavery was constitutional. Indeed, at the time of the Dred case even in some so-called 'Slave States' of the US; selected persons of African descent had the vote and were recognized as US citizens.[33] Once again, this time in *Dred,* we discover that 'rule of law' in theory disconnected in practice from *substantive rights implicated by respect for human dignity*[34] results in (a) non-democratic rulings and inadequate implementation of Fifth Amendment procedural safeguards such as in *Dred Scott*, and (b) rulings often markedly tainted by discrimination in precluding the extension, in practice, of *inherent fundamental rights* to the most vulnerable in society.

Had the United States Supreme Court Dred Scott majority relied on the constitution's substantive due process rights, grounded as they are on the *dignity of all human beings,*[35] Dred Scott the man, a human being residing within the jurisdiction of the United States, could *not* have been considered as slave/property by that Court in the first instance. This regardless in which State of the United States he was habiting let alone be it in Wisconsin, a free State. The natural *a priori* right of Dred Scott to freedom as opposed to enslavement, and that right independent of any consideration of the question of his US citizenship status, would have been apparent to the Dred US Supreme Court under a true substantive due process analysis.[36] This is evident also from the preamble of the Declaration of Independence (1776)[37] which affirms the equality of all people and the inalienable right of all to be free.[38] Instead, the Dred Scott United States Supreme Court majority erroneously let the Missouri Supreme Court response to the political discretionary question of who, at the time, qualified as a US citizen arbitrarily and improperly dictate (a) the foundational basic human rights question of who qualifies as a human being (as opposed to property) entitled to exercise their *inherent* fundamental rights (i.e. liberty) and (b) what should be the interstate social policy and legislative implications, if any, across States in the US of prohibitions on slavery in any particular States(s) in the United States.

The question in *Dred* then was more foundational than who could become a member of the US political community as a citizen. That core question inquired

[33] *Dred Scott v Sanford* (1857) Justice Maclean dissent http://www.let.rug.nl/usa/documents/1826-1850/dred-scott-case/justice-mclean-dissenting.php (Accessed August 16, 2024).

[34] For a discussion about human dignity see, for example, Grover (2009), pp. 615–622.

[35] The notion of the dignity of all human beings was not foreign to the United States Supreme Court at the time of *Dred Scott* in that at the time Wisconsin and Illinois had outlawed slavery.

[36] For a discussion of whether any substantive due process rights are owed to non-US citizens especially when within US jurisdiction see, for example, Cole (2003).

[37] National Constitution Centre: The influence of the Declaration of Independence on the US Constitution https://constitutioncenter.org/news-debate/podcasts/the-declaration-of-independence-and-its-influence-on-the-constitution?gclid=CjwKCAiAhKycBhAQEiwAgf19ev_8pAJ0IQbvM5GyLaWZIGbji4qD1VM-oR8CbofBbxmDHru9TQeXhhoC9f4QAvD_BwE (Accessed August 16, 2024).

[38] Declaration of Independence (July 4, 1776) https://docs.house.gov/meetings/GO/GO00/20220929/115171/HHRG-117-GO00-20220929-SD010.pdf (Accessed August 16, 2024).

rather as to whether any human being might be legitimately considered property such that the issue of US citizenship became moot.[39] This was *not* properly a discretionary question for the Missouri legislature in *Dred* but rather a fundamental rights/rule of law matter for the judiciary, including the Supreme Court of the United States, to determine.[40]

Justice Maclean rebuked the Supreme Court of the United States for its declining to acknowledge Dred Scott and his family as free persons and to acknowledge relevant context in the case. That context included the Act of Congress under which persons born in the United States were considered US citizens.[41] Thus Dred Scott, his wife and children were, Justice Maclean held, given the circumstances of their birth, free persons. Dred Scott and his wife Harriett were both born in the United States (Virginia) as were their children. Justice Maclean held that consequently Dred Scott was a citizen of the United States which by definition meant he was a free man. From that US citizenship, Maclean maintained further, emanated also the right to petition the US Supreme Court for redress regarding his continuing enslavement contrary to controlling relevant federal law (and so too for his wife and children).[42]

The Dred Scott United States Supreme Court majority attempted to rationalize its denial of the humanity of persons of African descent by claiming that this class of persons in the United States were by the framers regarded as "private property" and hence precluded from *US citizenship*.[43] The latter purportedly being the case regardless of whether they were under municipal (State) law enslaved or free. Further, on that basis, according to the Dred Scott majority US Supreme Court, supposedly these persons did not enjoy the privileges and immunities of the Fifth Amendment granted

[39]National Archives Milestone Documents Dred Scott Justice Taney majority ruling (1857) *Dred Scott v Sanford* https://www.archives.gov/milestone-documents/dred-scott-v-sandford (Accessed August 16, 2024) "This is certainly a very serious question, and one that now for the first time has been brought for decision before this court. ...The question is simply this: Can a negro whose ancestors were imported into this country, and sold as slaves, become a member of the political community formed and brought into existence by the Constitution of the United States, and as such become entitled to all the rights and privileges and immunities guaranteed to the citizen? One of which rights is the privilege of suing in a court of the United States in the cases specified in the Constitution".

[40]Compare *Dred Scott v Sanford* (1857) Justice Maclean dissent http://www.let.rug.nl/usa/documents/1826-1850/dred-scott-case/justice-mclean-dissenting.php (Accessed August 16, 2024).

[41]The Missouri Appeal Court had also disregarded the Act of Congress and the Constitution of Illinois under which Dred Scott and his family were considered free persons See *Dred Scott v Sanford* (1857) Justice Maclean dissent http://www.let.rug.nl/usa/documents/1826-1850/dred-scott-case/justice-mclean-dissenting.php (Accessed August 16, 2024).

[42]*Dred Scott v Sanford* (1857) Justice Maclean dissent http://www.let.rug.nl/usa/documents/1826-1850/dred-scott-case/justice-mclean-dissenting.php (Accessed August 16, 2024).

[43]National Archives Milestone Documents *Dred Scott v Sanford* (1857) majority opinion IV (4) "The Constitution of the United States recognises slaves as property and pledges the Federal Government to protect it. And Congress cannot exercise any more authority over property of that description than it may constitutionally exercise over property of any other kind." https://www.archives.gov/milestone-documents/dred-scott-v-sandford (Accessed August 16, 2024).

to United States citizens (i.e., such as standing to petition the Federal Courts, as in the case at bar, for relief for harms imposed by a US State suffered or continuing to be suffered such as with Dred Scott and his wife's enslavement). There is, however, nothing in the Declaration of Independence (that set out the democratic values of the new Republic) to indicate that persons of African descent were to be excluded from the natural right to liberty afforded all under US jurisdiction and to its pursuit through legal means.

Chief Justice Taney who delivered the majority opinion in *Dred Scott,* on the view here, ignored the Declaration of Independence admonition that substantive injustices and oppressive practices against The People by government must be recognized as such and rejected and government altered or modified as need be to ensure justice.[44] It is arguably then also the role of the Courts to affirm democratic aspirations and initiatives when the proper case comes before them. That constitutional reform may be required (i.e., through constitutional amendments) would also be apparent where the Court addresses constitutional provisions that perpetuate nondemocratic laws (as in *Dred Scott* the majority could have, but did not, find the implicitly slave-affirming clauses of the US Constitution contrary to the democratic values and natural rights it was intended to protect). This as a necessary part of sustaining and perpetuating the democracy. Instead, Justice Taney did not properly rely on the values articulated in the Declaration of Independence in his interpretation of the Constitution and hence disregarded the fundamental natural liberty right of all human beings.[45] It is here respectfully argued then that Justice Thomas in *Dobbs* errs spectacularly in his assertion that it is the judiciary's reliance in a democracy on substantive due process rights that increases inexorably the risk for unspeakable harms. This rather than holding the converse; namely that it is the judiciary's very disregard of substantive due process that commonly produces that excessive injurious result.

---

[44]Declaration of Independence (July 4, 1776) https://docs.house.gov/meetings/GO/GO00/20220929/115171/HHRG-117-GO00-20220929-SD010.pdf (Accessed August 16, 2024).

[45]National Archives Milestone documents *Dred Scott v Sanford* (1857) majority opinion para 9: "The change in public opinion and feeling in relation to the African race, which has taken place since the adoption of the Constitution, cannot change its construction and meaning, and it must be constructed and administered now according to its true meaning and intention when it was formed and adopted." https://www.archives.gov/milestone-documents/dred-scott-v-sandford (Accessed August 16, 2024).

1.3 Selected Comparative Law Cases in Which the Court Rejects Reframing of Fundamental Rights Issues as Purely Political Questions

In this section we consider two selected comparative law cases concerning asserted substantive (fundamental) rights issues. These cases are instructive in the various judicial approaches to addressing government's efforts to transform the fundamental human rights question at issue into a purely political (a) one to be ignored (thus maintaining the status quo) or (b) returned to the legislature for resolution. In both comparative law cases discussed in this introduction (one concerning a New Zealand Supreme Court judgment and the other a European Court of Human Rights judgement); the courts in question ruled in a manner so as to protect both (a) one of the fundamental democratic rights of citizenship at issue in the case (the right to vote or the right to stand for election) and (b) to safeguard the fundamental human right to free expression or of free association infringed by the specific government involved.

1.3.1 Sejdic & Finci v. Bosnia and Herzegovina, European Court of Human Rights (Applications Nos. 27996/06 and 34836/06) Grand Chamber Judgement 22 December 2009

Sejdic & Finci v. Bosnia and Herzegovina involves exclusion, to a degree, of certain identifiable groups from the polity of a nation based on discriminatory grounds relating to ethnicity.[46] The case involves rendering members of particular groups precluded in respect of their fundamental right as citizens of the State (nation) in question to stand for particular political office. The case addresses the Constitution of Bosnia-Herzegovina which was an annex to the 1995 peace agreement signed 14 December 1995. That Constitution affirmed that Bosnia-Herzegovina was constituted of the Federation of Bosnia and Herzegovina and the Republika Srpska. The Preamble to that Constitution delineated who, according to that text, comprised the 'constituent peoples' of the State of Bosnia-Herzegovina; namely Bosniaks, Croats and Serbs, Certain power sharing and other arrangements ensured that it would be "impossible to adopt decisions against the will of the representatives of any of these so-called 'constituent peoples'."[47] All persons belonging to other ethnic or minority groups, even though citizens, were *not* considered 'constituent peoples' of the State. Note that the purported 'constituent people' groups were the majority with Bosniaks

---

[46] *Sejdic & Finci v. Bosnia and Herzegovina* European Court of Human Rights (Applications nos. 27996/06 and 34836/06) Grand Chamber Judgement 22 December 2009 para 7, p. 3.

[47] *Sejdic & Finci v. Bosnia and Herzegovina* European Court of Human Rights para 7 p. 3.

and Croats being the majority within the Federation of Bosnia and Herzegovina, and Serbs within the Republika Srpska.[48]

Both applicants had held, and current to the applications held, prominent public positions. At the time the applications were heard by the Grand Chamber of the European Court of Human Rights Mr. Sejdic, who described himself as of Roma descent, was the Roma Monitor of the Organization on Security and Cooperation in Europe (OSCE) Mission to Bosnia and Herzegovina. Mr. Finci, who described himself as of Jewish descent, was the Ambassador to Switzerland for Bosnia and Herzegovina. Since neither were members of the designated 'constituent peoples' specified in the 1995 Constitution; they were held ineligible both to stand for election to the second chamber of the State Parliament or to the Presidency of the State of Bosnia and Herzegovina.[49]

This explicit exclusion in certain respects of some groups from the polity though the Constitutional text was a compromise brokered with the help of international mediators. At the same time, these mediators ensured inclusion in the Constitution per the following paragraph affirming fundamental rights:

> The rights and freedoms set forth in the European Convention for the Protection of Human Rights and Fundamental Freedoms and its Protocols shall apply directly in Bosnia and Herzegovina. These shall have priority over all other law.[50]

The core issue in this case then was the viability in practice of the limitation on discrimination set out in the 1995 Bosnia-Herzegovina Constitution in the paragraph above. If the limitation were honored the Court would need to declare that the restriction on Roma and Jews running for public office -specifically for a seat in the second chamber of the State Parliament (the House of Peoples) or for the Presidency-would violate the *European Convention on Human Rights* and aspects of its Protocols. The applicants contended that their exclusion from the polity in the specific manner described above violated (a) the *European Convention on Human Rights* Article 14 prohibition on discrimination in according the rights of the

[48] *Sejdic & Finci v. Bosnia and Herzegovina* European Court of Human Rights para 19, p. 14 (Citing The Concluding Observations on Bosnia and Herzegovina of the Committee on the Elimination of Racial Discrimination document CERD/C/BIH/CO/6 of 11 April 2006, paragraph 11).

[49] Arguably the discrimination against Mr. Finci could be characterized as both ethnically and religiously based but the applicant pleaded only ethnic discrimination. Note that *The International Convention on the Elimination of All Forms of Racial Discrimination* (entered into force in respect of Bosnia and Herzegovina on 16 July 1993) defines racial discrimination as "any distinction, exclusion, restriction or preference based on race, colour, descent, or national or ethnic origin which has the purpose or effect of nullifying or impairing the recognition, enjoyment or exercise, on an equal footing, of human rights and fundamental freedoms in the political, economic, social, cultural or any other field of public life." https://www.ohchr.org/en/instruments-mechanisms/instruments/international-convention-elimination-all-forms-racial (Accessed August 16, 2024).

[50] *Id. Sejdic & Finci v. Bosnia and Herzegovina* European Court of Human Rights para 14, pp. 8–9 Citing Article II para 2 of the 1995 Constitution of Bosnia-Herzegovina.

Convention[51](b) Article 3 of Protocol No. 1 to the Convention (right to free elections which includes the right to stand for election)[52] and (c) Article 1 of Protocol No. 12 to the Convention (a prohibition on legislated discrimination).[53] These violations they held constituted unjustified direct discrimination.

The Grand Chamber, relying on *The International Convention on the Elimination of All Forms of Racial Discrimination*[54] found that ethnic discrimination is a form of racial discrimination. Importantly the Court held that such discrimination is a particularly egregious kind of discrimination that threatens democracy and must be quashed.[55] *Thus although the 1995 Constitution of Bosnia-Herzegovina*[56] *was quite literally enmeshed in politics (this given that the Constitution was part of a peace treaty to end the conflict in the former Yugoslavia), the European Court of Human Rights still ruled on the substantive rights issues in the case.* This rather than relegating the discrimination condoned in the Constitution matter to politicians to address, if at all, at their discretion.

The European Court of Human Rights concluded that maintaining the discriminatory provisions in the Constitution was not a proportional response to achieving a legitimate objective (peace) post the Dayton Agreement (or using the terminology of the US Constitution one could say that the Grand Chamber found that the substantive due process rights of the applicants had been violated by their exclusion as part of the 'constituent peoples' and their being denied certain fundamental democratic rights as a result).[57] The Court concluded that "the applicants' continued ineligibility to stand for election to the House of Peoples of Bosnia and Herzegovina lacks an objective and reasonable justification and has therefore breached Article 14 of the European

[51] European Convention on Human Rights (hereafter 'The Convention') Article 14 "The enjoyment of the rights and freedoms set forth in [the] Convention shall be secured without discrimination on any ground such as sex, race, colour, language, religion, political or other opinion, national or social origin, association with a national minority, property, birth or other status." https://www.echr.coe.int/documents/convention_eng.pdf (Accessed August 16, 2024).

[52] European Court of Human Rights Guide to Article 3 of Protocol No. 1 to the European Convention on Human Rights (right to free elections): Article 3: "The High Contracting Parties undertake to hold free elections at reasonable intervals by secret ballot, under conditions which will ensure the free expression of the opinion of the people in the choice of the legislature." https://www.echr.coe.int/Documents/Guide_Art_3_Protocol_1_ENG.pdf (Accessed August 16, 2024).

[53] Article 1 of Protocol No. 12 to the European Convention general prohibition on discrimination: "1. The enjoyment of any right set forth by law shall be secured without discrimination on any ground such as sex, race, colour, language, religion, political or other opinion, national or social origin, association with a national minority, property, birth or other status. 2. No one shall be discriminated against by any public authority on any ground such as those mentioned in paragraph 1." http://www.worldlii.org/int/other/treaties/COETS/2000/3.html (Accessed August 16, 2024).

[54] *The International Convention on the Elimination of All Forms of Racial Discrimination* https://www.ohchr.org/en/instruments-mechanisms/instruments/international-convention-elimination-all-forms-racial (Accessed August 16, 2024).

[55] *Sejdic & Finci v. Bosnia and Herzegovina* European Court of Human Rights Para 43, p. 32.

[56] That Constitution *precluded* Jews and Roma and also additional groups designated "Others" within that jurisdiction being considered 'constituent peoples' who had full political rights.

[57] *Sejdic & Finci v. Bosnia and Herzegovina* European Court of Human Rights para 48–50 at p. 34.

Convention on Human Rights taken in conjunction with Article 3 of Protocol No. 1."[58] In light of the preceding finding the Court held it unnecessary to determine if there had also been a breach of Article 3 of Protocol No. 1 taken alone or under Article 1 of Protocol No. 12 as regards the House of Peoples.[59] With regard to the general prohibition against discrimination articulated in Article 1 of Protocol No. 12 (in relation to "any right set forth by law") the Court found Article 1 Protocol No. 12 violated by the bar against the applicants standing for election to the Presidency.[60]

The Court did *not* find that the applicants had been treated in a degrading fashion since the objective of the Constitution as part of the Dayton Peace Agreement had been to achieve peace between the constituent peoples who had been involved in the conflict in the former Yugoslavia. Other groups such as the Roma and Jews were not represented at the negotiations but there was, according to the Court, no intent to denigrate these other groups and hence there was no violation of Article 3 of the European Convention. The Court also rejected the claim that there had been a violation of the applicants' right to domestic remedy since the contested provisions were part of the Bosnia-Herzegovina Constitution.[61] The point of note, however, is that the European Court of Human Rights in this case affirmed the right of the applicants to, in essence, substantive due process rights relating to the liberty to stand for office. Here the applicants' right to non-discriminatory treatment in terms of their right to stand for election to the House of Peoples or the Presidency was affirmed by the Court. This notwithstanding the applicants being citizens but not members of the so-called 'constituent peoples' referenced in the Bosnia-Herzegovina Constitution. The judicial declarations regarding certain violations of the *European Convention on Human Rights and Freedoms* was held by the Court to be a sufficient remedy regarding any non-pecuniary damages.

1.3.2 New Zealand Youth Voting Rights Case

1.3.2.1 Introduction to *Make It 16 Incorporated v. Attorney General*

We discuss next the Supreme Court of New Zealand judgment in *Make it 16 Incorporated v. Attorney General*: a breakthrough ruling in which the Court resisted the temptation to skirt its obligation to rule on a question of fundamental rights. The case concerned whether or not a vulnerable minority, children of age 16 and 17, should have the right to vote in elections for their legislative representatives and in the national election for the Prime Minister.

[58] *Sejdic & Finci v. Bosnia and Herzegovina* European Court of Human Rights para 50 at p. 34.

[59] *Sejdic & Finci v. Bosnia and Herzegovina* European Court of Human Rights para 51 at pp. 34–35.

[60] *Sejdic & Finci v. Bosnia and Herzegovina* European Court of Human Rights para 56 at pp. 35–36.

[61] *Sejdic & Finci v. Bosnia and Herzegovina* European Court of Human Right para 60, p. 37.

The Make it 16 case more specifically addressed inconsistency between (a) the New Zealand Bill of Rights (1990) s. 19 which guarantees non-discrimination against persons based on age with regards to those aged 16 years and over and (b) the New Zealand 1993 Electoral Act (re federal elections) and the 2001 Local Electoral Act which sets a minimum voting age of 18 years. Make it 16 plaintiffs were comprised of a representative group of children in the contested voting age eligibility group petitioning the New Zealand Supreme Court (on appeal) for a Declaration affirming that the inconsistency is present. Previous New Zealand Supreme Court case law had established that such Declarations of Inconsistency between the New Zealand Bill of Rights and certain statutory legislation were within the jurisdiction of the New Zealand courts to issue. Following one such landmark case; legislation was enacted setting out the procedures to be followed by the legislature and Executive in response to such a Declaration of Inconsistency.

The New Zealand Supreme Court formulated the questions to be addressed in the case as follows (using the current author's rephrasing):

- **Question One:** Whether the Court's inquiry into the matter of child voting rights at age 16 (minimum voting age eligibility of 16) based on the implication of the New Zealand Bill of Rights s. 19 non-discrimination on the basis of 'age' provision (age being defined for these purposes as 16 or over) is within the Court's jurisdiction.
- **Question Two:** Whether the guarantee at s. 12 of the New Zealand Bill of Rights of voting rights for those New Zealanders aged 18 years and older in general elections overrides the s. 19 New Zealand Bill of Rights age-related non-discrimination guarantee (requiring non-discrimination in respect of those 16 and over).
- **Question Three:** Whether the inconsistency between (a) the non-discrimination based on age provision (for children aged 16 and over) at s. 19 of the New Zealand Bill of Rights with (b) electoral law setting the voting eligibility age at 18 for general elections[62] can be justified in a free and democratic society as per the requirement of s. 5 of the New Zealand Bill of Rights.

1.3.2.2 History of *Make It 16 Incorporated v. Attorney General* in the New Zealand Lower Courts

The New Zealand High Court, amongst other things, had ruled that setting voting age eligibility at 18 served a legitimate purpose, was proportionate in the burden it created; and was rationally connected to the governmental objective. That alleged

[62] S. 12 of the New Zealand Bill of Rights guaranteeing the vote to New Zealanders 18 and over does not apply to local body elections, but the New Zealand Supreme Court held that this was not a bar to the plaintiffs seeking a minimum voting age of 16 for both general and local elections See *Make it 16 Incorporated v. Attorney General* [2022] NZSC 134 para 39.

legitimate purpose was held to be "to implement the basic democratic principle that all qualified adults (as opposed to children) should be able to vote."[63]

The New Zealand Court of Appeal disagreed with the High Court's quite broad characterization of the alleged legitimate objective of having age 18 years as the eligible voting age. According to the Court of Appeal a proper justification under s. 5 of the New Zealand Bill of Rights required a *compelling rationale* in terms of the presumed social good (that is for why specifically the minimum age for voting eligibility was set so as to exclude 16 and 17-year-olds). The Court of Appeal held that as voting is a fundamental right in a democracy; simply having a voting age that was one of several reasonable options for a minimum voting eligibility age did *not* meet the s. 5 New Zealand Bill of Rights justification test for unequal treatment under the law in this bedrock rights domain. The New Zealand Court of Appeal thus held that s. 19 of the New Zealand Bill of Rights had been infringed *without* a s 5 justification. Yet the Court of Appeal declined to issue a Declaration of Inconsistency between the s. 19 anti-age discrimination guarantee of the New Zealand Bill of Rights and the New Zealand statutory election law governing local or general elections. Instead *the Court of Appeal essentially turned the question of the fundamental human rights of sixteen and seventeen-year-old New Zealanders in respect of voting rights into a discretionary legislative political matter*. This by the New Zealand Court of Appeal holding that the Court could properly exercise restraint and decline to offer relief in the form of a Declaration of Inconsistency "for reasons of comity among or deference towards other branches of government."[64] In doing so then the New Zealand Court of Appeal punted on a fundamental human rights question. The Court of Appeal denied relief (a Declaration of Inconsistency) where in fact its own legal analysis would suggest that some at least preliminary form of relief for the plaintiffs through the Courts was justified and perhaps overdue.

That contentious fundamental human rights issues are often framed as 'culture war' themes subject to heated public debate, it is here contended, does *not*, from a legal perspective, thereby transform those issues into simply political questions. Nonetheless the New Zealand Court of Appeal, on the reading here, asserts just such a scenario when it characterizes minimum voting age as "… an intensely and quintessentially political issue involving the democratic process itself and on which there are a range of reasonable views" such that [therefore] "we choose to exercise restraint and decline the application for declarations."[65] Yet the Court of Appeal itself held a legal perspective (noting the lack of an articulated compelling governmental purpose in excluding 16 and 17-year- olds from the vote); on the view here, incompatible with the failure to issue a 'Declaration of Inconsistency.' That is,

---

[63] *Make It 16 Inc v Attorney-General* [2020] NZHC 2630, [2020] 3 NZLR 481 (Doogue J) [HC judgment] para 95–96.

[64] *Make It 16 Inc v Attorney-General* [2021] NZCA 681, [2022] 2 NZLR 440 (French, Miller and Courtney JJ) [CA judgment]. Para 61.

[65] *Make It 16 Inc v Attorney-General* [2021] NZCA 681, para 62.

the Court of Appeal found that the Attorney-General had *not* demonstrated a justified basis in a free and democratic society for the age-based discrimination against New Zealand 16 and 17-year-olds in the right to vote. At the same time, the Appeal Court ruled that "The decision rests not on a positive finding that discrimination on grounds of age cannot be justified but on what we have held to be a failure to attempt to justify the existing age limit."[66] That the Court nonetheless declined to issue a Declaration of Inconsistency, on the view here, was (a) to fail to affirm a key substantive due process right for an identifiable group of New Zealand citizens (freedom of expression through the vote) and (b) to do so notwithstanding the s. 19 New Zealand Bill of Rights non-discrimination provision. This, on the current author's respectful view, was to abrogate the Court's duty.

Deference to other branches of government (as in the New Zealand Court of Appeal *Make it 16* youth voting decision) is not, it is here contended, an acceptable rationale in a democracy for the courts (a) declining to rule to clarify or affirm fundamental rights under a Bill of Rights as here (or, as the case may be, a constitution) and (b) the failure to better create the conditions for those rights being respected through legislation. It is here argued that it is the duty of the courts to affirm fundamental human rights when they are under threat or infringed and reasonable relief is feasibly available if judicially granted.

The Court of Appeal in *Make it 16*, however, it seems to the current author, with respect, inappropriately minimizes the consequences of its failure to issue a Declaration of Inconsistency in this case when it states:

> A declaration of inconsistency is not a declaration of a legal right and the usual presumption of a remedy where a wrong has been established in the judicial review context does not apply with the same force.[67]

The aforementioned *Make it 16* Court of Appeal statement, it is here argued, is technically correct as to the Declaration of Inconsistency in and of itself but not its implications. A Declaration of Inconsistency in *Make it 16* would have, by implication, given the facts and the Court's reasoning (as to the Attorney General's lack of justification for the voting age discrimination against 16- and 17-year-olds) (a) further clarified and affirmed that there was no legal basis to undemocratically deny 16 and 17-year-olds the vote and (b) thereby would have possibly, at least implicitly, affirmed their right to vote. Further, the Declaration of Inconsistency arguably would have served to better highlight the need for a legislative remedy for the inconsistency between the New Zealand electoral law stipulated age eligibility for the vote of 18 and the non-discrimination rights guarantees for 16 and 17- year-olds incorporated in the New Zealand Bill of Rights at s. 19.

As will next be discussed; the New Zealand Supreme Court took a different tact. The New Zealand Supreme Court *resisted* sidestepping the fundamental human rights issue and the temptation to frame the issue as a purely political one calling

---

[66] *Make It 16 Inc v Attorney-General* [2021] NZCA 681, para 62.

[67] *Make It 16 Inc v Attorney-General* [2021] NZCA 681, para 60.

for deference to other branches of government such that a Declaration of Inconsistency should not be issued.

1.3.2.3 The New Zealand Supreme Court Ruling in *Make It 16* (*Make It 16 Incorporated v. Attorney General* [2022] NZSC 134)

The New Zealand Supreme Court rejected the Attorney-General's position that since Parliament had set out a procedure for changing the minimum voting age[68] the Courts should not enter the fray and make a preemptive decision that might impact the public's view. The New Zealand Supreme Court held that the making of such a Declaration of Inconsistency was consistent with the role of the courts in New Zealand "particularly where fundamental rights are involved."[69] In fact the New Zealand Supreme Court emphasized its view (concurrent with that of the New Zealand High Court in the matter) that where fundamental human rights are at issue, as with the minimum voting age question; the matter cannot be conceptualized as entirely political.[70] The New Zealand Supreme Court held in the *Make It 16* case that (a) it must fulfill its responsibility to declare what the law is pertaining to the issue at hand and (b) if a Declaration of Inconsistency is issued by the Court then Parliament has the responsibility under New Zealand statutory law to respond to that Declaration and ensure that a debate in Parliament on the matter be held.

The New Zealand Supreme Court further highlighted the critical point that in declaring, in a particular instance, the inconsistency between certain New Zealand statutory law and particular provisions of the New Zealand Bill of Rights or with the *European Convention on Human Rights*; the Court does *not* usurp the power and function of Parliament. It remains still for Parliament to decide if and how it will respond.[71] The 'Declaration of Inconsistency', however, on the view here, sets out the incompatibility of the contested law with democratic values and principles thus (a) educating the public on whether their rights are being properly protected by government and (b) laying bare what is at stake in the government's response to the Declaration. In that sense it would be reasonable, it is here suggested, to contend that a Declaration of Inconsistency increases the chance for public pressure on government to act democratically and resolve the inconsistency in such a way as to protect the fundamental human right(s) at issue.

The New Zealand Supreme Court further noted that the Bill of Rights s. 12 guarantee of the right of all New Zealanders to the vote who are 18 or over does *not*

---

[68] To change the minimum voting age for general elections would require a super-majority in Parliament or support for the new minimum age for general elections through a referendum of eligible voters aged 18 and over *Make it 16 Incorporated v. Attorney General* [2022] NZSC 134 para 27 The process for changing the minimum voting age in local elections is more straightforward as that age is not entrenched.

[69] *Make it 16 Incorporated v. Attorney General* [2022] NZSC 134 para 28.

[70] *Make it 16 Incorporated v. Attorney General* [2022] NZSC para 28.

[71] *Make it 16 Incorporated v. Attorney General* [2022] NZSC para 32.

at all preclude a minimum voting age being lowered to 16 years. Hence (a) s. 12 and s. 19 of the New Zealand Bill of Rights are *not* incompatible on the New Zealand Supreme Court view and (b) s. 12 is not a bar to lowering the minimum voting age to 16.[72] Note also that the evidence before the Zealand Supreme Court was that 16 and 17-year-olds are competent to vote and the New Zealand Attorney-General offered nothing in rebuttal on that point.[73]

For the New Zealand Supreme Court then the question remaining was whether 18, being one of a number of reasonable options for a minimum voting age, can be justified as the arbitrary selection in a democratic and free society such as New Zealand. The New Zealand Supreme Court held that given s. 19 of the New Zealand Bill of Rights (barring discrimination based on age for those 16 and over) the Attorney-General had to show "why 18 was chosen as opposed to 16 or 17" as the legislated minimum voting age.[74] The Attorney-General, however, had not sought to show why 16 and 17- year-olds should be barred from the vote but only argued, as mentioned, that 18 was a reasonable choice given that, for instance, (a) several other countries have adopted that minimum voting age, and (b) 18-year-olds assume new legal rights such as the right to enter into contracts.[75] When considering restrictions on fundamental human rights, however, (as the then Chief Justice of the Canadian Supreme Court, Justice McLachlin states) it is to be understood that "*core democratic rights … do not fall within* a *'range of acceptable alternatives' among which Parliament may pick and choose at its discretion* (emphasis added)."[76]

The New Zealand Supreme Court issued the Declaration of Inconsistency affirming that there is an inconsistency between (a) the anti-age discrimination clause s. 19 of the New Zealand Bill of Rights (where age is defined as 16 and older) and (b) the New Zealand electoral law minimum voting age of 18.[77] The New Zealand Supreme Court based its decision to do so in large part, though not exclusively, on the following: "that the case involves "…the protection of the fundamental rights of a minority group."[78] The New Zealand Supreme Court maintained that since children aged 16 and 17 are a vulnerable minority; the Courts may be the only avenue realistically available to seek a form of relief (the Declaration of Inconsistency) on the minimum voting age issue for this identifiable group.

---

[72] *Make it 16 Incorporated v. Attorney General* [2022] NZSC para 36 and 40.

[73] *Make it 16 Incorporated v. Attorney General* [2022] NZSC paras 53, 56, 57.

[74] *Make it 16 Incorporated v. Attorney General* [2022] NZSC para 45.

[75] *Make it 16 Incorporated v. Attorney General* [2022] NZSC paras 44 and 45.

[76] *Make it 16 Incorporated v. Attorney General* [2022] NZSC at para 51 Citing *Sauvé v Canada (Chief Electoral Officer)* 2002 SCC 68, [2002] 3 SCR 519 at para 13. Yet it is to be noted that Canada has declined to lower the voting age to 16 without demonstrable evidence that 18 as the minimum voting age ensures a compelling legitimate government objective while 16 does not.

[77] See *Make it 16 Incorporated v. Attorney General* [2022] NZSC 134 para 72 for the exact wording of the Declaration of Inconsistency in this case.

[78] See *Make it 16 Incorporated v. Attorney General* [2022] NZSC 134 para 67.

Then Prime Minister of New Zealand, Jacinda Ardern had committed to the government drafting legislation to establish a minimum voting age of 16 and to bringing the bill to Parliament to decide. However, subsequently the Prime Minister Jacinda Ardern resigned, and the new Prime Minister has tabled the issue for the time being. Thus, the New Zealand Supreme Court's finding that the child plaintiffs' civil/political fundamental right is violated by the minimum voting age set at 18 (a proxy for adulthood) has led to the New Zealand government formally being alerted to the compelling issue of a fundamental rights violation. Whether a failure of Parliament to address the matter, if such be the case, comes at any political cost remains to be seen.[79]

1.4 Concluding Comment

As the cases discussed in this introduction illustrate; both enumerated and non-enumerated fundamental rights notions; especially as affects vulnerable groups; are under threat when (a) courts reframe, arguably capriciously, contested fundamental human rights issues into purely political questions and/or (b) decline to determine whether the government has violated the principles and values of *democratic rule of law* which is grounded first and foremost on respect for the human dignity of all persons. The peril of such an approach to democracy hauntingly echoes, on the view here, in Justice Taney words when he wrote the discredited majority ruling in *Dred Scott* and stated: "It is not the province of the court to decide upon the justice or injustice…of these laws."[80] (referring to the State laws that ostensibly stripped enslaved persons of African descent (an identifiable group) of all rights and privileges under the Fifth Amendment of the US Constitution).

It is apparent, however, that in declaring what is the law the Court is simultaneously deciding whether it meets the threshold of legitimacy as law in a democracy. The Courts in a democracy affirm then not simply rule of law but *democratic rule of law*. The latter distinguishes itself in its being grounded on substantive human rights. In that sense the courts in a democracy then in deciding on the constitutionality of the law speak *ipso facto* to whether justice is served by the law at issue. Indeed, Taney did address the justice issue despite his disclaimer of alleged neutral legal analysis. Taney (himself a slaveowner) tragically, however, defended the misguided fantastical justness of property rights over human beings of African descent

[79]McClure, Tess (2022) Ardern promises bill to lower voting age to 16 in New Zealand after discrimination ruling *The Guardian* Mon 21 Nov 2022 04.27 GMT https://www.theguardian.com/world/2022/nov/21/voting-age-of-18-is-discriminatory-new-zealand-supreme-court-rules (Accessed August 16, 2024).

[80]National Archives Milestone Documents Dred Scott majority ruling (1857) *Dred Scott v Sanford* https://www.archives.gov/milestone-documents/dred-scott-v-sandford (Accessed August 16, 2024).

notwithstanding the natural inherent right to freedom and dignity of the enslaved as for all other peoples.

The Dred Scott United States Supreme Court majority thus adopted a non-democratic interpretation of the Constitution inconsistent with the values of the Declaration of Independence that preceded and inspired it. Justice Taney, however, in *Dred Scott* rejected that notion of inconsistency between the Constitution's slave affirming clauses and the Declaration of Independence affirmation of the liberty rights of all men. Justice Taney thus, based on his worldview, abandoned originalism in that regard and rejected the plain meaning of the Declaration's text that "... all men are created equal...endowed ...with certain unalienable Rights, that among these are Life, Liberty and the pursuit of Happiness"[81] as words that "embraced the whole human family."[82] This he based *not* on legal analysis but on the fact that (a) those who signed the Declaration of Independence were, amongst them, also slave holders and (b) erroneously maintaining, in essence, that the architects of the Declaration of Independence were somehow immune from the possibility of committing acts of oppression and cruelty.

It has been held by some constitutional scholars, such as Nikolas Bowie of Harvard Law, that *Dred Scott* is evidence that "what makes something constitutional is not its substantive justice but the ability of someone to justify it using constitutional vocabulary."[83] What Bowie refers to, however, is of course but *perceived* constitutionality too often wrongly based. It is the responsibility then of 'We the People' to challenge as unconstitutional such judicial rulings that would undermine or ignore substantive justice matters and ultimately then democracy itself grounded on that justice. This monograph hopefully is a small but valuable contribution in that regard.

Materials

Declaration of Independence (July 4, 1776) https://docs.house.gov/meetings/GO/GO00/20220929/115171/HHRG-117-GO00-20220929-SD010.pdf (Accessed August 16, 2024)

European Convention on Human Rights https://www.echr.coe.int/documents/convention_eng.pdf (Accessed August 16, 2024)

European Court of Human Rights Guide to Article 3 of Protocol No. 1 to the European Convention on Human Rights (right to free elections) https://www.

[81] Declaration of Independence (July 4, 1776) https://docs.house.gov/meetings/GO/GO00/20220929/115171/HHRG-117-GO00-20220929-SD010.pdf (Accessed August 16, 2024).

[82] National Archives Milestone Documents Dred Scott majority ruling (1857) *Dred Scott v Sanford* https://www.archives.gov/milestone-documents/dred-scott-v-sandford (Accessed August 16, 2024).

[83] Gersen (2021).

echr.coe.int/Documents/Guide_Art_3_Protocol_1_ENG.pdf (Accessed August 16, 2024)

Legal Information Institute, Cornell Law School, Rational Basis Test https://www.law.cornell.edu/wex/rational_basis_test (Accessed August 16, 2024)

McClure, Tess (2022) Ardern promises bill to lower voting age to 16 in New Zealand after discrimination ruling *The Guardian* Mon 21 Nov 2022 04.27 GMT. https://www.theguardian.com/world/2022/nov/21/voting-age-of-18-is-discriminatory-new-zealand-supreme-court-rules. (Accessed August 16, 2024)

National Archives Milestone Documents *Dred Scott* Justice Taney majority ruling (1857) *Dred Scott v Sanford* https://www.archives.gov/milestone-documents/dred-scott-v-sandford (Accessed August 16, 2024)

National Constitution Centre: The Declaration of Independence and its Influence on the US Constitution https://constitutioncenter.org/news-debate/podcasts/the-declaration-of-independence-and-its-influence-on-the-constitution?gclid=CjwKCAiAhKycBhAQEiwAgf19ev_8pAJ0IQbvM5GyLaWZIGbji4qD1VM-oR8CbofBbxmDHru9TQeXhhoC9f4QAvD_BwE (Accessed August 16, 2024)

Protocol No. 12 to the European Convention Article 1 General prohibition on discrimination http://www.worldlii.org/int/other/treaties/COETS/2000/3.html (Accessed August 16, 2024)

The International Convention on the Elimination of All Forms of Racial Discrimination (entered into force in respect of Bosnia and Herzegovina on 16 July 1993 https://www.ohchr.org/en/instruments-mechanisms/instruments/international-convention-elimination-all-forms-racial (Accessed August 16, 2024)

US Congress Modern Doctrine on Privileges or Immunities Clause, Constitution Annotated https://constitution.congress.gov/browse/essay/amdt14-S1-2-2/ALDE_00000815/#essay-1 (Accessed August 16, 2024)

United States Supreme Court Case Law

Dred Scott v Sanford 60 U.S. 393 (1857) Excerpts from the Majority and Dissenting Opinions (United States Supreme Court) Bill of Rights Institute https://billofrightsinstitute.org/e-lessons/dred-scott-v-sanford-1857-excerpts-from-majority-and-dissenting-opinions (Accessed August 16, 2024)

Roe v Wade 410 U.S. 113 (1973) (United States Supreme Court) Decided January 22, 1973

Thomas E. Dobbs, State Health Officer of the Mississippi Department of Health et al. v Jackson Women's Health Organization et al United States Supreme Court No. 19-1392. October term 2021 Decided June 24, 2022

Canadian Case Law

Sauvé v Canada (Chief Electoral Officer) (Supreme Court of Canada) 2002 SCC 68, [2002] 3 SCR 519

European Case Law

Sejdic & Finci v. Bosnia and Herzegovina European Court of Human Rights (Applications nos. 27996/06 and 34836/06) Grand Chamber Judgement 22 December 2009

New Zealand Case Law

Make it 16 Incorporated v. Attorney General [2022] NEW ZEALAND SC [SC judgment 14/2022 (Supreme Court of New Zealand) https://www.courtsofNewZealand.govt.NewZealand/assets/cases/Case-synopses/NEWZEALAND SC/20220704-Make-it-16-synopsis.pdf (Accessed August 16, 2024)

Make It 16 Inc v Attorney-General [2021] NEW ZEALAND CA 681, [2022] 2 NEW ZEALAND LR 440 (French, Miller and Courtney JJ) [CA judgment] (Court of Appeal of New Zealand)

Make It 16 Inc v Attorney-General [2020] NEW ZEALAND HC 2630, [2020] 3 NEW ZEALAND LR 481 (Doogue J) [HC judgment] (High Court of New Zealand)

References

Chemerinsky E (1999) Substantive due process. Touro Law Rev 15:1501–1534

Cole D (2003) Are foreign nationals entitled to the same constitutional rights as citizens? Georgetown University Law Center. https://scholarship.law.georgetown.edu/facpub/297/. Accessed 16 Aug 2024

Gersen JS (2021) The importance of teaching Dred Scott. The New Yorker, 8 June 2021. https://www.newyorker.com/news/our-columnists/the-importance-of-teaching-dred-scott. Accessed 16 Aug 2024

Grover SC (2009) A response to Bagaric and Allan's "the vacuous concept of dignity". Int J Hum Rights 13(4):615–622

Chapter 2
Litigating the Politics of Religious Conservatism in Public Life

Abstract In *303 Creative* the plaintiff claims that her First Amendment right to free speech/free expression would be violated by the State of Colorado under its public accommodation statute if she were required to offer her planned custom wedding web design service also to same-sex couples. This, on her view, would amount to being compelled to communicate, contrary to her sincerely held religious belief, that same-sex marriages are *bona fide* in every way (compelled speech). Plaintiff requested *pre-enforcement relief* through an exemption (based on an alleged compelled speech First Amendment ground) such that she could lawfully deny the custom wedding web service to same-sex couples. The government held that it is the service and not speech that would be compelled given that the service was stipulated to be a public accommodation. The State argued that in this case the couple's status (as same sex) is inextricably linked to why plaintiff wishes an exemption from providing her expressive custom wedding web service to that protected group. That fact, the State maintains, runs afoul of public accommodation law requirements. *303 Creative* highlights the culture war surrounding the LGBTQ plus community and its, to some conservatives, being a perceived threat to religious conservatism.

2.1 303 Creative, Lori Smith v Aubrey Elenis et al. (United States Supreme Court)

The case *303 Creative*[1] concerns a web designer, Lori Smith, who hoped to expand her business to include a custom wedding web design service. It is important to understand that it was stipulated by the parties that the anticipated custom wedding web design business would be a public accommodation. The issue was whether

[1] 303 Creative, Lori Smith v Aubrey Elenis et al. (hereafter also referred to as *Creative* or 303 Creative or *Creative LLC* Argued December 5, 2022 Case Documents https://www.supremecourt.gov/search.aspx?filename=/docket/docketfiles/html/public/21-476.html (Accessed August 20, 2024) Oral Argument United States Supreme Court audio C-Span https://www.c-span.org/video/?524449-1/303-creative-llc-v-elenis-oral-argument (Accessed August 20, 2024).

S. C. Grover, *Litigating the Politics of Human Rights*, Ius Gentium: Comparative Perspectives on Law and Justice 121, https://doi.org/10.1007/978-3-031-82463-0_2

Ms. Smith would be entitled to an exemption from compliance with the Colorado public accommodation law such that she would not need to design wedding websites that announced same-sex weddings thus excluding same-sex couples as clients. Ms. Smith would then be declining to provide her custom wedding web design service to an entire protected class (namely all same-sex couple members of the LGBTQ plus community who wished to use her service to announce their wedding). This request for an exemption was based on the fact that same-sex weddings are inconsistent with Ms. Smith's sincerely and deeply held religious beliefs and her interpretations of Christian scripture.

Ms. Smith alleges that the Colorado Anti-Discrimination Act would compel her to create speech on her custom wedding web pages that celebrates same-sex marriage when in fact her faith rejects the sanctity of same-sex marriage. Ms. Smith, it was agreed by the parties, *is* willing to offer services to members of the LGBTQ plus community should the website contracted for *not* relate to the issue of same-sex marriage. The example was given that she would be agreeable to creating a website, for example, for a gay client promoting an animal shelter through the website.[2] Further Ms. Smith wishes to post a statement on the planned wedding website that she will create web pages that celebrate heterosexual marriage and is unable for religious reasons to create wedding web pages that also honor and celebrate same-sex marriage. However, Ms. Smith fears the disclaimer would run afoul of the State of Colorado's Anti-Discrimination Act (specifically its Communications Clause) and hence holds she would need to be silent and not post a disclaimer or risk legal penalty. In fact, such a disclaimer would have run afoul of the State of Colorado's Anti-Discrimination Act at the time of the case.

In framing the issue in terms of her First Amendment free expression rights, Ms. Smith argues that she does not seek to discriminate against any identifiable class of protected persons (i.e., same-sex couples) in her custom wedding website service. She argues that she rather is merely advancing her right to exercise her free speech/free expression First Amendment rights as an artist. The current author argues, in contrast, however, that Ms. Smith's First Amendment right to free speech/free expression would not have been undercut by the State of Colorado's Anti-Discrimination Act (i.e., should Ms. Smith have failed to receive the exemption she sought). Rather it is Ms. Smith who, on this respectful analysis, exhorts the State (through her requested exemption based on alleged 'compelled speech') to suppress the free speech rights of same-sex couple otherwise prospective clients of her custom wedding web service. This in that an exemption to the State of Colorado's Anti-Discrimination Act for Ms. Smith would mean that *same-sex couples would not be permitted to speak on her custom wedding website.* Thus, those same-sex couples would have been denied the opportunity to freely express, on Ms. Smith's proposed

---

[2]Robinson, S (2022) Free Speech Case Tests Whether Anti-Discrimination Laws Can Compel Artistic Work *Maine Wire* (5 December, 2022) https://www.themainewire.com/2022/12/free-speech-case-tests-whether-anti-discrimination-laws-can-compel-artistic-work/ (Accessed August 20, 2024).

custom wedding web pages (a public accommodation), *their* celebratory sentiments about getting married. On the view here then the jeopardy is to the free expression rights of same-sex couple otherwise prospective clients of Ms. Smith's custom wedding design service as a result of Ms. Smith petition for an exemption (which as will be discussed was held by the US Supreme Court to be in order).

The government argued that Ms. Smith was free to custom design her wedding websites as she pleased. The wedding web designs could all, for instance, be religiously based quoting the Bible or even touting heterosexual marriage as the only valid marriage. However, as a public accommodation that service would still have to be accessible to same-sex couples as well. The government's position in *303 Creative* is then that the entrepreneur may choose what are the contours of their service and the range and type of product they sell. However, if that service or product is offered to the public then the service or product must be offered to all and not exclude protected classes i.e., if the custom wedding web service on all of the website pages quotes scripture blessing marriage, then same-sex couples must be able to access that custom wedding design service also if they wish to do so.

This author is in accord with the government's position in the case that since the entrepreneur decides the contours of the service or the type and range of product offered, and also if it should involve speech, there is no compelled speech. Rather there is 'compelled service' insofar as the inability to deny access to statutorily protected classes of persons.[3] That is; if the entrepreneur is willing to offer the speech as part of the service to heterosexual couples but will not offer the *same speech* (same message of celebration of a wedding, expressions of love etc.) to a same-sex couple then the service violates public accommodation law.[4] The State is not requiring Ms. Smith to create or communicate any message on her custom wedding web pages she would not be offering to heterosexual couples. In short, the Colorado public accommodation law reflects the State's interest in quashing discrimination in public accommodation. This in order that protected classes can also be full participating members of the community and access products and services that the prospective clients maintain impact the quality of their lives. As to the First Amendment issue, the State also argued that Ms. Smith sought to define her service in terms of protected status. The latter such that she would refuse to craft speech that she would normally craft and custom design as an artistic element in a wedding

---

[3] Colorado argued in *303 Creative* that any impact on speech in this case (such as mentioning on the website the names of the couple such that the indication is that they are a same-sex couple) due to application of the anti-discrimination law is legally permissible. This since that impact on speech is incidental to the neutral generally applicable public accommodation regulation requiring all businesses that are public accommodations to allow access to members of protected groups. In any case, all the speech Ms. Smith objects to would not be to convey *her* message/sentiments but that of the same-sex couple and would be perceived as such by viewers of the wedding website.

[4] Ms. Smith insists that she seeks the exemption not based on who the client couple is but rather the message she is being asked to create though arguably the wedding message is essentially the same for same-sex and opposite-sex couples in content (a celebration of the marital union).

announcement/story if that speech were a message to be conveyed at the behest of a same-sex prospective client couple instead of a heterosexual couple.

On the view here (*as was also argued in the case by the government*), it would be the sentiments/message of the same-sex couple conveyed on the custom wedding website. However, that message would be crafted in an artistic form in part through speech/words as also an artistic element designed by Lori Smith. It is in part then that artistic service she would wish to decline for same-sex couples. *Hence the message at issue here is that of the client-its artistic form given shape by Ms. Lori Smith.* Justice Jackson pointed out that in the case at bar no facts had been adduced showing that anyone would perceive the content of the couple's wedding announcement and wedding story as anything but the same-sex couple's sentiments rather than that of the web designer. On the respectful analysis here, the State of Colorado would *not,* in enforcing its public accommodation law, be compelling *Ms. Lori Smith's speech* in any way. Nor would the State be dictating how Ms. Smith would give artistic form to the sentiments that her same-sex and heterosexual client couples wish to convey on the custom wedding website they contract with her. The State under its public accommodation law is only concerned with accessibility of the service also to members of protected classes given that the commercial service in question is being offered to the public.

The view on the current author's analysis is that there would be harm to members of a protected group (the LGBTQ plus community) if Ms. Lori Smith can lawfully decline to create custom wedding webpages for a same-sex couple. This where that refusal is based on the professed claim that such a custom wedding announcement expressing the same-sex couple's loving sentiments is 'compelled speech' that offends her (Ms. Smith's) conscience. If it is lawful for Ms. Smith to refuse service on an alleged compelled speech ground where the message is that of the same-sex couple client (as this author contends it is) then it is arguably Ms. Smith who succeeds in silencing the same-sex couple's free expression. The latter discrimination (on the analysis here) *in effect* then would occur under the State's imprimatur through the grant of an exemption to the Colorado Anti-Discrimination Act. This by Ms. Smith successfully entreating the State of Colorado to allow her to decline to communicate same-sex couples' wedding announcements and wedding stories via her custom designed wedding website despite that service being offered to the public.

That same-sex couple's message on the Smith custom wedding website most probably would involve content expressing the same-sex couple's love for each other and joy in their upcoming wedding. The latter content then would be analogous generally in that way to the proposed custom wedding website content of the heterosexual couple clients. Thus, ultimately even if for the same-sex couple the custom wedding message content *per se* is quite comparable overall to that for a heterosexual client couple; the former would be denied service. *It is then the fact of the union being same sex, the client identity, that the plaintiff holds transforms the speech (as art) into compelled speech that violates her conscience.* Ms. Smith objects then on religious grounds to granting the prospective same-sex client couple access to her custom wedding website design service to announce their same-sex wedding. However, the *meaning content* of the same-sex couple's wedding announcement/story is the *client couple's message.* Ms. Smith has but given the wedding announcement/story artistic form, including with selected words as graphic and symbolic design elements, and provided an internet site. Thus Ms. Smith's speech, on the view here, is *not* compelled.

The web designer (as pointed out in one of the hypotheticals discussed by the US Supreme Court Justices in the case) could, furthermore, include a disclaimer marked as a message from the web designer. That disclaimer could lawfully express (as discussed by the Dissenting US Supreme Court Justices in the case) the position that 303 Creative, consistent with the proprietor's religious perspective, considers only heterosexual marriage as valid marriage though same-sex couples may access the service. It is here suggested that such a disclaimer could even include explicit wording saying that Creative's hosting also same-sex couples on the custom wedding website should not be interpreted as an endorsement of same-sex marriage. Such a disclaimer would in all likelihood *not* have run afoul of Colorado's public accommodation law 'communications clause' even at the time the case was brought. This since the disclaimer would not say the custom wedding web service would, on religious grounds, be denied to same-sex couples and same-sex couples would not in fact be denied access to the service. Nor would same-sex couples be told that they are unwelcome as 303 Creative custom wedding web design clients.

On the view here, the claims by certain amici (for example the Centre for Constitutional Jurisprudence, Claremont Institute)[5] that Ms. Smith is being compelled to speak a message and/or affirm a message that she fundamentally disagrees with while her own speech is being censored, are erroneous. Such claims are fundamentally inconsistent with the pre-enforcement case specifics as framed by the plaintiff. Here speech *attributed to the web designer* can be fully aligned with her religious/ideological and political perspective. On the analysis here, consistent with Colorado's position, it would appear that *Creative* would under Colorado's Anti-Discrimination Act simply not be permitted by the State to use an unsupported allegation of compelled speech as a shield for discrimination in denying a public accommodation with that denial being in fact based on a specific protected status (sexual orientation).

If the same-sex couple wanted wording on the custom wedding website such as "God blesses this union"; according to Colorado's argument in *303 Creative*, this service could lawfully be denied only if it can be shown that the website designer would refuse to speak that message for anyone (a couple who are members of the LGBTQ plus community or a couple who are members of the heterosexual community). The business is permitted under Colorado public accommodation law to indicate its values and beliefs and communicate these to the public and shape its

[5]Amicus Brief, Centre for Constitutional Jurisprudence, Claremont Institute, United States Supreme Court In 303 Creative LLC et al. v Aubrey Elenis et al. https://www.supremecourt.gov/DocketPDF/21/21-476/198003/20211028133149710_21-476%20CCJ%20ISO%20Cert.pdf (Accessed August 20, 2024).

service in that way as it wishes. At the same time, however, as a public accommodation the service, in whatever form, must be available to all. The custom wedding website business offered as a public accommodation is *not* permitted then to deny service on the basis of objection to the *perceived* expressive message being, in Ms. Smith's opinion, *ipso facto* shaped by client status. Here Ms. Smith wishes to be exempt from offering her planned custom wedding web service to same-sex couples on the contention that (1) the client's protected status (identity) shapes the message the client wishes to convey and which she is crafting as an art piece and posting and (2) thus this scenario, she alleges, constitutes 'compelled speech' that relays a message that violates her deeply held religious beliefs. Yet, even if the plaintiff is correct on the view that the same-sex couple's sexual orientation shapes in some way whatever message announces their nuptials; nonetheless that message is *not* Ms. Smith's but that of the client as was previously discussed. Therefore, the 'compelled speech' claim arguably is, on the view here, again defeated. Further the identity of couples as heterosexual, on Ms. Smith's view, also shapes the message and she does not plan to bar them from her custom wedding web design service. So too, on the analysis here, gender identity or sexual orientation (both prohibited grounds of discrimination) cannot lawfully be a bar for prospective same-sex couple clients to accessing Ms. Smith's public accommodation custom wedding website design business.

It would appear that the plaintiff does not rely on objective criteria as indicia of what constitutes 'compelled speech' but rather her subjective experience. As a result then, on the plaintiff's view, any commercial service offered to the public that involves (1) some form of artistic expression of a message/meaning *the client* wishes to convey and (2) uses some form of speech, graphics, or symbolic speech *as design elements* crafted by the artist in consultation with the client to artistically convey *the client message* could be held by the creator of that artistic expression to be 'compelled speech' (i.e., on the grounds of religious or conscientious objections) as opposed to 'compelled service.'[6] In this instance (on the analysis here) the artistic creator, Ms. Smith, the custom wedding website designer, disapproves of the member of the protected class (a same-sex couple) having the free expression right to convey *their* wedding message through Smith's custom wedding web design business (a public accommodation). This no matter how innocuous the message (i.e., the message 'you are invited to come and celebrate our love at our wedding service') would appear to be. Ms. Smith's planned custom wedding web design business was to be a commercial business offering to the public the very service (artistically custom designed wedding web pages using selected speech and other graphic artistic elements) she contends need not in her case be offered to same-sex couples.

[6]The plaintiff seems to hold that alleged 'compelled speech' becomes an issue only in respect of artistic expression where there is speech or symbolic speech involved as an artistic design element in the context of *artistic expression* offered as a service. This since then the artist's First Amendment free expression right is purportedly engaged. This though it is here argued that there would be no violation of the artist's First Amendment free speech right under Colorado Anti-Discrimination Act on the facts of the 303 Creative case.

Note that (as the dissenting justices in Creative argued) many services could also be conceptualized as communicating a message through 'symbolic speech.' So interpreted then, on Ms. Smith's analysis, a vast range of artists could then potentially decline to offer a public accommodation service to selected protected groups on the alleged ground of 'compelled speech'. The Creative case then, on the view here, involves a plaintiff attempting to ensure that public accommodation laws cannot compel any artist/content creator *to offer a service* to a client where the identity of the client allegedly shapes the expressive message in a way that offends the provider's religious or ethical/moral values. This being the case here even though the message meaning conveyed is itself objectively comparable to that communicated by client couples (heterosexual couples) whose identity (sexual orientation) Ms. Smith does not find problematic in the context of her custom wedding web design business.

In oral argument Ms. Smith's representative erroneously (on the respectful view here) characterized the situation as one in which another party was shaping what message Ms. Smith was creating through *her speech* thus compelling *her speech.* In opposition to the latter characterization by the plaintiff, it is to be emphasized, however, that the artistic form (a form that may include selected words and other graphics) is chosen by Ms. Smith *in consultation with the client* (as is the routine in her business) to *convey the client's message.* Hence the speech is *not* Ms. Smith's insofar as its intent and meaning is to convey the client's and not Ms. Smith's emotive message. Therefore, on the analysis here, Ms. Smith's First Amendment right as an artist is not in any way interfered with by government pursuant to Colorado's public accommodation anti-discrimination regulations. Rather it is, on the view here, Ms. Smith's ability to discriminate against the LGBTQ plus community in denying the same=sex couple members of that community access to her custom wedding website design service that is blocked by the Colorado public accommodation law.

On the analysis here, it is access to Ms. Smith's custom designed wedding website to host *not* Ms. Smith's message but rather that of the same-sex couple's (a message *artistically designed* by Ms. Smith) that is at the heart of the case. Therefore, it is, on the respectful view here, erroneous to argue, as the plaintiff does, that Colorado has wrongly framed (alleged) 'compelled speech' as 'compelled service.' On the view here then it is Ms. Smith (through her sought-after exemption to the public accommodation law notwithstanding the fact that her custom wedding website is a public accommodation business service with other than a primary religious purpose) who seeks to silence, with the State's backing, the same-sex couple*'s* ability to communicate *their* wedding announcement on her website. This even though the message would be comparable to those wedding announcements/stories for heterosexual couples. The State of Colorado, in contrast, seeks to affirm its right to compel Ms. Smith *to provide that public accommodation service equitably* regardless of the protected class status of the prospective client. At the same time, the State holds that Ms. Smith is free to laud the biblical foundations of heterosexual marriage on her custom wedding website in any artistic form she wishes, in speech, graphics and symbolic speech.

The State argues that Colorado's public accommodation law compels equity in access to any service that is offered to the public. That is, a commercial service offered to the public, including those where meaning messages are conveyed, has no exemption from public accommodation law. The State of Colorado essentially maintains that it has in Ms. Smith's case no legitimate basis for silencing the lawful messages of same-sex couples who wish to make a wedding announcement through Ms. Smith's custom wedding web design public accommodation service. Same-sex couples after all also enjoy the First Amendment right to free expression and equal protection of the law generally.

Recall that the United States Supreme Court analyzed *303 Creative* as plaintiff framed her case; that is in terms of (a) Ms. Smith's First Amendment right to free expression (which in this instance is informed also by her religious views/conscientious beliefs) and (b) with reference to the notion of 'compelled speech.' The case was *not* analyzed by the Court through the lens of religious liberty (i.e., freedom to practice one's religion without government interference). Further there was agreement between the parties that 303 Creative custom wedding web sites would be a public accommodation and a service offered to the public *without a primary religious purpose*. Given the latter it would seem that a 'compelled speech' argument grounded here, as it is, on Ms. Smith's sincerely held religious beliefs is beyond the scope of permissible considerations in assessing the validity of any restrictions on access to the service as a public accommodation for same-sex couples.

Justice Ketanji Brown Jackson, Associate Justice of the United States Supreme Court, points out that, for example, beliefs about interracial marriage also are often informed by religious views (sincerely held religious beliefs). Hence if a business offering an artistic expressive service or product to the public can exclude members of the LGBTQ plus community; the business can potentially also exclude members of other protected classes as well based on religious beliefs. The consequence would be that equity in service and access to products offered by public accommodation enterprises would be jeopardized in varied contexts for diverse protected groups. Note that in contrast to Justice Jackson's analysis; some legal scholars (on the view here misguidedly), in support of Ms. Smith's position, contend that *303 Creative* does *not* in fact concern gay rights. Rather they argue that the case raises a different more limited legal question and formulate their position, for instance, as follows: "*303 Creative* was not a case centering on gay rights or gay marriage, though it undeniably has implications for both… The sole legal question was whether the state had the power to enforce antidiscrimination laws that compelled businesses serving the public to engage in speech at odds with their own beliefs."[7] Clearly implicit in the latter question is the particular context in which the case arises. That context is the quandary that Ms. Smith perceives for herself (given her religious views) around the issue of being *compelled to offer* her planned public accommodation custom

[7]Ross, Catherine J. The Real and the Phantom *303 Creative*: Which Is More Dangerous? *The George Washington Law Review* July 25, 2023 https://www.gwlr.org/303-creative-elenis-response/ (Accessed August 20, 2024).

wedding web design *service* to same-sex couples. The case thus clearly concerns the right of same-sex couples, under Colorado public accommodation law, to convey *their* wedding message using Ms. Smith's custom wedding web design service.

What is rather unique here is that the Smith custom wedding web design business did *not* exist at the time of the case (this then was a *pre-enforcement* challenge to Colorado's Anti-Discrimination Act). This as Colorado had *not* enforced the Act upon Ms. Smith's wedding web business since the 303 Creative custom wedding web design public accommodation service had not yet materialized. Hence there were as yet no facts regarding refusal of service to same-sex couples underlying the case. Arguably the latter situation unfortunately makes it easier to create (on the view here) *the illusion* that the case *303 Creative* does not concern gay rights. This though the decision would, in practice, profoundly impact those rights such as the right to be full participants in the community and in the marketplace without suffering discrimination. Furthermore, gay rights are at the heart of another central question in the case; namely whether the case involves compelled service to a particular protected group at issue (as Colorado contends) or compelled speech for a proprietor of a public accommodation artistic expression service (as Ms. Smith maintains). That question hinges in large part on whose message is being conveyed in artistic form-Ms. Smith's or that of the same-sex couple. This attempt then by some legal scholars to disentangle gay rights (here the right of same-sex couples to public accommodation services on an equitable basis) from the contested 'compelled speech' question in *303 Creative* is, on the view here, a legal fiction. It is a legal fiction, on the analysis here, which serves to undermine equal protection of the law in this area for same-sex couples and does so using an illegitimate façade of legality.

On the analysis of the current author the meaning message to be conveyed is that intended by the same-sex client couple. Ms. Smith is hired *to translate that client couple's meaning message* into *an artistic form* which, in consultation and agreement with the client, may include graphics, selected words and/or symbolic speech as design elements. Kindly contemplate, therefore, the following less than prefect analogy. Consider a sign interpreter translating into spoken English, for the benefit of a hearing person (the target audience), what it is that a profoundly deaf person communicated in American Sign Language. The translator is *not* conveying his or her own message but rather communicating the meaning (the message) that the profoundly deaf person wishes to convey. Moreover, the translator is conveying that message in a different surface form using the phonemes and distinct grammatical structure of English to convey a meaning message originally communicated by the deaf person in American Sign Language. The sign translator will choose the particular English words and phrasing to use to communicate the gist of the deaf person's message. This as American Sign Language cannot be translated word-for-word into spoken English in that its grammatical structure is much different from that of English. Likewise in *303 Creative*, the web designer would be (1) conveying the meaning message of another -namely that of the same-sex client couple and (2) using an *original artistic form* that reflects Ms. Smith's creativity. However, all users of the website will understand that the couple's wedding web pages (whether announcing a heterosexual or a same-sex wedding) reflect the thoughts and emotions/meanings that the couples wish to convey relying on Ms. Smith's artistry to do so. In regard to the latter point, it is essential to appreciate that Ms. Smith's wedding web design business *as a public accommodation* means that she is *in effect* but an artistic translator for her clients' messages. That is the very nature of her public accommodation service. Just because her service involves artistic expression in *form* does *not* support the conceptual conflation of the artistic form (Ms. Smith's *in consultation with the client*) with the meaning content of the message (the meaning messages the client couple wishes to convey). It is then, on the view here, grossly misleading and erroneous to characterize the issue as involving "the right of a business owner whose services involve her own expression not to be compelled to use her art to celebrate a same-sex marriage."[8]

The 303 Creative custom wedding web design business was envisioned, according to the stipulations in the case, as a public accommodation *without a religious exemption* and would *not* involve a specific religious purpose. Thus Ms. Smith's artistic translation service *to convey client messages* must be accessible also to protected groups. Giving *artistic form* to the *client's message* does not constitute 'compelled speech' even if that artistic form (agreed to by the client couple) may, in part, include the artist's selected words as graphic design elements. In this regard then the current author would dispute the United Sates Supreme Court majority's implied view that the speech; -selected words used as part of the art form on the wedding custom design website, reflects Ms. Smith's message and not just her art. As it is Ms. Smith's decision to have her custom wedding website enterprise as a public accommodation and not a business/service with a specific religious purpose, it is clear (on the analysis here) that she is not exempted under the Colorado Anti-Discrimination Act from serving same-sex couples. It is also evident therefore that the messages conveyed on the custom wedding website do not necessarily relate to a religious perspective (Christian or otherwise) unless the particular client couple requests the same. On the view here, however, the US Supreme Court majority in *303 Creative* in endorsing Ms. Smith's compelled speech argument (as will be discussed) has (a) afforded Ms. Smith the opportunity to reap the benefits of having her custom wedding website design business classed a public accommodation while, at the same time, (b) impermissibly allowing it to function in fact as a business with a specific religious purpose that can lawfully decline service on religious grounds to a particular protected group (same-sex couples).

It is important to highlight that Ms. Smith had not and, on the understanding here of her case, would not plan to file for a religious exemption to the Colorado Anti-Discrimination Act for her planned (at the time of the case) custom wedding web design service.[9] This presumably as the business would not qualify for a religious

[8] Ross, Catherine J. The Real and the Phantom *303 Creative*: Which Is More Dangerous? *The George Washington Law Review* July 25, 2023 https://www.gwlr.org/303-creative-elenis-response/ (Accessed August 20, 2024).

[9] 303 Creative custom wedding web design is at the time of writing operational and, pursuant to the United States Supreme Court decision in the case, Ms. Smith need not offer the service to same sex couples.

exemption given the specifics of the purpose of her custom wedding website business as a non-religious commercial enterprise offered to the public. It may be that this in part explains the choice of the plaintiff to argue 'compelled speech' rather than State interference with religious liberty. On the view here, Ms. Smith sought to *in effect* circumvent Colorado's anti-discrimination statute through creating United States Supreme Court case law precedent which she in fact did. This even though her proposed custom wedding website design service would be, as she envisioned it at the time, a commercial service *without* a specific religious purpose and offered to the public. The Colorado Anti-Discrimination Act then, on the view here, would not compel or silence Ms. Smith's speech or her form of artistic expression. Rather the Colorado Anti-Discrimination Act would protect, in this instance, the First Amendment rights of same-sex couples to express their sentiments regarding their wedding through Ms. Smith's custom artistic wedding web design service offered to the public (a public accommodation). As will here be discussed, however, Ms. Smith prevailed at the United States Supreme Court and same-sex couples hence were blocked in accessing her custom artistic wedding web design service notwithstanding the Colorado antidiscrimination statute relating to public accommodation businesses or services.

In oral argument Ms. Smith's representative explained that the custom artistic wedding web pages that her client would create would include both words she selects *as art* and graphics and that these would be incorporated as web design. The custom design wedding website service thus, it was explained, combined technological skills with art. It is here contended, as discussed, in opposition to Ms. Smith's 'compelled speech' argument that such wedding websites would be perceived by those viewing them as speech and art that expressed the *sentiments (message content)* of the same-sex couple client *not* that of the artistic designer of the web pages, Ms. Smith. This would be the public perception also for any such similar wedding website service. Furthermore, Ms. Smith, as any such web designer, would consult closely with her client couples regarding what is the *couple's vision* for their wedding website in terms of what overall message *they* hoped to convey with their wedding announcement. Framing the case as a First Amendment free speech case implicating Ms. Smith's speech (as did the plaintiff), while a useful legal tactic is, it is here argued, misleading and a complete mischaracterization of (a) the core issue at bar and (b) a misconstrual of whose free speech rights are actually at risk and how. The same-sex couple after all is not requesting that Ms. Smith adopt their views on same-sex marriage and laud it *on her own behalf.* They are requesting a service-both artistic and technological in nature-a custom designed wedding website where they can speak regarding *their* thoughts and feelings about their impending union as a married same-sex couple. When Ms. Smith as an artist uses both words as art and graphics to give artistic form to the sentiments the same-sex couple wishes to express; she is conveying her client's message/meaning content not her own but with her artistic imprimatur. Colorado thus is *not* compelling Ms. Smith to create a speech message *as her own* that is misaligned with her faith, Rather Colorado is requiring that Ms. Smith not discriminate based on sexual orientation such that barriers are created for same-sex couples who would wish to access her proposed custom wedding website design public accommodation service. The latter to express sentiments that are universal when couples celebrate their marriage.

On the analysis here, it is irrelevant (for the purposes of assessing the viability of Ms. Smith's claim that her First Amendment rights are violated by Colorado's anti-discrimination requirement) whether the overall message conveyed on the wedding webpages would be inherently different where the names of the couple are clearly perceived as denoting two males or two females as opposed to a heterosexual couple. This is the case in that the *message* is (in both the case of a perceived same-sex couple and a heterosexual couple) understood by the viewers of the web pages as that conveyed by the couple planning marriage and not that of the artistic designer of the wedding website (the latter using both words and non-word graphics as design elements to convey *her client's message content*).[10] Ms. Smith further argued, erroneously on the view here, that Colorado was treating *her speech* as a public accommodation. However, it is here contended that instead it was her anticipated wedding website design art and technology *service* that was being regarded as a public accommodation that should be equitably available to members of any protected class.

As discussed above, using in part *speech as art*[11] along with other design elements, Ms. Smith is conveying a message that goes beyond that communicated by the selected few words-a message that is *not hers* but rather her client couple's. Thus, although Ms. Smith *selected certain of the words as artistic elements* along with other graphics to enable the couple to artistically express the sentiments *they* wished to express; the message conveyed is not Ms. Smith's and would not be perceived as hers by viewers of the wedding website. Hence the *words as art* selected by Ms. Smith (in consultation with her client couple) do *not* qualify as 'compelled speech.'

In this regard recall also that it was a fact stipulated to by both parties in the case that Ms. Smith is willing to design web sites for same-sex couples or individual members of the LGBTQ plus community that convey messages on topics other than an upcoming nuptial of a same-sex couple. However, on the analysis here, the latter does not excuse Ms. Smith from her obligations under Colorado human rights law not to discriminate against same-sex couples by refusing them access to her planned custom wedding website business. Further, it is here contended that it is no answer to

[10]Ms. Smith, through her representative, argued before the USSC that she would be the victim of having her speech compelled if she were required by State public accommodation law to also design custom wedding websites for a same-sex couple clients. That design would include selected words as themselves a design element/artistic element along with other graphics. Ms. Smith maintains that she was thus *not* making arguments about any objection she might have to any implicit *perceived* endorsement of same-sex marriage that could potentially arise due to her creating/designing custom wedding websites also for same-sex couples but rather relying on the 'compelled speech' argument *per se.*

[11]The reference here is to plaintiff's (Ms. Lori Smith's) characterization of aspects of her work that involves selecting particular words for the website presented *as design elements* along with other graphics.

argue (as did Ms. Smith before the United States Supreme Court) that a custom web designer who is a member of the LGBTQ plus community would have the same right (under Ms. Smith's vision of the Colorado public accommodation law) to decline, even where there was no religious exemption, to convey a message which *that* web designer found offended the web designer's religious convictions/conscientious beliefs. The issue here is rather whether a service offered to the public (a) where no religious or conscientious belief exemption has been requested but yet 'compelled speech' contrary to religious belief is alleged and (b) that service in part involves selected speech or symbolic speech *as art to convey a client message* can be denied to members of a protected group. This denial being based on the contention that the lawful message content to be communicated is directly or indirectly connected to/shaped by the identity of the protected class of which the client is a member (in the case at bar the message to be conveyed involves a same-sex wedding announcement and thus connects to the identity of the client couple as members of the LGBTQ plus community). On the current author's analysis, Ms. Smith prevailing on the 'compelled speech' argument in this context (as occurred before the United States Supreme Court and will be here discussed) constitutes an unjustified violation of the Colorado public accommodation law and of the free expression rights of the same-sex client couple to convey *their* wedding message. It may be that the identity of the client couple-a same-sex couple-is implicitly or explicitly referenced in the wedding message that the couple wishes to convey. However, it is here contended, in opposition to plaintiff's position, that the aforementioned fact is not a basis for State authorized discrimination. Further it is to be noted, as discussed, that the overall meaning content of the wedding message the same-sex couple wishes to convey is likely analogous to that of heterosexual couples.

Respectfully, on the view here, in sum then Ms. Smith's 'compelled speech' argument is misguided. This in that it is *not* communication of *her* message regarding marriage on the planned custom wedding website that is at issue nor a perception by viewers that it is *her* message. In contrast, the speech (as graphic elements) at issue would have to be communicated to and perceived by viewers or listeners as constituting Ms. Smith's vision of marriage to be considered 'compelled'. The same-sex couple's message would not, however, be perceived as being the religious custom wedding web designer's message. This is clear in that all the clients who would be using Ms. Smith's custom wedding web service are couples who are communicating *their* wedding story as *they* believe and understand it to be. It is then rather the meaning message of the same-sex couple and their free expression right to express their wedding announcement and story as a same-sex couple that is the issue. That free speech right of the same-sex couple prospective client is violated, it is here argued, since Colorado is required (as a result of the Supreme Court ruling in *303 Creative*) to grant an exemption to the Colorado Anti-Discrimination Act in this case and like cases. That decision, on the analysis here, sets a very injurious precedent for the rights of the LGBTQ plus community in regard to public accommodation law.

It is to be emphasized that it is the plaintiff who highlights client protected status (here in terms of sexual orientation) as the relevant factor underlying her request for an exemption (based on alleged ‘compelled speech’) from the Colorado public accommodation law regarding her custom wedding website service. *It is (on the view here) clearly instead the First Amendment free speech right of the same-sex couple and not that of Ms. Smith that is at the core of the case.* An exemption here is an acceptance by the State that where the protected status (identity) of a prospective client is alleged to change or be the message; a public accommodation service can be denied. This then silences the voices of members of the protected group at issue and does so with the State’s blessing.

In this specific situation involving a custom wedding web designer Colorado’s public accommodation law serves to protect (1) the same-sex couple’s right to equity in accessing a particular commercial business service offered to the public and (2) their right to equality under the law in terms of protection of their First Amendment free expression right. Were Colorado to have taken the position that Ms. Smith may lawfully decline the same-sex couple’s wish to access her custom wedding web design service; the State would, it is here contended, be violating the couple’s First Amendment right to free expression as well as their right to equality under the law in accessing a commercial business service offered to the public. Yet the United States Supreme Court ruling in *303 Creative* for the Plaintiff in fact, on the analysis here, places Colorado precisely in that position.

Ms. Smith at the time of filing her case had ample notice and understanding that the real-world implication of the Colorado Anti-Discrimination Act is that the State would compel equitable access to her public accommodation service in regard to her planned custom wedding website design business.[12] That Ms. Smith’s custom wedding website design service includes speech (words) as an artistic design element along with other graphic elements, on the view here, would not, as explained here, relieve her of her obligation to provide equitable access. Furthermore, in all instances of custom wedding website pages Ms. Smith planned to design for various clients she would, on the analysis here, be conveying *the client couple’s message* not her own (from the wedding announcement itself to all other sentiments relating to the couple’s wedding that the client couple wished to express). If the message is lawful there is then no basis, it is here argued, for Ms. Smith to discriminate against a particular protected class in denying them the service. This is especially the case in that Ms. Smith, as discussed, had *not* sought a religious exemption to Colorado’s public accommodation law and her business was *not* framed as one with a specific religious purpose. Nevertheless, Ms. Smith, arguably in contradictory fashion, argued before the Courts that her custom wedding website design service was envisioned as a virtual site for the celebration of heterosexual marriage. One could

[12]During oral argument before the United States Supreme Court in *Creative* (Lori Smith v Aubrey Elenis et. al.); Justice Sotomayor asked the representative for Ms. Smith whether she was arguing that the issue was *compelled speech* as opposed to *compelled service* The counsel for the plaintiff appeared to respond that the argument concerned the ‘compelled speech’ that was being alleged.

contend reasonably then, it is here held, that Ms. Smith managed with her success at the United States Supreme Court to (1) reap the commercial benefits of having her custom wedding web design service considered a public accommodation while (2) at the same time, ironically, *in effect* receiving a religious exemption though no formal specific religious purpose enterprise application for an exemption was ever advanced. This by being permitted to decline access to her wedding web service to same-sex couples on an alleged religiously informed 'compelled speech' ground. The latter denial of service arguably amounts to a religious exemption in practice.

In fact, it would appear, based on Ms. Smith's filings in court and her counsel's arguments, that Ms. Smith wished to advocate, at least implicitly through her refusal of the custom wedding web design service to same-sex couples, for heterosexual marriage as the only true form of marriage. This as a tenet of Christian faith such that her custom wedding website design business could in fact, on the view here, then not properly be considered to be secular. With the State of Colorado required by law to allow an ostensibly secular commercial business offered to the public to decline service to same-sex couples (based on a Christian tenet of faith or any other sincerely held belief system basis); the State is arguably promoting potential unlimited discrimination in the provision of goods and services against a protected class (or a range of protected classes).[13] This discrimination would be further promulgated then (as a consequence of the 303 Creative United States Supreme Court majority decision) by a potential host of other entrepreneurs also designated as expressive artists conveying meaning messages in part through symbolic speech. The 303 Creative United States Supreme Court decision in favour of Ms. Smith, on the analysis here, thus creates foreseeable practical harms in the lives of the members of the targeted protected class and establishes those members *in effect* as second-class class citizens.

While Ms. Smith would not but for the Colorado Anti-Discrimination Act contemplate announcing on her planned custom design wedding website a wedding *on her client's behalf* of a same-sex couple; she is, it can be appreciated, yet not being compelled to speak *their* message as if it were her own. Rather the requirement is that she provide equitable access to her anticipated custom design wedding website design service. The latter in order that same-sex couples in the instance may speak and convey *their* message as is in accord with *their* free expression right. The message, even if it implicitly endorses same-sex marriage, not being that of the web designer, is not 'compelled speech' nor would the message, as discussed, even be perceived as *hers* (Ms. Smiths) speech by those who access the website. In any case, it is to be highlighted that Ms. Smith's arguments did *not* rely on an 'implicit endorsement of same-sex marriage' contention but rather squarely on an alleged 'compelled speech' claim and on the notion that the identity of the couple as same-sex allegedly shaped the message. Protected classes cannot, however, on the analysis

---

[13] This as a result of the United States Supreme Court majority ruling in *303 Creative, Lori Smith v Aubrey Elenis et al.* Argued December 5, 2022 Case Documents https://www.supremecourt.gov/search.aspx?filename=/docket/docketfiles/html/public/21-476.html (Accessed August 20, 2024).

here, be legitimately denied equitable access to a *secular commercial service* freely offered to the public by the proprietor simply on the basis that the service involves an element of artistic expression. This irrespective of whether that artistic expression makes use in part or in whole of speech/words as art or other expressive elements.

The so-called liberal Justices of the United States Supreme Court, dissenting in the 303 Creative case, struggled during oral argument with where the line would then be if Ms. Smith's 'compelled speech' argument were accepted in denying service to same sex couples and potentially also to certain other protected classes. This since so many businesses involve an element of artistic expression (i.e., photography, custom baking, hairdressing, clothes design etc.) which could be considered protected under the First Amendment. In each case, however, the *custom design* is crafted according to what the client wishes to convey while the designer gives that message artistic form.

Colorado held simply that Ms. Smith, since (a) she wished to offer a service combining art and technology to the public (a public accommodation) and (b) she had *not* applied for nor received an exemption from Colorado anti-discrimination law based on an available exemption (here for religious organizations or enterprises with a religious purpose) cannot lawfully choose to reject for access to that service members of the LGBTQ plus community. The latter denial of service being on the basis of a religiously informed conscientious objection to same sex marriage but the objection being instead framed as a 'compelled speech' matter. To allow the same would be both to suppress (through a State law exemption) the First Amendment right to free expression of the same-sex prospective client couple and their right to be afforded, through law, equity in the provision of a service (here the custom wedding website service) offered to the public. Hence Colorado did *not* intend to compel Ms. Smith's speech as the State had no interest *per se* in the expressions of affection and admiration that the partners in a same-sex relationship wish to express but only in their right to equitable access to a public accommodation (here a planned custom wedding web design private business offering service to the public). That discrimination in access would be based on the sexual orientation of the same-sex client couple is evident in part, it is here argued, from the fact that the custom-designed artistic elements (selected words as graphic elements along with other graphic design features) *conveying essentially the same message* (positivity relating to a couple's union), if designed for a heterosexual couple, would not then, in Ms. Smith's view, constitute for her so-called 'compelled speech.' It is not then Ms. Smith's right to use particular word design elements as artistic expression but who is to be afforded the wedding website design service that is at the core of the plaintiff's case. Put somewhat differently; it is not the message *per se* conveyed both by the selected words (speech) as art and other graphics (expressing *the couple's message* of love, excitement, joy, gratitude to have found each other) that is problematic for Ms. Smith. Instead, it is on the view here (1) the identity in terms of sexual orientation of the client couple that is the difficulty for Ms. Smith as well as (2) the requirement under Colorado law at the time the case was advanced that, should she start her wedding website design business, in offering the service to the public she do so without discrimination relating to any of Colorado's recognized human rights legislated protected classes of persons.[14]

Ms. Smith maintains that on Colorado's analysis the government could compel political speech. She gave the example during oral argument before the United States Supreme Court of a democratic publicist being compelled to create speech for public consumption (a press release) for a republican. The purported analogy falls short however in that political affiliation or ideology and the distinct group so created is *not* a protected class under Colorado human rights law. Thus, private commercial businesses can discriminate on that basis while the government may not do so as there exists First Amendment protection in that regard.[15] Further, as Colorado pointed out, speech writers (and presumably then also publicists) are not in all cases public accommodations in any meaningful sense (they are not always services or products offered to the public more generally).

The State of Colorado 's grant (given the United States Supreme Court decision in *303 Creative*) of Ms. Smith's request for an exemption from public accommodation law based on alleged 'compelled speech' (in respect of her not wishing to custom design wedding announcements/stories on her web platform for same-sex couples), on the view here, constitutes government interference with the free speech of the same-sex couple. Arguably, in addition, insofar as the wedding announcement of a same-sex couple is considered political speech *per se*, an exemption for Ms. Smith (based on alleged compelled speech grounds) would *in effect* mean (a) the government permitted *Ms. Smith's political speech* through her wedding website (via the denial of service to same sex couples and presumably a disclaimer on the site regarding the business offering service only to heterosexuals) while (b) denying the political speech of a prospective client same-sex couple through their wedding announcement. In addition, the exemption is the government speaking for the plaintiff Ms. Smith. Thus, the government would have, in this circumstance, suppressed the alleged political speech that is inextricably bound to protected sexual orientation status were a same-sex couple denied access to announce their nuptials on the Smith custom wedding website due to their particular protected status identity.[16] In summary then it is here contended that by refusing to do a custom

---

[14]The Colorado Anti-Discrimination Act prohibits discrimination based on disability, race, creed, color, sex, *sexual orientation*, gender identity, gender expression, marital status, national origin or ancestry. In respect of public accommodations "Coloradans are entitled to the full and equal enjoyment of all goods, *services*, facilities, privileges, advantages, or accommodations offered to the public, regardless of protected class…Places of public accommodation do not include a church, synagogue, mosque or other place that is principally used for religious purposes (emphasis added)." Colorado Department of regulatory Services (Civil Rights Division) https://ccrd.colorado.gov/discrimination (Accessed August 20, 2024).

[15]Consider that in the hypothetical a Democrat publicist working for a Republican to create a news release is creating a message that is communicated and perceived as that of the client (the Republican). The political affiliation of the publicist is thus a sidenote and irrelevant to the message or service provided to the client and received by the audience.

[16]Members of the LGBTQ plus community are very unlikely to hold that same-sex marriage is antithetical to the proper interpretation of religious values. Further their posting on the Smith

wedding web site for a gay couple, and notwithstanding that the web site is offered to the public, Ms. Smith would be expressing *her* political view. The same-sex couple, however, would be silenced by the State through the exemption the plaintiff requested and was granted. That exemption, it should be recalled, is *not* ostensibly held by the Plaintiff to be a religious one (which is contestable) but rather one granted to avoid placing her in a situation allegedly requiring compelled speech.

The same would be the result (silencing of a message inextricably bound to protected status), it is here contended, if the web designer declined a same-sex couple's wish to have the words "God blesses this union" appear on the site (a hypothetical that was discussed by the Justices). The current author holds that it would again not be the web designer who would be perceived as making that statement as a third party but rather the same-sex couple as to their belief that the statement reflects a truth about their marriage. The upshot is that the wedding web designer is prepared to create the words "God blesses this union" as a design element for the web page of a heterosexual couple to announce their wedding but not provide the service with or without that speech element for same-sex couples to convey the very same sentiments objectively speaking.[17] The latter denial of service based on status is contrary to the requirements for a business offered to the public. On the analysis here, and it would appear consistent with Colorado's position; status and message are *inseparable (confounded) from the perspective of Ms. Smith's religious worldview*. Colorado thus held that the basis for Ms. Smith wishing to decline to announce same-sex weddings on her custom wedding web pages (whether with or without creative elements like the words 'God blesses this union') is due to the message, in Ms. Smith's eyes, being imbued with meaning through the identity status of the client couple as same-sex. Hence status protections in public accommodation are triggered. Ms. Smith however, in contrast, argued that (a) her request for an exemption was based on message alone not status (i.e., she would serve LGBTQ plus clients and design other types of websites for them, (b) that status changes the message *when it comes to same-sex wedding announcements and stories* and (c) this would result in her being compelled to create speech she objects to on religious grounds.

In regard to this issue of 'compelled speech' consider then Justice Jackson's point that *an artist for hire* (here Ms. Smith is providing a public accommodation custom wedding website service for hire) is one who is communicating *others' sentiments*

---

custom wedding website arguably conveys that a same-sex marriage is a true marriage in the couple's view.

[17]The current author would argue that the *essential or core meaning* of a message does *not* necessarily change with the identity status of the speaker in all instances. The example was raised in *Creative* during oral argument of an anti-vaccine proponent and an abortion rights proponent and the meaning of the words "my body my choice" The essence of the message meaning is the same, this author argues, in both instances, namely the right to bodily integrity and to personal and bodily autonomy. The situational context is different in each case and clarifies that the discussion regarding bodily autonomy relates to a particular scenario (informed voluntary decisions about abortion vs decisions about vaccine).

through art. In contrast, an artist who expresses their own views and opinions through their art and then sells the product is in a different category. The distinction then has implications as to whether or not 'compelled speech' is in fact an issue in *303 Creative.* The Supreme Court majority in *Creative,* however, held that Ms. Smith in creating *a custom* wedding website where the selected words and other graphics are chosen by her (albeit in consultation with the client couple) creates a website that purportedly represents Ms. Smith's speech (*her* expression). In part on that basis the United States Supreme Court majority in *Creative* held that Ms. Smith's 'compelled speech' argument is supportable should she be required to provide the custom wedding web design service to same-sex couples. On the analysis here, however, that reasoning and conclusion are fatally flawed. This in part in that were Ms. Smith to convey her own message about same-sex marriage through *her* independently selected words and graphics; it hardly would be expected to meet the expectations of the same-sex client couple given her views on same-sex marriage. Rather the words selected as a graphic element are understood by all viewers to have been selected by the artist (in consultation with the client) to best represent the client couple's message about their wedding plans and about their individual and unique marriage story.

The presumed relevant context here is defined by Ms. Smith, the plaintiff, in terms of status of the prospective client couple; namely a same-sex couple. She is the one, on the view here, who has highlighted the sexual orientation of the couple (a protected status) as *the* relevant context to her request to be exempted from having to offer her custom wedding web service, a public accommodation, to a particular protected group. It is Ms. Smith then who has inextricably linked status (sexual orientation of the couple) to the message to be conveyed respecting a custom wedding announcement and story. That service Ms. Smith declines to offer to this protected group (same-sex couples).[18] She does the latter then rather than, for example, linking a *non-status* contextual element (i.e., her perception of whether the prospective client couple is a 'committed couple') to the decision as to whether to offer the custom wedding web service to a particular prospective client couple.

It is argued here that it is Ms. Smith's religious ideological viewpoint that (a) same-sex status defines/is the message and (b) unacceptably does not comport with "biblical truth" which plaintiff communicates through a State granted exemption. This is the result though it should be noted that Ms. Smith argued through her representative at the United States Supreme Court that she did not seek to send a message through her conduct other than that her website business reflects the religious perspective of the owner. Colorado in granting an exemption (pursuant to the 303 Creative United States Supreme Court ruling in the case), on the analysis here, however, prioritizes a particular religious viewpoint condoning status discrimination over the right to equity of same-sex couples to a particular public

[18] In Colorado's view, the plaintiff links same-sex status of prospective client couples to her anticipated conduct; namely her refusal to offer the planned custom wedding web service to the designated group (same-sex couples).

accommodation service. This outcome, it is here argued, is antithetical to the values of a democratic inclusive society.

The State of Colorado in *303 Creative* argued as lawful *a prohibition* against both (a) non-religious exemptions from public accommodation law that would permit discrimination against any particular protected group and (b) censorship of communication pursuant to the protected status (identity) of the communicator (here censorship of the same-sex couple's wedding announcement and wedding story neither of which is, objectively speaking, inherently political on its face any more than would be the case were the couple heterosexual). The vital State interest at play here then is to support the democratic participatory rights of members of protected status groups. The concern is also that, on Ms. Smith's analysis, any protected status could in other instances by other plaintiffs be held to define the message and hence allegedly justify discrimination. Justice Sotomayor raised the example in *303 Creative* of plaintiffs who might object to inter-racial marriage or the marriage of disabled persons for instance. Exemption to public accommodation law in those instances based on a sincerely held belief would result in discrimination based on race or disability respectively. The State of Colorado does *not* find that protected status is a relevant contextual factor for the grant of an exemption. The State would thus hold the same presumably whether the exemption request was based on a religiously or other inspired 'compelled speech' argument denying *a public accommodation service* based on race, disability, sexual orientation or any other protected status of the prospective client held to allegedly 'change the message'.

Let us consider a hypothetical case where the plaintiff would likely *decline* to create words as art to convey a *client message* to the effect of 'God blesses both same-sex and heterosexual marriages' on her custom wedding website. This even if the client couple who hired her to do so were a heterosexual client couple. In that hypothetical, the heterosexual couple is an ally of same-sex couples speaking the same message that they (same-sex couples) might have wished to convey explicitly on the custom wedding website if permitted to do so.[19] Here (in this hypothetical as set out), the heterosexual couple (an LGBTQ plus community ally) is then, on the analysis here, being treated by the custom wedding web designer *in effect* as a *de facto* member of the LGBTQ plus community whose message would constitute alleged 'compelled speech' for Ms. Smith. Hence Ms. Smith's anticipated denial of a public accommodation service to the heterosexual couple in this hypothetical scenario would, on the analysis here, also violate the Colorado Anti-Discrimination Act. This in that, *from Ms. Smith's religious perspective*, it would seem that anyone conveying the message that 'God blesses both heterosexual and same sex marriages' would be perceived to be so aligned with the protected same-sex couple group as to

[19]Colorado argued that plaintiff would not need to design speech saying 'God blesses same-sex unions' even if hired by a heterosexual couple to do so *as long as she could show that her refusal was not connected to the status of the couple who hired her for her custom wedding design web service.* The current author argues here that the refusal *is* connected to *perceived status* in both cases. That is, the refusal would be linked to the status of being a heterosexual couple ally of the LGBTQ plus community or that of a same-sex couple.

have, for purposes of allegedly justifying discrimination[20] no distinction therefrom (i.e. even if the client couple is heterosexual). On the view here then the heterosexual couple in the described hypothetical properly could be extended public accommodation protection based potentially on *both* (a) their *perceived* identity status (perceived as *in effect*, given their allyship to the LGBTQ plus community, to be tantamount to being members of that community) and (b) based on political ideology (their support of the LGBTQ plus community then being considered part perhaps of a liberal political ideology).[21] However, note that very few locales in the US have public accommodation laws that include political affiliation or political ideology as a ground for protected status. In such instances as in the aforementioned hypothetical, message and status are intertwined for both members of the LGBTQ plus community and their close allies and cannot be dissected the one from the other.

There seems to be no basis that this author can discern for accepting the plaintiff's claim that her focus is on message and not client status. In *303 Creative* the message, according to Ms. Smith, is in fact tied up with status in that *the message is in part the very fact of the same-sex union* existing separate and apart from the couple's sentiments about their union and their upcoming nuptials. However, any burden on speech in requiring the custom wedding web designer to also serve same-sex couples (i.e., having to mention first names that indicate the couple is same sex), Colorado contends, is incidental to the prohibition on discriminating in denying access to a public accommodation service based on a couple's sexual orientation (protected status).[22] The current author holds that in fact there is no incidental burden on Ms. Smith's speech in that that speech is perceived to convey the client's message not hers.

Let us consider political ideology once more, this time in relation to a hypothetical posed in *303 Creative* by the United States Supreme Court's Justice Alito.

---

[20]That discrimination would be in terms of declining access to her public accommodation custom wedding web design service based on the sexual orientation status of the prospective client couple.

[21]Volokh, Eugene (2021) Can Places of Public Accommodation Exclude People Based on Their Politics? It all depends on where you are. The Volokh Conspiracy (a legal blog) https://reason.com/volokh/2021/04/08/can-places-of-public-accommodation-exclude-people-based-on-their-politics/ (Accessed August 20, 2024).

[22]The representative for Colorado argued before the United States Supreme Court that the case at bar, *Creative*, is different from any case in which an expressive artist was simply compelled by the State to engage in expressive speech that the artist fundamentally disagreed with on ideological grounds (i.e., a Muslim filmmaker compelled to create a film promoting Scientology). This is evident, Colorado argued, in that *no content-neutral law* (such as Colorado's public accommodation law) can be crafted that would require such a direct burden on speech. Also, Colorado argued that even if status is connected to the message this is not status discrimination in the way that is involved in denying service to same-sex couples. This author would hold that the difference is that with same-sex couples, their very existence as a same-sex couple is perceived by some as the message. That is the case over and above any specific meaning/message the couple wishes to communicate through the expressive features (words and other graphics) of the custom wedding website. Hence discrimination based on the same-sex couple's status *as such* allegedly shaping/being the message seems an unjustified basis for violation of public accommodation law and insufficient to make out a 'compelled speech' argument.

Justice Alito inquired of the representative for Colorado whether a Santa photography service in a mall offering photos of Santa with children as a public accommodation would require a "black Santa" to take a photo with a child in a Ku Klux Klan (KKK) outfit. The representative for Colorado replied that KKK outfits are not protected under Colorado public accommodation law so the black Santa would not be required to take that photo. One might consider the KKK outfit as an expression of political ideology (most likely expressed by the child's caregivers through the child's outfit and not by the young child). However, as mentioned previously political ideology does *not* define a protected class in Colorado. As was made clear in oral argument were this to have occurred in a US State that has some statutory protections under public accommodation law for political ideology then the so-called black Santa may have been required to take the photo.

In *303 Creative* Ms. Smith, on the analysis here, is *not* being compelled to create a message, political or apolitical, as her own that is not her own. She instead would have been required under Colorado's Anti-Discrimination Act (absent the *303 Creative* majority ruling by the United States Supreme Court) to provide artistic expression through her custom wedding website design services to the public in a manner that would not discriminate against the LGBTQ plus community. This by making the same custom wedding design service also accessible to same-sex couples. The message to appear on the custom design web wedding pages is dictated by the client couple (whether same-sex or heterosexual) to convey the meaning the couple wishes. It is the *custom artistic form* that is chosen by Ms. Smith the web designer in consultation with the client couple.

Ms. Smith's custom wedding web design business was, as discussed, not intended for a specific religious purpose, and unsurprisingly then she had stipulated that it would be a public accommodation. Yet she sought an exemption on an alleged free speech ground (informed by religion) to deny the service to same-sex couples since she ties message to status. Arguably the plaintiff *in effect* holds that the prospective client couple being a same-sex couple in the wedding context *is* the message. The State thus recognizes that Ms. Smith is free to express on her website, in a section recognized as expressing her position rather than her client's, her religious views on what constitutes a valid marriage. However, as a public accommodation under Colorado's Anti-Discrimination Act (had the US Supreme Court not ruled in her favor), she would have had to offer the public a service that does not discriminate against gay couples who wish to hire her for a custom wedding website. This regardless of her view that a message contrary to her religious perspective is sent by simple virtue of the couple client of her custom wedding website service being same sex.

Ms. Smith (on the analysis here as discussed) was not being compelled to speak the wedding message of the same-sex couple as her own. Other contextual indicia also reveal that the State of Colorado was not pressuring Ms. Smith to betray the tenets of her faith through 'compelled speech.' Firstly, she was not being compelled to have a commercial wedding web design service offered to the public. It was *her* choice to offer the service to the public as a secular non-religious public accommodation service. Hence it was her choice to create a business that clearly falls (on the view here) under the ambit of Colorado human rights anti-discrimination regulations where no exemptions apply to 303 Creative's custom wedding web design service. Secondly, Ms. Smith could have, under Colorado's Anti-Discrimination Act, lawfully added, for example, to the home page advertising her custom wedding websites, as discussed, a statement (disclaimer) expressing her religious views regarding what allegedly constitutes a valid marriage (biblically). That disclaimer would clearly be interpreted as her own by those who view the 303 Creative home page. Thirdly, it would appear that Ms. Smith had not requested a religious exemption from the Colorado agency regulating compliance with Colorado's Anti-Discrimination Act. Yet Ms. Smith sought an exemption on religiously informed free speech grounds. This notwithstanding that her custom wedding web design business would be a public accommodation (not one for solely a religious purpose) and (on the view here) there was, as discussed, no basis for claiming a 'compelled speech' burden; incidental or otherwise.

Ms. Smith's 'compelled speech' claim is imbued with a particular religious view as to what is appropriate as to wedding announcements/stories on her site. It is arguably the case then that Ms. Smith confounds two disparate bases for requesting an exemption: free speech and a religious belief. Ms. Smith makes the 'compelled speech' claim, despite the fact that (on the view here) the message conveyed is that of her client and would be perceived as such. Ms. Smith's religious perspective holds, it would appear, that the identity of the same-sex couple as a same-sex couple *is* the message in this context overriding any other aspect of the wedding message. Further Ms. Smith contends that since her wedding web design is custom (with original expressive elements involving words, graphics and other features) the same -sex wedding message might be misperceived as hers. However, it is clear that it would be the client couple who would have to concur that (a) the artistic expression accurately reflected the sentiments *they* wished to convey, and that (b) the artistic form would be interpreted by the target audience as the couple's true thoughts and feelings about the upcoming marriage and their wedding story. Viewers of the custom wedding website for a same-sex or for a heterosexual couple would surely understand this.

Ms. Smith in fact did argue that the status of the client couple (same sex) changes the message in this same-sex marriage context. However, *if* that is correct; it would be only in the religious/political interpretation of Ms. Smith and perhaps others with the same overall world view but arguably not for all viewers of the wedding website. Objectively the speech and message, a wedding announcement and a personal 'wedding story' of mutual affection, is the same for same-sex and heterosexual couples. It is that very sameness of ultimate message meaning, it is here suggested, that contributes in part, it would appear, to the plaintiff's self-perceived need to request an exemption to public accommodation law in this case. The sameness of the message is the very thing that is potentially most, one might surmise, threatening to a certain religious perspective. That sameness in essential message content when it comes to the same-sex couple's personal wedding story and sentiments (compared to that of a heterosexual couple) undermines the 'othering' of same-sex married couples. An exemption from the public accommodation law for the 303 Creative plaintiff (as was made possible by the United States Supreme Court majority ruling in the case), on the analysis here thus, *erroneously* (a) implicitly affirms that same-sex status of the client couple in this context automatically dictates an alleged possibly subversive objectionable message (or metamessage) about the sanctity of same-sex marriage and (b) *in effect* puts the State's imprimatur on approval of status discrimination in public accommodations whenever (1) the expressive business claims that the protected status of the client *is* the message and (2) the message is therefore *ipso facto* objectionable or at least that the status of the client unacceptably alters the message in a way that offends the artist entrepreneur's sincerely held beliefs. Colorado had argued in opposition that essentially Ms. Smith is free to design her product/service as she wishes with the limitation that she may not define the product/service in terms of the protected status of a prospective client to be excluded from access.[23] Unfortunately the United States Supreme Court ruling in *303 Creative* in fact permitted just the latter; that is the defining of a product/service offered to the public in terms of the protected status of a prospective client to be *excluded* from access.

Ms. Smith represented to the Court through her representative in oral argument before the United States Supreme Court that it was her sincere religious belief that same-sex marriages are *not true marriages*.[24] The State of Colorado grant of the requested exemption then (pursuant to the United States Supreme Court decision in *303 Creative*) arguably speaks a disparaging message regarding the sanctity and validity of same-sex marriages. That negative message disputing the legitimacy of same-sex marriage from a particular biblical perspective may, in the public perception, it should be understood, easily morph into unjustified disparagement also of the very identity of the protected group. However, there is no claim here that the latter is or ever was plaintiff's intent.

Furthermore, the State *in effect* appearing ostensibly to agree with the plaintiff's arguments (given the grant of an exemption to Colorado's anti-discrimination law that was required as a consequence of the United States Supreme Court ruling in *Creative*) is to concur that status in terms of sexual orientation automatically defines the message when it comes to artistic expression relating to same-sex weddings/marriages. This in that the central issue in the case (on the analysis here) is Ms. Smith's *claim* that the very fact of the couple being same sex (their status or identity) in and of itself changes the wedding message to one that is, in her view, unacceptable on religious grounds. This even though the message content *objectively* would be a client couple wedding announcement and personal wedding story as is the case for the heterosexual client couples as well with analogous sentiments being expressed. The State had argued unsuccessfully that any impact on speech, if it

[23] For further detail on Creative see Scotus Blog https://www.scotusblog.com/case-files/cases/303-creative-llc-v-elenis/ (Accessed August 20, 2024).

[24] 303 Creative, Lori Smith v Aubrey Elenis et al. (hereafter also referred to as *Creative* or 303 Creative or *Creative LLC* Argued December 5, 2022 Oral Argument United States Supreme Court audio C-Span https://www.c-span.org/video/?524449-1/303-creative-llc-v-elenis-oral-argument (Accessed August 20, 2024).

did exist, was minimal and incidental and less compelling than the overriding need to allow members of the LGBTQ plus community to have equal access to the public accommodation at issue.

Thus (same-sex versus heterosexual) couple status, on Ms. Smith's perspective, defines the message and, she argues, would thus constitute 'compelled speech' were she required to offer the custom wedding web design service also to same-sex couples. Colorado held in opposition that an exemption would not be consistent with the intent of public accommodation law to ensure equity in the marketplace also for consumers from protected classes who wish to access certain products and services offered to the public. Public accommodation law then seeks to affirm respect for members of protected groups such that they are shielded from discrimination in the marketplace.

The United States Supreme Court Majority in *303 Creative* found for the plaintiff Ms. Smith by a vote of 6 to 3 in her favor.[25] The Majority accepted (misguidedly on the view here) plaintiff's argument that Colorado's public accommodation law would unconstitutionally compel Ms. Smith's speech (contrary to her religious views) if she were required to make her custom wedding web design service available also to same-sex couples. On the analysis here, the Majority appears to inappropriately confound the *client's message/sentiments* with *Ms. Smith's artistic expression* insofar as her art form includes selected speech (her own and the client's) along with non-speech graphics.[26] For the reasons then here previously discussed (i.e., Ms. Smith is but giving artistic form to the *client's* message) the current author maintains that the First Amendment free speech clause was *not* triggered in this case for the Plaintiff. The Plaintiff in *Creative* then cannot properly ground the case on but a mirage (on the view here) of 'compelled speech.' Plaintiff is free to have a disclaimer on the custom wedding website proclaiming her religious views on marriage. For that reason amongst others it is arguably erroneous to claim, as the United States Supreme Court Majority in *Creative* does, that the government is attempting to compel its "preferred" speech on the issue of same-sex marriage. Further the current author concurs with the dissent that *303 Creative* is a step toward, practically speaking, nullification of public accommodation anti-discrimination law.

[25] 303 Creative, Lori Smith v Aubrey Elenis et al. (United States Supreme Court) No. 21-476 Argued December 5, 2022, Decided June 30, 2023.

[26] "...the wedding websites Ms. Smith seeks to create involve *her* speech; a conclusion supported by the parties' stipulations..." See 303 Creative, Lori Smith v Aubrey Elenis et al. (United States Supreme Court) No. 21-476 Argued December 5, 2022, Decided June 30, 2023, Syllabus at p. 5.

2.2 Comparative Law Perspectives on Free Expression and Internet Site Access

Let us consider then a few cases from the European Court of Human Rights that, though not analogous necessarily on all basic facts, nevertheless speak to some relevant core principles of free expression/free speech and diversity of religious/ideological/political viewpoint. Those core principles are, on this author's view, important to keep in mind when also considering the facts, issues, and arguments in the United States Supreme Court *Creative* case.[27]

2.2.1 Lee v United Kingdom (Application No. 18860/19) European Court of Human Rights Judgment of 23 March 2020

In *Lee v United Kingdom*[28] the complainant, Mr. Lee (a resident of Belfast, Northern Ireland), hired a bakery (Ashers) to bake a cake with a design in the icing that Mr. Lee would choose. The bakery had published a notice of this service that made no mention of religiously based limitations to the type of icing designs the bakery was willing to create. Mr. Lee communicated to the bakery that he wished a cake design in the icing that was (a) a picture of Bert and Ernie (Sesame Street children's show characters) and (b) with the wording also "Support Gay Marriage" and the logo[29] of a particular non-profit ('Queer Space') that supported same-sex marriage and was hosting a private party. The bakery took his order, and it was paid for. Subsequently, Ashers informed Mr. Lee that due to the proprietors' religious beliefs the bakery would not be willing to fill the order after all and the bakery refunded his money. Mr. Lee brought a discrimination claim based on sexual orientation and on political/religious opinion under certain non-discrimination domestic statutes that set out protected groups.

The bakery owners (the McArthur's) argued that baking the cake with the design requested would have been to communicate support for the political campaign at the time to legislate recognition of same-sex marriage in Northern Ireland. The bakery

---

[27] 303 Creative, Lori Smith v Aubrey Elenis et al. (hereafter also referred to as *Creative* or 303 Creative or *Creative LLC* Argued December 5, 2022 Case Documents https://www.supremecourt.gov/search.aspx?filename=/docket/docketfiles/html/public/21-476.html (Accessed August 20, 2024).

[28] Lee v United Kingdom (Application no. 18860/19) European Court of Human Rights, 23 March 2020 https://hudoc.echr.coe.int/fre#{%22itemid%22:[%22001-202151%22]} (Accessed August 20, 2024).

[29] Lee v United Kingdom (Application no. 18860/19) European Court of Human Rights 23 March 2020 p. 3 https://hudoc.echr.coe.int/fre#{%22itemid%22:[%22001-202151%22]} The Order at p. 2 (Accessed August 20, 2024).

proprietors objected to that political initiative based on their Christian beliefs that viewed same-sex marriage as unacceptable. The County Court Judge found that the bakery owners had *not* been compelled to "support, promote or endorse" Mr. Lee's point of view on same-sex marriage[30] and hence Article 10 of the *European Convention on Human Rights* on freedom of expression for the owners had *not* been triggered. Further, the County Court Judge held that the McArthurs' sincerely held religious beliefs was *not* a sufficient basis to overcome the need to enforce the law designed to affirm equity in access (non-discrimination) *in public accommodations* (here for the LGBTQ plus community) as is consistent with democratic values. Hence the County Court found that Convention Article 9(2) setting out what are the *lawful limitations* on freedom of thought, conscience and religion came into play in this case. The Court concluded that (a) Ashers bakery is a public accommodation service and not a religious organization entitled to a religious exemption from public accommodation anti-discrimination requirements and that (b) Ashers' owners could not lawfully infringe on the rights of others (i.e., set out in domestic anti-discrimination law) based on their Christian beliefs.[31]

The County Court Judge held that (a) Mr. Lee had been directly discriminated against based on sexual orientation and (b) directly discriminated against also based on his political belief (relating to his support for legal recognition of same-sex marriage in Northern Ireland) or his religious belief. These were the holdings though the County Court Judge did *not* find that the bakery had refused service based on Mr. Lee's actual or perceived sexual orientation *per se. The Court instead concluded that sexual orientation (protected status) could not be dissociated in this case from Mr. Lee's message (that he wished to convey via the cake's icing) and hence this resulted in discrimination by the bakery through the refusal of service.*

The Court of Appeals affirmed the lower Court decision that providing the cake icing as designed by Mr. Lee would *not* have constituted the bakery supporting or promoting same-sex marriage ('compelled speech' in essence). Hence, the Court of Appeals found that the bakery owners' Convention Article 9 freedom of thought, conscience and religious rights would *not* have been infringed were they required to bake the cake with the 'support gay marriage' message design given that the bakery offered services to the public. The Court of Appeals concluded further that no new issue arose under Convention Article 10 (freedom of expression) in the case that was not already covered under Convention Article 9 (freedom of thought, conscience,

---

[30] Lee v United Kingdom (Application no. 18860/19) European Court of Human Rights 23 March 2020 p. 3 https://hudoc.echr.coe.int/fre#{%22itemid%22:[%22001-202151%22]} (Accessed August 20, 2024).

[31] The County Court further held that to the extent the complaint was against the bakery and not the owners, "... as a limited company it [Ashers] could not itself invoke the protection afforded by Article 9 of the Convention." See *Lee v United Kingdom* (Application no. 18860/19) European Court of Human Rights 23 March 2020 para 17. https://hudoc.echr.coe.int/fre#{%22itemid%22:[%22001-202151%22]} (Accessed August 20, 2024).

and religion). The Appeals Court found in this case *direct associative discrimination* based on sexual orientation of the LGBTQ plus community.[32]

The Court of Appeals held that the same analysis regarding *proportionate limitations* (stipulated in statutory law and the Convention) on the bakery owners' ability to discriminate in a public accommodation (due to their sincere religious beliefs regarding same-sex marriage) would apply to discrimination against Mr. Lee's due to his religious or political belief (his support for same-sex marriage being regarded as a political opinion or belief). However, the Appeals Court did not delve into the latter question. The Court of Appeals expressed concern about the possibility that businesses could refuse a wide range of services to persons based on sexual orientation if this were permissible based on the sincerely held religious belief of the service provider.[33]

The Supreme Court[34] held that the bakery was *not* refusing service to Mr. Lee because of his actual or perceived sexual orientation or because he supported same-sex marriage but instead due to the support gay marriage message *per se* that Mr. Lee proposed for the cake icing design. The Supreme Court contended then that Ashers Bakery had declined to serve Mr. Lee (in terms of baking the cake with the pro same-sex marriage design in the icing) only because the bakery owners sincerely disagreed, on religious grounds, with the message the design was to convey. The Court determined that Ashers' bakery would have declined service to anyone who wished to convey that pro same-sex marriage message and that the latter appeared to be a stipulated fact. There was no evidence that the bakery had discriminated against homosexuals in employment or service in the past. *The Court concluded that there was no confounding of message objected to by the bakery and protected status of the customer in this case.* Hence the Court concluded that no discrimination based on sexual orientation of the customer or based on his association with the LGBTQ plus community (i.e., at Queer Space) had occurred. The Supreme Court held further that it was ruling in favor of the bakery owners to affirm their rights under Convention Article 9 guaranteeing freedom of thought, conscience, and religion.[35]

[32]Direct associative discrimination is less favorable treatment of a person due to that person's association with another individual(s) who is discriminated against due to a protected characteristic that the other person(s) has. An example is a mother of a disabled child treated less favorably due to her son's disability *See Coleman v Attridge Law* (Case C-303/06) [2008] ICR 1128, in the European Court of Justice https://eur-lex.europa.eu/legal-content/EN/TXT/PDF/?uri=CELEX:62006CJ0303 (Accessed August 20, 2024).

[33]For details on the procedural history and findings of the various domestic courts in *Lee* see Lee v United Kingdom (Application no. 18860/19) European Court of Human Rights 23 March 2020 p. 3 https://hudoc.echr.coe.int/fre#{%22itemid%22:[%22001-202151%22]} (Accessed August 20, 2024).

[34]*Lee v Ashers Baking Company Limited and Others, Reference by the Attorney General for Northern Ireland* Judgement Date: 10 Oct 2018 (Case ID UKSC 2017/0020) [2018] UKSC 49.

[35]The Supreme Court held also that *if* any infringement occurred of Mr. Lee's political free expression, the McArthurs could nonetheless not be 'compelled' to speak as if (allegedly) it were their own message supporting gay marriage *Lee v Ashers Baking Company Limited and Others,*

It is accurate to contend that Ashers Bakery would have declined to do the cake with the 'support gay marriage' message also if a heterosexual person or couple would have ordered it. On the analysis here, however, that fact does *not* evidence that message and status (sexual orientation of the customer) were not confounded and were dissociable here. This also being the case even if the Ashers' employee who took the order did not know the sexual orientation of the customer. Rather message and status *are* confounded, it is here contended, in that a 'support gay marriage' message is first and foremost a declaration on the rights of same-sex persons and an expression of the demand for a particular right *from that community* (the LGBTQ plus community) and understood as such by the public. This fact is *not* diminished by the additional fact that the LGBTQ plus community has outside allies and advocates who are also committed to that community's struggle for recognition of their rights. In addition, such allies may be perceived as tantamount to members of the LGBTQ plus community for the purpose of identifying the target for discrimination hence leading to 'direct associative discrimination' (to use the wording from the Appeals Court in *Lee*).

Consider a hypothetical in which the customer asks for a cake icing design that reads 'Ban Gay Marriage' or 'Stop the Legalization of Same-Sex Marriage and of Same-Sex Civil Unions.' Though the latter messages are *consistent* with the McArthurs' (owners of Ashers Bakery) religious views; let us imagine that Ashers *declined* service in that case also.[36] The refusal of service here (less favorable treatment) likely implicates the perceived conservative religious views *of the customer* that leads him to reject same-sex marriage. However, Convention Article 9(2) allows for limitations on expression of those religious rights when they interfere significantly with the rights of others. On the hypothetical facts of the latter scenario, the bakery arguably could justify the refusal of service. The latter in that such disparaging messages likely contribute to a climate of hostility toward the LGBTQ plus community, a *protected status community.* Such fomenting of hostility toward a protected vulnerable community is contrary to democratic values that underly equity in public accommodation law.

A *pressing* case might also be one where Ashers could prove that the refusal of service was justified based on the constraints on expression articulated at Convention Article 9(2) (i.e., a situation where the customer is linked to a group that promotes violence or hate against same-sex couples or the customer expressed violent or hateful sentiments towards the LGBTQ plus community while ordering the cake). It should be noted that the claim that a baker would refuse the cake order with the 'Ban Gay Marriage' message based on the message regardless of who ordered the cake is thus plausible. The disparaging anti-gay marriage message could have

---

Reference by the Attorney General for Northern Ireland Judgement Date: 10 Oct 2018 (Case ID UKSC 2017/0020) [2018] UKSC 49 para 36.

[36]Let us consider the hypothetical in terms, for example, of the McArthurs not wishing to engage in the political controversy regarding the movement at the time to legalize same-sex marriage in Northern Ireland.

various authors and whether or not the author (customer) belongs to another protected group or not is not the issue. Rather the issue in the "Ban Gay Marriage" message scenario is whether the message violates the bounds of free expression as set out in the Convention which requires respect for everyone's basic human rights (i.e., the message contributes to hostility toward a protected group).

Suppose for the purposes of another hypothetical that another bakery had *agreed* to bake cakes with the anti-gay marriage messages while, at the same time, *declining* service to a perceived heterosexual or homosexual customer wanting to order a cake with a pro same-sex marriage message. The customer in *Lee* was in fact requesting a pro same-sex marriage message cake design. In doing so the customer (Mr. Lee) here is arguably speaking a political message on behalf of the LGBTQ plus community including allies and a pro LGBTQ plus rights NGO ('Queer Space'). The message is the LGBTQ plus community's demand for realization of full rights to marriage/family; it is a pro fundamental human rights message. Thus, the message is here inherently confounded with protected status also of the customer as *a member (based on sexual orientation or gender identity) or, alternatively, simply ally* of the LGBTQ community. A refusal of service to anyone who authorized the order of this cake design is thus, on the view here, a refusal based on message confounded with status.[37] This though there is no basis in law why the religious views of the bakery owners should limit the rights, in these circumstances (i.e., no religious exemption in place), of someone to access a public accommodation bakery. That is; the free expression rights of a customer here who, based on the cake message ordered, is likely perceived as associated with the LGBTQ community have been infringed.

The LGBTQ plus community includes, as here discussed, also allies who are, practically speaking, perceived by those who discriminate against the community to be a part of that LGBTQ plus community. The pro-gay marriage message on the Ashers' cake would, furthermore, likely be perceived by those who attended the private party in support of same-sex marriage and were familiar with the Queer Space logo as a message (a) authored by and (b) requisitioned by a representative for or ally of the LGBTQ plus community and Queer Space *not* Ashers' Bakery.[38] Thus the protected status of the customer[39] is confounded with the message.

---

[37] Contrast this analysis with that of Lady Hale of the UK Supreme Court in her commentary on the United States Supreme Court judgment in *Masterpiece Bakery*. See *Lee v Ashers Baking Company Limited and Others, Reference by the Attorney General for Northern Ireland* Judgement Date: 10 Oct 2018 (Case ID UKSC 2017/0020) [2018] UKSC 49 at pp. 17–19, para 59–62 (Postscript).

[38] Ashers was concerned that its logo *on the box* might be associated with the message and taken as an indicator of endorsement of the 'Support Gay Marriage' message if it fulfilled the cake order. However, Ashers' logo was only on the box while the Queer Space logo was on the cake as part of the message design in the icing. Therefore, it is here argued that Queer Space and not Ashers would be perceived as author of the message. This while Ashers would be understood to be the bakery which baked the cake and produced the design in the icing *per the instructions of the cake order supplied by the customer, a member or ally of the LGBTQ plus community.*

[39] Customer here refers to Mr. Lee who endorsed the pro gay marriage message or in other similar cases whoever authorizes the payment and endorses the message.

Ashers was *not* contracted by Mr. Lee to create a Bert and Ernie icing design with the 'Queer Space' logo and "Support Gay Marriage" wording to reflect Ashers' sincerely held political and religious belief regarding same-sex marriage. Rather *Mr. Lee contracted Ashers to give artistic form to his own message and that of Queer Space.* In a true 'compelled speech' case, in contrast, the person compelled is forced to utter speech *as if their own* though they fundamentally disagree with the message. That compelling of speech occurs often in the hopes the person so compelled will internalize the message (i.e., cases in which children are forced to themselves directly recite aloud a prayer in public school or routinely say aloud in concert with other schoolchildren a scripted pledge of allegiance).[40]

In the case at bar (*Lee v United Kingdom*)[41] the facts (i.e., the 'Queer Space' logo on the cake) make clear that the bakery is *not* author of the implied message objective (the success of same-sex marriage legal recognition initiatives in Northern Ireland) nor of the meaning content of the message wording more generally ('Support Gay Marriage'). The bakery is perceived as authors/creators only of the artistry of the cake and the *artistic elements* of the design in the icing such as the font used in the wording and the likeness of Bert and Ernie on the cake to the TV characters. There is then *no violation* of the bakery owners' right *not* to express an opinion they disagree with (a right against 'compelled speech' held to be derivative of the Convention Articles 9 and 10 freedom of expression rights though not expressly stipulated).[42]

Whether the refusal of service regarding the pro gay marriage message on the cake was factually to a homosexual or heterosexual customer is, on the current author's analysis then, irrelevant. It is irrelevant since, for those who share the Ashers' religious and political perspective, it would seem likely that allies of the LGBTQ plus community (i.e., on the pro same-sex marriage message) are considered, as discussed, part of the opposition. Thus, in that regard, for all intents and purposes, allies of the LGBTQ plus community are perceived and treated (in the denial of service when they wish to speak a pro same-sex marriage messages) as part of the protected status group, here the LGBTQ plus community. On the view here, where the State and/or courts designate as lawful such refusal of service in a public accommodation linked to a protected status then discriminatory *attitudes* are permitted to manifest both in terms of inequity and exclusion in an undemocratic fashion.

To recap then, the Supreme Court in *Lee* maintained that having to design the cake with a pro same-sex message would amount to 'compelled speech'; specifically

---

[40] Criss, D CNN online Here's why students don't have to recite the Pledge of Allegiance Published 5:54 PM EST, Tue February 19, 2019 https://www.cnn.com/2019/02/19/us/pledge-of-allegiance-explainer-trnd/index.html (Accessed August 20, 2024).

[41] *Lee v United Kingdom* (Application no. 18860/19) European Court of Human Rights 23 March 2020.

[42] *Lee v Ashers Baking Company Limited and Others, Reference by the Attorney General for Northern Ireland* Judgement Date: 10 Oct 2018 (Case ID UKSC 2017/0020) [2018] UKSC 49 at pp. 15–16, para 51–52.

compelled political speech. This as support for gay marriage was held by the Court to be a political opinion. The Court held that there was no confounding of protected status regarding political opinion and the message here. That is, the Supreme Court of the United Kingdom found (erroneously on the view here) that Mr. Lee was not refused service due to his personal pro-gay marriage political opinion nor his association with those who shared that view. Rather the Supreme Court in *Lee* held that the denial of service by Ashers was due to the McArthurs not wishing to promote or be seen as endorsing a pro same-sex marriage position. According to the Supreme Court then, the denial of service was because of the message *per se* and not the protected characteristics of Mr. Lee (i.e. his personal political opinion or inferred sexual orientation or a perceived allyship with the LGBTQ plus community). The current author, in contrast, concurs with the lower courts in this case that baking a cake with a pro same-sex message for any customer conveys and is understood to convey the customer's message not the bakery owner's message. This is just, for instance, as with a retirement cake thanking someone for their long years of service is perceived as the customer's message not the bakery owner's message. The baker may not even know the person retiring or have any knowledge of their work service. *The message is the customer's speech* given *artistic form* through the bakery's service. The *message content* is *not* (on the view here) thereby *ipso facto* perceived by others as (or in fact) necessarily supported or endorsed by the Christian bakery owners.[43] In the case at bar, furthermore, it was the customer Mr. Lee who chose the specific words to be used in the message and who indicated through the 'Queer Space' logo (to also be part of the design in the icing of the cake) who were the authors of the message.[44] The authors (Mr. Lee/Queer Space) of the message and the message itself are thus inextricably intertwined (Mr. Lee endorsed pro same-sex marriage as part of the political community that supports LGBTQ plus rights).[45] On the view here, service was denied then based both on the 'what' (the message) and the 'who' (supporters of a pro-gay marriage political initiative in Northern Ireland).

As discussed, the Supreme Court in *Lee* held that requiring Ashers to bake the cake with the pro same-sex marriage *customer message* would be 'compelled speech' involving *political opinion* allegedly unconnected to Mr. Lee's protected status. However, arguably, such a ruling opens the possibility of designating as 'compelled speech' any commissioned expressive work from a public accommodation service provider that includes some type of pro human rights *customer message*.

---

[43] It should be noted that in any case there is a diversity of opinion among Catholics on the issue of legal recognition for same-sex marriage and of same-sex civil unions See Diamant, J Pew Research Centre *How Catholics around the world see same-sex marriage, homosexuality* 2 November 2020.

[44] The bakery owners had argued that they were not aware of Mr. Lee' political opinion or religious beliefs but the District Judge had rejected that proposition. It would seem they likely would have known at least of Mr. Lee's political opinion both through his requested pro-gay message cake design and the Queer Space NGO logo he wished on the cake.

[45] Someone who held the opposing political opinion (one that was against legalizing same-sex marriage or civil unions) would presumably not ask for a cake with a pro same-sex marriage message.

The right to marry for non-incestuous consenting persons of age is recognized in international human rights law as a basic right. Hence, on the analysis here, framing the issue in *Lee* as one of mere political opinion *unconnected to the customer's protected status* or to *a vulnerable protected community's fundamental rights* is a red herring, an unnecessary and inapplicable diversion from the deeper issues (i.e. an undemocratic limitation on the protected status customer's freedom to self-advocate for fundamental rights).

To deny service regarding a public accommodation on an alleged 'compelled speech' justification and sincere religious belief ground when the facts clearly indicate who is the author of the message (Mr. Lee/Queer Space) is, on the analysis here, unjustified. The denial of service in *Lee*, on the view here, is a denial of the free expression rights of Mr. Lee regarding his lawful views and conscientious political opinion or belief. For the courts and/or the government to abide such a refusal of service in these circumstances is to undermine Mr. Lee's protected status (in terms of assurance to equity in a public accommodation) and his freedom of expression Convention rights. The Supreme Court in *Lee* held remarkably, however, that to the degree that political discrimination had occurred; there was still *no justification for denying an exemption* and instead purportedly compelling speech (requiring the bakery to create the icing design on the cake as requested). It is here argued in contrast that (a) as previously discussed; there is no compelled speech as the message is clearly perceived as that of Mr. Lee and the NGO 'Queer Space' and *not* that of the bakery owners and (b) hence such political discrimination against Mr. Lee (suppressing the expression of his positive view of same-sex marriage) should not be validated by the State through an exemption from anti-discrimination public accommodation law. *Given the facts in Lee, on the view here, to grant the State's imprimatur on the MacArthur's declination of service undermines the values of a pluralistic democratic society.* Also, it is the contention here that an exemption would be damaging to the greater integration of the LGBTQ plus community into the larger society in Northern Ireland generally.[46]

Further Convention Article 9(2) recognizes that there can in law be narrow limits on freedom of expression of religious beliefs where they *disproportionately* adversely affect the rights of others in a manner inconsistent with democratic values. On the current author's view, the latter is precisely the situation here (violation of Mr. Lee's Convention rights under Convention articles 9 and 10) and with Mr. Lee's

[46]The Supreme Court of the United Kingdom itself acknowledged that conveying the support gay marriage message would have a benefit also for relatives of the same-sex couples planning marriage including their children, friends and allies See *Lee v Ashers Baking Company Limited and Others, Reference by the Attorney General for Northern Ireland* Judgement Date: 10 Oct 2018 (Case ID UKSC 2017/0020) [2018] UKSC 49 at p. 10 The Attorney General intervened to question the validity of the legislation that created civil liability for declining what he saw as compelled speech (being allegedly compelled to express a political or public policy view contrary to one's religious beliefs) See *Lee v Ashers Baking Company Limited and Others, Reference by the Attorney General for Northern Ireland Id. supra* at p. 3 Available at https://www.supremecourt.uk/cases/uksc-2017-0020.html (Accessed August 20, 2024).

freedom of expression being suppressed regarding his political view and his conscientious thought or belief regarding same-sex marriage. Expression of *Mr. Lee's political opinion* on same-sex marriage is suppressed by his inability to convey a message through a cake design blocked by Ashers, a public accommodation service. It should be noted that Mr. Lee was able to hire another bakery to design the cake as he wished. However, this, on the view here, does not justify tightening the public marketplace options for Mr. Lee and creating an additional burden on him as a result. This not to mention also his having to suffer the indignity of the previous refusal of service by a public accommodation business.

It is here argued that where, as in *Lee,* religious or political views are expressed; the message is often confounded with the protected status of the speaker. The government and the courts, on the view here, should be reluctant to grant exemptions to equity laws in such circumstances. This in that to do so is to undermine a secular democratic society and foster exclusion of marginalized groups and, in certain cases, to stigmatize, through official channels, certain political or social policy views. In addition, on the analysis here, the Lee case is a cautionary tale regarding proper adjudication concerning whether or not the case actually involves 'compelled speech' as is alleged.

Mr. Lee appealed to the European Court of Human Rights. He maintained that (a) his rights had been breached and interfered with due to the ruling of a public authority, the Supreme Court of the United Kingdom and that (b) there had been no breach of statutory duty under the domestic anti-discrimination laws (relating to the purported 'compelled speech' issue) in his case. Mr. Lee claimed violations resulting from the Supreme Court judgment of Convention Article 8 (right to respect for private life), Article 9 (freedom of thought, conscience and religion) and Article 10 (freedom of expression), both alone and in conjunction with Article 14 (prohibition of discrimination). Unfortunately for the complainant and the LGBTQ plus community, the European Court of Human Rights ruled[47] that the Lee case was inadmissible. This in that Mr. Lee had not, according to the European Court of Human Rights, expressly pled violations of the *European Convention on Human Rights*[48] in the domestic courts such that they would have had an opportunity to fully consider such alleged breaches. The European Court of Human Rights thus held that Mr. Lee had not exhausted the domestic remedies.

---

[47]Lee v United Kingdom (Application no. 18860/19) European Court of Human Rights 23 March 2020 https://hudoc.echr.coe.int/fre#{%22itemid%22:[%22001-202151%22]} (Accessed August 20, 2024).

[48]The Government in *Lee v Ashers*, before the European Court of Human Rights, argued that "Although the defendants invoked their rights under Articles 9 and 10 of the Convention, *the applicant*, who had access to extensive legal expertise throughout the proceedings, did *not* submit that his Convention rights should be balanced against theirs (emphasis added)." See Lee v United Kingdom (Application no. 18860/19) European Court of Human Rights 23 March 2020 at para 53 https://hudoc.echr.coe.int/fre#{%22itemid%22:[%22001-202151%22]} (Accessed August 20, 2024).

Importantly, the European Court of Human Rights has held in its case law that one of the conditions to its accepting to hear a Convention complaint is that "it [Convention rights alleged infringements] must have been aired, *either explicitly or in substance*, before the national courts (emphasis added)."[49] Arguably Mr. Lee did raise Convention rights violations "in substance" in the national courts. This by way of his arguments regarding his right to equitable access to a public accommodation service (a bakery) which would allow him to *freely express* his views regarding same-sex marriage through a cake design. The Government, however, argued before the European Court of Human Rights in *Lee* that (a) the applicant raising his Convention rights "in substance" was not sufficient and that (b) this was the case even if the domestic courts on that basis could have considered those rights.[50] The European Court of Human Rights in *Lee* attempted to navigate this issue by holding that the equity rights to free expression and private life under domestic public accommodation (consumer) law are limited and do not refer to the broad substantive rights guaranteed under Convention articles 8, 9, and 10.[51] However, respectfully, it would appear that the European Court of Human Rights may have erred on that point. This in that the issue is arguably whether the Convention rights are raised 'expressly' or 'in substance' in the domestic courts and *not* whether, for instance, the free expression rights under consumer law are in some ways narrower than those under the Convention (i.e. the former applying as they do only to a particular public marketplace context).

In the next case here discussed, *Gachechiladze v. Georgia*; the European Court of Human Rights ruled that the State in giving priority to a particular religious view (by interfering with the free expression of those who hold views inconsistent with that perspective) is violating the free expression rights of the dissenters.

---

[49] Lee v United Kingdom (Application no. 18860/19) European Court of Human Rights 23 March 2020 at para 68 https://hudoc.echr.coe.int/fre#{%22itemid%22:[%22001-202151%22]} (Accessed August 20, 2024).

[50] Lee v United Kingdom (Application no. 18860/19) European Court of Human Rights 23 March 2020 https://hudoc.echr.coe.int/fre#{%22itemid%22:[%22001-202151%22]} at para 54 (Accessed August 20, 2024).

[51] Lee v United Kingdom (Application no. 18860/19) European Court of Human Rights 23 March 2020 https://hudoc.echr.coe.int/fre#{%22itemid%22:[%22001-202151%22]} at para 70 (Accessed August 20, 2024).

2.2.2 *Gachechiladze v. Georgia (Application 2591/19) European Court of Human Rights, Judgment of 22 July 2021*

Gachechiladze v. Georgia[52] speaks to the need for tolerance of views that may be contrary to prevailing religious sentiments or religious orthodoxy.[53] *Gachechiladze v. Georgia* concerns in part an issue of access to the web for communication of a symbolic message that an entrepreneur wished to send. The message was inherent in the product the entrepreneur wished to sell. She was prohibited from access to the web for selling of certain of those products. The businessperson sold condoms with designs on the packaging. Some of the images on the packaging involved same-sex relationships. The complainant businessperson held that she wished to dispel certain stereotypes about same-sex relationships and facilitate public debate. She also wished, with respect to the design featuring same-sex relationships, to mitigate negative attitudes about the LGBTQ plus community.

The government maintained that certain of the messages (communicated via the condom package design), such as that depicting same-sex relationships, (a) could be interpreted as a dissident challenge to religious orthodox tenets and as (b) contrary to public morals and therefore the advertising of the product on the web was deemed unethical. Thus, in *Gachechiladze* the entrepreneur wished to open up the marketplace to more diverse views while in *Creative* the entrepreneur wished to deny access to her custom wedding web service for same-sex couples wishing to announce their wedding and tell their wedding story. The European Court of Human Rights in *Gachechiladze* found that the complainant businessperson's condom brand was intended to foster *political debate* and that the product was, in part, a *social and political commentary* and not entirely reflective of a commercial enterprise. The European Court of Human Rights ruled for the complainant on three of the four contested condom packaging designs holding that (a) there was no basis in a pluralistic democratic society to maintain that the Georgian Orthodox Church's views on values and ethics should take precedence, (b) the Georgian Orthodox Church's views on same-sex marriage etc. could not be the basis to silence the plaintiff's expressive speech through certain of her condom packaging designs (designs that offered political and social commentary on particular religious perspectives) and (c) as several of the condom designs could be viewed as social or political commentary; the product should be allowed in the marketplace given democratic principles concerning the value of diverse viewpoints. The Court found there to be a violation of the *European Convention on Human Rights and*

---

[52] *Gachechiladze v. Georgia* European Court of Human Rights, Judgment of 22 July 2021 https://hudoc.echr.coe.int/eng#{%22itemid%22:[%22001-211123%22]} (Accessed August 20, 2024).

[53] Peter Noorlander, Latest *Developments in the Case Law of the European Court of Human Rights on Freedom of Expression*, Bulletin No. 3 (2021) (Report Funded by the European Union and the Council of Europe) at p. 8.

Fundamental Freedoms Article 10, Freedom of Expression.[54] At the same time, the Court held that their ruling did not support products or services as protected that were *gratuitously offensive* to the Church or to mainstream public values.

Recall that in the United States case, *Creative*, the plaintiff (Ms. Smith) argued on religiously informed free speech grounds that requiring her, under public accommodation law, to give a same-sex couple access to her planned custom wedding web site (a web design service offered to the public) to announce their wedding and tell their wedding story would be to allegedly compel plaintiff's speech. That 'compelled speech', she maintained, would involve her communicating a message contrary to Christian teaching and plaintiff's sincerely held religious values. In this way, by her own admission, on the view here, plaintiff in *Creative* wished on her custom wedding website to censor any potential for wedding speech ('marriage talk' so-to-speak) by prospective same-sex client couples. Ms. Smith represented to the Court through her counsel in oral argument, as discussed, that her request for an exemption to Colorado's public accommodation law arose from her sincere religious belief that same-sex marriages are not genuine marriages according to biblical teaching. Thus, the businessperson in *Creative*, intentionally or unintentionally, arguably would be playing a role, even if small, in *shrinking or narrowing* the marketplace in terms of the possibility of communications concerning same-sex weddings.

In both *Gachechiladze* and *Creative* the businessperson complainant wishes to be free to shape their product or service as they see fit. In *Creative*, however, the businessperson, Ms. Smith, seeks to decline to custom design and host on her wedding website the *same-sex couple's wedding message*. This declination being based in *Creative* on the status (sexual orientation) of the client couple (a same-sex couple). The plaintiff contends that client status defines or shapes the message where the couple is same-sex such that Ms. Smith's religious sensitivities regarding same-sex marriage support an exemption. Colorado rejected the alleged justification for an exemption to a public accommodation here. That is, the State held that the petitioner's purported basis for the exemption request being grounded as it is on the notion that status (of the client couple) defines or alters the message in a way that is objectionable to the businessperson's sincerely held religious beliefs is not an appropriate basis for the exemption. Colorado then contended, it will be recalled, that though Ms. Smith could carve out her service as she wished to promote her Christian values; that service could not be denied to a prospective client based on status (membership in a protected group) or status held to be inextricably intertwined with message. If Ms. Smith is correct that status changes the wedding message, then Colorado held that she could nevertheless *not* exclude the wedding announcement and wedding story of same-sex couples on that rationale. This in that overall, the issue here is (protected) status discrimination. In the latter regard it is relevant to note that in the United States same-sex marriages are considered valid both in existing

[54]European Convention on Human Rights https://www.echr.coe.int/documents/convention_eng.pdf (Accessed August 20, 2024).

United States Supreme Court case law[55] and statutory law[56] and by a significant percentage of the public.[57]

2.2.3 *Case of Cengiz and Others v Turkey (Applications 48226/10 and 14027/11) European Court of Human Rights Judgement of 1 December, 2015*

In *Cengiz and Others*[58] various academics from different universities were blocked from accessing YouTube. These academics regularly, prior to the blocking, had used YouTube in their teaching and research by using YouTube's political and social commentary content. The government had blocked access on the basis that YouTube had made available ten videos that were critical of one of the founding fathers of Turkey. The complainant's argued that this bar on their use of You Tube violated their freedom of expression under the *European Convention on Human Rights* Article 10.

The blocking order as issued by a Turkish criminal court (the Ankara Criminal Trial Court) was a blanket block of YouTube and had not specifically targeted the complainants. The Turkish domestic courts on that basis held that the complainants had no legal standing to challenge the blanket YouTube blocking order. The blocking of YouTube in Turkey however constrained Turkish citizens' access to much political and social commentary. The Turkish Constitutional Court, in contrast to the Turkish lower courts, did accept that the complainants, though not specifically targeted by the blanket ban on You Tube, were victims of the block. This since, for professional reasons, they were avid users of YouTube prior to the blocking order. The Constitutional Court thus held that the complainants had legal standing to bring their case.

The European Court of Human Rights held that the interference with complainants' access to YouTube could be framed as an interference with *European Convention on Human Rights* Article 10 on free expression which covers both freely

---

[55] *Obergefell v Hodges*: "The Fourteenth Amendment requires a State to license a marriage between two people of the same sex and to recognize a marriage between two people of the same sex when their marriage was lawfully licensed and performed out-of-State." pp. 3–28. https://www.law.cornell.edu/supct/pdf/14-556.pdf (Accessed August 20, 2024).

[56] Kinery, E Biden signs bill to protect same-sex and interracial marriages (published 13 December, 2022) https://www.cnbc.com/2022/12/13/biden-signs-respect-for-marriage-act-to-protect-same-sex-interracial-marriages.html (Accessed August 20, 2024).

[57] Pew Research Centre, About six-in-ten Americans say legalization of same-sex marriage is good for society (published 15 November, 2022) https://www.pewresearch.org/fact-tank/2022/11/15/about-six-in-ten-americans-say-legalization-of-same-sex-marriage-is-good-for-society/ (Accessed August 20, 2024).

[58] Case of Cengiz and Others v Turkey (Applications 48226/10 and 14027/11) European Court of Human Rights Judgement of 1 December, 2015 (Accessed 23 December 2023).

imparting and receiving information. The European Court of Human Rights held that blanket bars to internet sites due to selected objectionable content were not consistent with Turkish law at the time though after the case at bar the law was amended to include that possibility.

In *Creative*, the plaintiff, Ms. Smith, requests the imprimatur of the State to effectuate a blanket ban on access for an entire *targeted protected group* (same-sex couples) to a particular internet platform; namely her custom wedding website service-a public accommodation. The plaintiff argues that the same-sex status of the client couple in and of itself changes the message content in, for her, an unacceptable fashion. Thus, plaintiff in *Creative*, it appears, requested an exemption from State anti-discrimination law to allow for a *blanket bar* on any same-sex couple having access to her proposed custom wedding website. The latter regardless of the specific details of the custom wedding web design for a wedding announcement and wedding story that any particular such couple might envision. At the same time, plaintiff argues she would provide access to a same-sex couple to create for them a custom website on a topic other than their same-sex marriage. This though the meaning content-a wedding announcement and personal wedding story- is substantively the same as the messages of heterosexual couples whose custom designed communications would appear on the Creative custom wedding website.

It seems to the current author that, possibly with some exceptions,[59] *blanket bars* prohibiting a certain class of persons (i.e. a protected status group) or all of the public access to an internet platform (especially but not exclusively when based in part or in whole on unjustified discriminatory attitudes or beliefs about members of the particular consumer group) are likely to constitute an unjustified violation of the freedom of expression of the person(s) wishing to impart or receive information via that platform.

2.2.4 *Orlandi and Others v Italy European Court of Human Rights (Application No. 26431/12) Judgment of 14 December 2017 and Vallianatos and Others v Greece European Court of Human Rights (Applications 29381/09 and 32684/09) Grand Chamber Judgment of November 7, 2013*

The issue of the validity of same-sex marriages has arisen in the European Court of Human Rights jurisprudence. In *Orlandi and Others v Italy*,[60] for instance, the Court

[59] Those exceptions might include for instance bars against children accessing certain internet sites that pose a grave risk to the mental health of children.

[60] *Orlandi and Others v Italy European Court of Human Rights* (application no. 26431/12) 14 December, 2017 https://www.echr.coe.int/documents/fs_sexual_orientation_eng.pdf (Accessed August 20, 2024).

found that Italy had violated the right to respect for family and private life (Article 8 of the *European Convention on Human Rights*) since Italy did not recognize or allow registration of the marriages of the same-sex couple complainants. The couples involved had been legally married abroad but Italy did not recognize their marriages or offer them any protection as a married couple prior to the date Italy legislated recognition of same-sex *civil unions*. Thus, the European Court of Human Rights affirmed in *Orlandi and Others* that same-sex marriages are true relationships that must be legally recognized though individual nation states are granted leeway as to whether to recognize such relationships as legal marriages or legally as civil unions. This position was further bolstered in *Vallianatos and Others v Greece*.[61] That case concerned same-sex couple complainants who had been denied having their stable committed same-sex relationships legally recognized as a civil union. This in that Greece, at the time, reserved recognition of civil unions for only heterosexual couples. The European Court of Human Rights found that this approach violated Article 14 of the *European Convention on Human Rights*' prohibition on discrimination as well as Convention Article 8 on respect for private and family life.

Recall that in *Creative* the issue was plaintiff's request for an exemption to the public accommodation law in order that she be permitted to exclude same-sex couples as clients from her custom wedding website design service. This on the grounds that in her religious perspective such marriages were not true marriages. Though she did not speak to the issue; plaintiff presumably, on her religious view, would not also regard same-sex unions (i.e., a civil union) as properly legalized in any framework. Arguably a grant of such an exemption in *Creative,* (such as was required pursuant to the United States Supreme Court ruling in the case) would, in the public perception, assign the government's imprimatur (a) to the view of same-sex unions (whether a lawful marriage or legal civil union) as purportedly not true unions and (b) unions to be perceived by society at large as unacceptable. Indeed arguably it was, it would seem, that plaintiff feared what she regarded as participating in conveying a contrary message (should she provide the custom wedding website service to same-sex couples) and that prompted her to request an exemption from Colorado public accommodation law.

2.2.5 Concluding Comment

The cases discussed in this chapter were intended to encourage us to reflect anew on who in fact is being victimized in these scenarios and whose freedom of expression rights are being infringed. The argument was made in the case analyses here that it is

---

[61] *Vallianatos and Others v Greece* European Court of Human Rights (applications 29381/09 and 32684/09) Grand Chamber Judgment November 7, 2013 https://hudoc.echr.coe.int/fre#{%22itemid%22:[%22002-9224%22]} (Accessed August 20, 2024).

those wishing to express certain dissenting political or social views that may clash with religious orthodoxy who in fact have too often had their voices suppressed and their access to the marketplace public accommodation unjustifiably curtailed. The culture war framework here appears to be a smokescreen for a more fundamental struggle; that being the one to maintain the separation of Church and State as a feature of a pluralistic democratic State.

References

Materials

Amicus Brief Centre for Constitutional Jurisprudence, Claremont Institute, United States Supreme Court In 303 Creative LLC et al. v Aubrey Elenis et al. https://www.supremecourt.gov/DocketPDF/21/21-476/198003/20211028133149710_21-476%20CCJ%20ISO%20Cert.pdf (Accessed August 20, 2024)

Colorado Anti-Discrimination Act (CADA), Colorado Department of regulatory Services (Civil Rights Division) Discriminatory Complaints https://ccrd.colorado.gov/discrimination (Accessed August 20, 2024)

303 Creative, Lori Smith v Aubrey Elenis et al. (United States Supreme Court) Argued December 5, 2022 Oral Argument United States Supreme Court audio C-Span https://www.c-span.org/video/?524449-1/303-creative-llc-v-elenis-oral-argument (Accessed August 20, 2024)

Criss, D (CNN online) Here's why students don't have to recite the Pledge of Allegiance Published 5:54 PM EST, Tue February 19, 2019 https://www.cnn.com/2019/02/19/us/pledge-of-allegiance-explainer-trnd/index.html (Accessed August 20, 2024)

Diamant, J Pew Research Centre *How Catholics around the world see same-sex marriage, homosexuality* 2 November 2020 https://www.pewresearch.org/short-reads/2020/11/02/how-catholics-around-the-world-see-same-sex-marriage-homosexuality/ (Accessed August 20, 2024)

European Convention on Human Rights https://www.echr.coe.int/documents/convention_eng.pdf (Accessed August 20, 2024)

Kinery, E *Biden signs bill to protect same-sex and interracial marriages* (published 13 December, 2022) https://www.cnbc.com/2022/12/13/biden-signs-respect-for-marriage-act-to-protect-same-sex-interracial-marriages.html (Accessed August 20, 2024)

Noorlander, Peter (2021) Council of Europe *Latest Developments in the Case Law of the European Court of Human Rights on Freedom of Expression*, Bulletin No. 3 (Report Funded by the European Union and the Council of Europe) https://rm.coe.int/e-bulletin-04-english-with-covers-2753-0922-2918-1/1680a7ad0e (Accessed August 20, 2024)

Robinson, S (2022) Free Speech Case Tests Whether Anti-Discrimination Laws Can Compel Artistic Work *Maine Wire* (5 December 2022) https://www.

themainewire.com/2022/12/free-speech-case-tests-whether-anti-discrimination-laws-can-compel-artistic-work/ (Accessed August 20, 2024)

Ross, Catherine J. The Real and the Phantom *303 Creative*: Which Is More Dangerous? *The George Washington Law Review* July 25, 2023 https://www.gwlr.org/303-creative-elenis-response/ (Accessed August 20, 2024)

Scotus Blog: 303 Creative LLC v. Elenis https://www.scotusblog.com/case-files/cases/303-creative-llc-v-elenis/ (Accessed August 20, 2024)

Volokh, Eugene (2021) Can Places of Public Accommodation Exclude People Based on Their Politics? It all depends on where you are. https://reason.com/volokh/2021/04/08/can-places-of-public-accommodation-exclude-people-based-on-their-politics/ (Accessed August 20, 2024)

United States Supreme Court Cases

303 Creative, Lori Smith v Aubrey Elenis, Charles Garcia, Ajay Menon, Miguel Rene Elias, Richard Lewis, Kendra Anderson, Sergio Cordova, Jessica Pocock, Phil Weiser United States Supreme Court No. 21-476. Argued December 5, 2022—Decided June 30, 2023

Obergefell v Hodges Supreme Court of the United States No. 14-556. Argued April 28, 2015—Decided June 26, 2015 https://www.law.cornell.edu/supct/pdf/14-556.pdf (Accessed August 20, 2024)

European Court of Human Rights Cases

Case of Cengiz and Others v Turkey European Court of Human Rights (Applications nos. 48226/10 and 14027/11) Judgment 12 December 2015 (Accessed 23 December 2023)

Gachechiladze v. Georgia, European Court of Human Rights, Judgment of 22 July 2021 https://hudoc.echr.coe.int/eng#{%22itemid%22:[%22001-211123%22]} (Accessed August 20, 2024)

Lee v United Kingdom (Application no. 18860/19) European Court of Human Rights 23 March 2020 https://hudoc.echr.coe.int/fre#{%22itemid%22:[%22001-202151%22]} (Accessed August 20, 2024)

Orlandi and Others v Italy European Court of Human Rights (application no. 26431/12) 14 December 2017 (European Court of Human Rights Fact Sheet at p. 16) https://www.echr.coe.int/documents/fs_sexual_orientation_eng.pdf (Accessed August 20, 2024)

Vallianatos and Others v Greece (European Court of Human Rights) (applications 29381/09 and 32684/09) Grand Chamber Judgment November 7, 2013 https://hudoc.echr.coe.int/fre#{%22itemid%22:[%22002-9224%22]} (Accessed August 20, 2024)

European Court of Justice Cases

Coleman v Attridge Law European Court of Justice (Case C-303/06) [2008] ICR 1128 https://eur-lex.europa.eu/legal-content/EN/TXT/PDF/?uri=CELEX:62006CJ0303 (Accessed August 20, 2024)

United Kingdom Supreme Court Cases

Lee v Ashers Baking Company Limited and Others, Reference by the Attorney General for Northern Ireland Judgement Date: 10 Oct 2018 (Case ID UKSC 2017/0020) [2018] UKSC 49 Available at https://www.supremecourt.uk/cases/uksc-2017-0020.html (Accessed August 20, 2024)

Chapter 3
US Education Culture Wars: Freedom of Expression, Race, Gender and Revisionist History

Abstract This chapter discusses US 'education culture wars' in the context of debates about educational instruction regarding race/ethnicity and gender as well as intersectionality. In this regard, the Oklahoma federal case *Black Emergency Response Team et al. v John O'Connor (Attorney General of Oklahoma)* is examined. That case concerns an Oklahoma statute that impinges on educators' freedom of expression rights in addressing race and gender in the classroom. In addition, this chapter explores affirmative action in university admissions in the context of the United States Supreme Court case *Students for Fair Admissions, Inc. v President and Fellows of Harvard University*. The latter case represents a challenge to whether affirmative action relating to race/ethnicity in US university admissions is being fairly applied and whether or not the university admissions process reflects a meritocratic system. Both legal cases raise the issue of 'revisionist history' that is intended to minimize or even negate historical truths and their legacy, especially about race as a factor in US society. Also considered are relevant selected comparative law cases.

3.1 Barring Discussions of Critical Race Theory and Gender in the Classroom: Contributions to Revisionist History

3.1.1 Introduction

This chapter addresses the right to education as well as the First Amendment right to freedom of expression in the context of US culture wars concerning 'critical race theory' and gender discussions in the classroom. An Oklahoma federal case is discussed in which the plaintiffs challenge the constitutionality of an Oklahoma law that constrains the discussion of race and gender in the classroom. Plaintiffs contend that the contested statute is (1) overbroad with ill-defined notions and prohibitions and that it (2) unconstitutionally chills speech undercutting the possibility for in-depth critical instruction and informed thoughtful classroom discussion on race and gender. The law at issue, plaintiffs contend further, exacerbates

S. C. Grover, *Litigating the Politics of Human Rights*, Ius Gentium: Comparative Perspectives on Law and Justice 121, https://doi.org/10.1007/978-3-031-82463-0_3

discriminatory attitudes and behavior relating to race and gender. Also discussed here is the notion of 'revisionist history' implicating ethnicity, race and/or gender. The argument is made that revisionist history is arguably most often discriminatory or, in some cases, even reaches to the level of 'hate speech.' The latter where such revisionism seeks to grossly distort, minimize or even negate painful landmark historical truths and quash open and honest discussion of that true history and its legacy.

3.1.2 *Black Emergency Response Team et al. v John O'Connor, Attorney General of Oklahoma et al. US District Court for the Western District of Oklahoma Case No. 5:21-cv-1022-G (Before Hon. Charles B. Goodwin)*

The case to be discussed here *Black Emergency Response Team et al. v John O'Connor, Attorney General of Oklahoma et al.*[1] concerns an Oklahoma law hereafter referred to as "H.B. 1775" or "the Act" and its implementing regulations. The Act stipulates that mandatory gender or sexual diversity training, or counselling are prohibited in any Oklahoma institution of higher learning on the condition that voluntary counselling is not prohibited. Also prohibited are any orientation or requirement that involves alleged stereotyping or bias on the basis of race or sex.

Concepts that align with Oklahoma Academic Standards can be taught to schoolchildren but any requirement in a course or part of a course that includes one or more of the following notions or concepts is prohibited under the Act (a) any notion of one race or sex being superior to another; (b) the notion that a person can be inherently racist, sexist or oppressive, whether consciously or unconsciously, just by virtue of being a member of a certain identifiable group defined by race or sex; (c) the notion that race or sex of a target can justify in part or in whole discrimination or other adverse treatment of that targeted individual; (d) the notion that it is impossible and improper to treat others in a manner that pays no regard to race or sex; (e) the notion that moral character is inextricably and inevitably linked to or determined by race or sex; (f) the notion of group culpability holding that individuals belonging to a certain identifiable group defined by race or sex are responsible for past actions committed by others in their same group; (g) the notion that any individual member of a group defined by race or sex should experience any form of psychological distress due to the latter fact in and of itself; and (h) the notion that a belief in meritocracy (that effort and success are generally inevitably linked) are oppressive

[1]The Oklahoma case is but the first of such suits likely to follow in other US states concerning analogous laws. The case was argued December 4, 2023.

devices invented by members of a dominant class defined by race and/or sex.[2] Let us consider next then the lawsuit brought by the American Civil Liberties Union and others on behalf of Oklahoma students and educators in opposition to the Oklahoma Act (H.B. 1775) challenging its constitutionality.

3.1.3 The Oklahoma Law in Dispute That Constrains Discussion on Race and Gender in the Classroom

Plaintiffs' complaint argues[3] that H.B.1775 (the Act) is imposed without a valid pedagogical objective and mandates *unconstitutional censorship* on discussions regarding race and gender in classrooms. Plaintiffs contend that these unconstitutional limitations on free expression were, according to the Act, to be implemented across all educational levels from elementary to post-secondary institutions of learning upon pain of various severe penalties for non-compliance (i.e., loss of professional licenses or institutional accreditation). Exacerbating the matter is the fact that the Act allows any private person to file a complaint against a school board or the State Board of Education under the auspices of the Act. Plaintiffs contend that the Act violates both First Amendment free expression protections and the equity and due process provisions of the Fourteenth Amendment.[4] The complaint hence is not just against the State[5] but against particular Oklahoma educational institutions and certain representatives in their official capacity that are alleged to have harmed plaintiffs. The latter by allegedly infringing on certain of plaintiffs' constitutional rights. This in the latter defendants' efforts to comply with Oklahoma Act (H.B. 1775).[6] Plaintiffs argue then that they have standing due to the particularized harms they have allegedly suffered and continue to suffer due to Defendants'

[2]H.B. 1775 70 OK Stat § 70-24-157 (2021) Education; prohibiting certain training for students; prohibiting courses from including certain concept https://legiscan.com/OK/text/HB1775/id/2387002 (Accessed August 20, 2024).

[3]Black Emergency Response Team et al. v John O'Connor, Attorney General of Oklahoma et al. Amended Complaint at para 2 https://www.aclu.org/legal-document/amended-complaint-6 (Accessed August 20, 2024).

[4]Complainants held the court had subject matter jurisdiction under the First and Fourteenth Amendment and jurisdiction to provide declaratory relief. See Black Emergency Response Team et al. v John O'Connor, Attorney General of Oklahoma et al. Amended Complaint at para 31 https://www.aclu.org/legal-document/amended-complaint-6 (Accessed August 20, 2024).

[5]Black Emergency Response Team al. v John O'Connor, Attorney General of Oklahoma et al. Plaintiffs' Memorandum of Law in Opposition to Oklahoma University Regent's Motion to Dismiss https://www.aclu.org/legal-document/plaintiffs-response-opposition-ou-regents-motion-dismiss (Accessed August 20, 2024).

[6]Black Emergency Response Team et al. v John O'Connor, Attorney General of Oklahoma et al. Plaintiffs' Memorandum of Law in Opposition to Edmond Public School's Motion to Dismiss https://www.aclu.org/legal-document/plaintiffs-response-opposition-eps-defendants-motion-dismiss (Accessed August 20, 2024).

implementation of H.B. 1775 (the Act) including but not necessarily limited to (a) curtailment of their freedom of speech in the classroom in terms of disallowing certain key viable pedagogically important topics for discussion, restrictions in the permissible design of courses such that contested race and gender notions are off-limits, and elimination of mandatory training, orientation or coursework on sexual harassment, diversity, equity and inclusion and (b) threats of prosecution involving various professional penalties for educators triggered by violations of the Act's implementation regulations.[7]

The complainants further maintain that the allegedly vague language of the Act (such as universities being barred from offering any "orientation or requirement" that discusses "any form of sex or race stereotyping" or "bias on the basis of race or sex") is a significant threat to academic freedom in the university.[8] The University of Oklahoma, in an effort to comply with the Act, has removed from its previous mandatory offerings; sexual harassment training and coursework on diversity, equity and inclusion. The Act arguably reflects an implicit prohibition on mandatory teaching of fundamental human rights and of sociological notions relating to contested race and gender concepts. For instance, school teachers are barred under the Act from discussing with schoolchildren, as part of a course, a list of eight specified concepts relating to race and gender (here previously discussed). Plaintiffs pointed out that these eight concepts had been banned for classroom discussion under a Trump executive order in September 2020[9] which order was blocked in part as unconstitutionally vague[10] by a federal court.[11]

Plaintiffs allege that the result of the contested Oklahoma Act also includes, at all educational levels, 'chilled speech' in the classroom and the banning of books that raise contested issues of race or gender.[12] The impact of the Act in part is then that a diversity of authors and opinions about contemporary American society and on American history have been removed from the classroom at all educational levels.

[7]The Act (H.B. 1775) lists its prohibitions with the wording "shall" thus stipulating mandatory obligations for educators.

[8]Black Emergency Response Team et al. v John O'Connor, Attorney General of Oklahoma et al. Amended Complaint at para 2 https://www.aclu.org/legal-document/amended-complaint-6 (Accessed August 20, 2024).

[9]Trump Executive Order 13950 of September 22, 2020 https://www.federalregister.gov/documents/2020/09/28/2020-21534/combating-race-and-sex-stereotyping (Accessed August 20, 2024).

[10]Santa Cruz Lesbian & Gay Cmty. Ctr. V Trump (United States District Court Northern District of California), San Jose Division 508 F. Supp. 3d at 543.

[11]Trump Executive Order 13950 was also revoked and replaced by "Advancing Racial Equity and Support for Underserved Communities Through the Federal Government" a Biden Executive Order of 20 January, 2021 championing inclusiveness and equity See Office of Federal Contract Compliance Programs *President Biden Revokes Executive Order* 13950 https://www.dol.gov/agencies/ofccp/executive-order-13950 (Accessed August 20, 2024).

[12]Black Emergency Response Team et al. v John O'Connor, Attorney General of Oklahoma et al. Amended Complaint at para 3 https://www.aclu.org/legal-document/amended-complaint-6 (Accessed August 20, 2024).

Plaintiffs contend that the emergency measure (the Act) in fact represents the imposition of a particular political view that rejects notions of 'systemic racism' and 'implicit bias'. The Act then, the complainants contend, embodies a political perspective held by the Act's legislative supporters and imposed upon students and educators in the State along with content-based censorship barring competing views.[13] The complainants argue further that the Act fosters *undemocratic* attitudes and behavior.[14] The amended complaint goes so far in fact as to allege that "the Act's censorship … rests upon illicit motives and inflicts disparate harm: H.B. 1775 was enacted with the particular intent of harming historically marginalized students, and the Act has had its intended effect."[15]

Importantly the amended complaint also points to the relevance of and necessity for open and truthful discussions of Oklahoma history and how the latter continues to affect contemporary society in Oklahoma. That history includes shameful episodes such as (a) the so-called Indian boarding schools intended to separate indigenous children from their families and communities for at least some time and remake them in the European illusory then idealized model and (b) the Tulsa race massacre in which hundreds of persons of African descent in a prosperous black neighborhood were murdered.[16] According to the complainants, prior to the enactment of the Oklahoma Act at issue there were attempts in regards to such aforementioned history to "rectify…historic erasure and provide a fuller account of historical events, incorporating diverse opinions."[17] The cost of not discussing such history is in part that of not learning any lessons regarding the unacceptably high risk of not addressing racism and sexism today (as plaintiffs point out). However, there is also the real risk that such 'chilled speech' will inevitably lead to actual negating of such historical truths and the teaching of a revisionist history directly or constructively largely through omission. For instance, the admonition under the Act against discussing race superiority has chilled discussion even if to criticize and invalidate

[13] Black Emergency Response Team et al. v John O'Connor, Attorney General of Oklahoma et al. Amended Complaint at para 8 https://www.aclu.org/legal-document/amended-complaint-6 (Accessed August 20, 2024).

[14] Black Emergency Response Team et al. v John O'Connor, Attorney General of Oklahoma et al. Amended Complaint at para 4–5 https://www.aclu.org/legal-document/amended-complaint-6 (Accessed August 20, 2024).

[15] Black Emergency Response Team et al. v John O'Connor, Attorney General of Oklahoma et al. Amended Complaint at para 37 https://www.aclu.org/legal-document/amended-complaint-6 (Accessed August 20, 2024).

[16] Black Emergency Response Team et al. v John O'Connor, Attorney General of Oklahoma et al. Amended Complaint at para 6 https://www.aclu.org/legal-document/amended-complaint-6 (Accessed August 20, 2024).

[17] Black Emergency Response Team et al. v John O'Connor, Attorney General of Oklahoma et al. Amended Complaint at para 7 https://www.aclu.org/legal-document/amended-complaint-6 (Accessed August 20, 2024).

such historical perspectives grounded on racism and stereotypes.[18] That revisionist history likely would outright directly or indirectly minimize or deny the past and likewise the intergenerational suffering resulting from historical instances of systemic racism and sexism perpetrated against marginalized communities.

Legislation, in essence, supporting revisionist history, as arguably the Oklahoma Act does, intentionally or unintentionally (under the guise of being an anti-race and anti-gender discrimination initiative) is, on the view here, legislation that in fact violates the democratic norms of inclusion, equity and free speech. The current author leaves it to the reader to decide for themselves (a) whether such revisionist history is a foreseeable progeny of Oklahoma HB 1775 (the Act), (b) what the Act, if resulting in revisionist history and let stand, means for education rights, freedom of expression and the right to truth[19] for students and the public in the State as well as (c) whether Oklahoma, given the State's (and more generally America's) historical links to racist ideology and incidents that harmed masses of, for example, indigenous persons and persons of African descent, has a special moral duty to ensure that attempts at revisionist history in that regard are quashed.

We will consider next various comparative law cases on discrimination and freedom of speech. Some of these cases address also European Court of Human Rights designated 'hate speech' involving the minimization and negation of past historical wrongs or the otherwise untruthful revising of history. Such comparative law cases provide useful perspectives on various judicial approaches to the handling of revisionist history cases, and to racist and other hate speech and the weight assigned by the courts to such matters.

3.2 Comparative Law Perspectives on Freedom of Speech, Discrimination and Hate Speech

3.2.1 Carl Jóhann Lilliendahl v Iceland (European Court of Human Rights) (Application No. 29297/18) Judgment 11 June 2020

Lilliendahl v Iceland involves issues of LGBTQ plus rights and freedom of expression issues. In April 2015 the municipal council of an Icelandic town named Hafnarfjörður approved a proposal to strengthen education and counselling in elementary and secondary schools on LGBTQ plus community issues. The initiative was to be implemented with the collaboration of a national LGBTQ association named *Samtökin '78*. The decision of the municipal council was reported in the news

[18] Black Emergency Response Team et al. v John O'Connor, Attorney General of Oklahoma et al. Amended Complaint at para 48 https://www.aclu.org/legal-document/amended-complaint-6 (Accessed August 20, 2024).

[19] The 'right to truth' under international law is discussed here in the chapter conclusion.

and there was much public controversy and discussion about it. A radio show had callers call in and voice their opinion on the matter. There was later an article published in which there was diverse opinion expressed on some of the very derogatory comments made during the radio show about the proposal and about the LGBTQ plus community. The latter with allegedly little push back, if at all, from the radio show host. The applicant Mr. Carl Jóhann Lilliendahl wrote comments in response to the article which comments were posted and, arguably, from the viewpoint of the LGBTQ plus community, amounted to 'hate speech' regarding that community. Samtökin '78 reported the applicant's Mr. Carl Jóhann Lilliendahl's speech to the police. The police investigation led to indictment of Mr. Lilliendahl's for public threatening of and defamation of a group based on the members' sexual orientation and gender identity in violation of the relevant section of the General Penal Code. The District Court of Reykjavík, however, acquitted Mr. Lilliendahl. The District Court held that his comments were protected free speech and did not rise to the level required so as to trigger a penal code violation. This, the Court found, as there was purportedly no intent to violate the criminal code and it was not clear that the comments were intended to foster violence.

The acquittal was appealed to the Supreme Court of Iceland and was overturned. The Supreme Court found that Mr. Carl Jóhann Lilliendahl's speech engaged the limitations on constitutionally protected free speech stipulated both in Icelandic law and the *European Convention on Human Rights*. This, the Court found, in that his speech violated the rights of members of the LGBTQ plus community to respect for private life.

The applicant appealed to the European Court of Human Rights. The latter court found that the applicant's speech constituted a form of "hate speech" that slandered members of the LGBTQ plus community. The European Court of Human Rights concurred with the Icelandic Supreme Court that in order to ensure members of the LGBTQ plus community equal enjoyment of their rights, it was proper under the law (Icelandic law and the *Convention*) to find that the applicant's speech in this instance was not constitutionally protected. The European Court of Human Rights agreed with the Supreme Court of Iceland that the applicant's speech did *not* add to the public debate about or critique concerning the municipal council's decision to strengthen education and counselling in elementary and secondary schools on LGBTQ plus community issues. Rather the European Court of Human Rights concurred that Mr. Lilliendahl's speech was merely insulting, hurtful and defamatory. The European Court of Human Rights further found that the fine imposed with no prison term was proportionate and not at all excessive in the circumstance. The European Court of Human Rights thus found Mr. Carl Jóhann Lilliendahl's complaint to be manifestly ill-founded and inadmissible as a breach of Convention Article 10 on free expression or an infringement of Article 14 (discrimination based on political opinion) read together with Article 10.

3.2.2 *Pastors v Germany (European Court of Human Rights) (Application No. 5525/14) Judgment 3 October 2019*

In considering the Pastors case recall that in the United States (Oklahoma) case *Black Emergency Response Team et al. v John O'Connor et al.*[20] the issue of revisionist history was one of the central concerns. In the *Black Emergency Response Team et al. v John O'Connor et al.* case that revisionist history was alleged to be the result of specific legislation and its implementation. That legislation purportedly chilled speech about historical racism and sexism in America's past as well as chilling discussion of the legacy of that history. Pastors is a case involving revisionist history as *the* central issue and addresses the limits of free speech as well as positive State obligations around these matters.

Plaintiff in *Pastors* was a German parliamentarian and chairperson of the National Democratic Party of Germany in the Land Parliament of Mecklenburg-Western Pomerania. On 27 January 2010 a Holocaust Memorial Day was held in the Land Parliament, but no member of the National Democratic Party of Germany attended. The next day, the applicant, Mr. Pastors, gave a speech that included accusations that the Holocaust Remembrance Day was but political theatre and that any emotional concern about Germany's past in that regard displayed at that memorial was feigned.[21] Pastors further made inflammatory statements that the German Courts found amounted to *revisionist history*. These statements included, for instance, asserting that the Holocaust Remembrance Day was but part of a propaganda campaign that the democratic parties were imposing on the German people for political and commercial motives and that lies about Auschwitz were thereby also perpetrated.[22]

On the basis of his aforementioned speech, Mr. Pastor's immunity from prosecution as a parliamentarian was revoked by the Land Parliament of Mecklenburg-Western Pomerania on 1 February 2012. This in that such immunity did not provide a shield for the making of defamatory statements. On 16 August 2012 Mr. Pastors was convicted by the Schwerin District Court of violating the memory of the dead and convicted of defamation.[23] The German law held applicable by the German

[20] Black Emergency Response Team et al. v John O'Connor, Attorney General of Oklahoma et al. Amended Complaint https://www.aclu.org/legal-document/amended-complaint-6 (Accessed August 20, 2024).

[21] Pastors v Germany European Court of Human Rights (Application No. 5525/14) Judgment 3 October 2019 para https://hudoc.echr.coe.int/fre#{%22documentcollectionid2%22:[%22GRANDCHAMBER%22,%22CHAMBER%22],%22itemid%22:[%22001-196148%22]} (Accessed August 20, 2024).

[22] Pastors v Germany (European Court of Human Rights) (Application No. 5525/14) Judgment 3 October 2019 para 5 https://hudoc.echr.coe.int/fre#{%22documentcollectionid2%22:[%22GRANDCHAMBER%22,%22CHAMBER%22],%22itemid%22:[%22001-196148%22]} (Accessed August 20, 2024).

[23] Pastors v Germany European Court of Human Rights (Application No. 5525/14) Judgment 3 October 2019 para 7 https://hudoc.echr.coe.int/fre#{%22documentcollectionid2%22:[%22

District Court was Criminal Code: Article 187: Intentional defamation and Criminal Code: Article 189: Violating the memory of the dead.[24] Mr. Pastors was sentenced to 8 months' imprisonment, suspended on probation. Mr. Pastors appealed but lost his appeal. The Appeals Court held that Mr. Pastors speech of 28 January 2010 incorporated untruths about the Nazi perpetrated Holocaust and about the extermination of Jews at Auschwitz. The speech wrongly denied, the Appeals Court maintained, the systemic racially motivated mass extermination of Jews[25] that had taken place during the Third Reich. While recognizing that Mr. Pastors was free to express his opinion as to the Holocaust Remembrance Day in most respects, that freedom, the Court held, did *not* however extend so far as to protect *Auschwitz denial*. The Appeals Court found that the victims of Mr. Pastors' court-determined defamation were the Jewish victims of Nazi persecution, both the deceased victims and the survivors. The Appeals Court held further that the mass extermination of Jews at Auschwitz was an *historical fact* and hence Mr. Pastors' Auschwitz denial was an untruth that offended the personal dignity of Jews.[26] Mr. Pastors appealed to the Constitutional Court which declined, without providing reasons, to hear his plea. At that point Mr. Pastors appealed to the European Court of Human Rights for relief.

Mr. Pastors claimed that his Article 10 right to freedom of expression under the *European Convention on Human Rights*[27] had been violated with his prosecution for his court-determined defamation of Jewish victims and survivors of the Holocaust. The defamation, the German courts found, arose due to Mr. Pastors' Auschwitz denial in a speech to parliament which was also carried on the internet. Mr. Pastors claimed that the German courts had misconstrued his speech as Holocaust denial and that it was merely a critique of so-called German Holocaust remembrance culture. The European Court of Human Rights in *Pastors* found that the German Courts had properly prosecuted the appellant under the German criminal code for intentional defamation and defaming the memory of the dead. The European Court of Human Rights further held that the German Courts had properly assessed Mr. Pastors' entire contested speech of 28 January 2010 and properly concluded that he had (a) purposively included material in part of the speech that amounted to Holocaust denial notwithstanding the historical facts to the contrary and (b) wrongly and intentionally contended that democratic parties were using Holocaust remembrance

GRANDCHAMBER%22,%22CHAMBER%22],%22itemid%22:[%22001-196148%22]} (Accessed August 20, 2024).

[24]Pastors v Germany European Court of Human Rights (Application No. 5525/14) Judgment 3 October 2019 para 28 https://hudoc.echr.coe.int/fre#{%22documentcollectionid2%22:[%22GRANDCHAMBER%22,%22CHAMBER%22],%22itemid%22:[%22001-196148%22]} (Accessed August 20, 2024).

[25]The Holocaust involved also the mass extermination of other identifiable groups such as members of the LGBTQ community, Roma people and the disabled.

[26]Their personal dignity was offended in that the Holocaust is part of the history of the Jews and in that way part of the personal identity of this identifiable religious group.

[27]*European Convention on Human Rights* https://www.echr.coe.int/documents/convention_eng.pdf (Accessed August 20, 2024).

to oppress and exploit the German people. The latter fact especially, the European Court of Human Rights determined, triggered Article 17 of the *European Convention* which states:

> **European Convention on Human Rights: Article 17—Prohibition of abuse of rights**
> Nothing in this Convention may be interpreted as implying for any State, group or person any right to engage in any activity or perform any act aimed at the destruction of any of the rights and freedoms set forth herein or at their limitation to a greater extent than is provided for in the Convention.[28]

The European Court of Human Rights found that Mr. Pastors' objective was to use his freedom of expression protection (a protection that is even more stringent for parliamentarians) to (a) promote notions that contradict the democratic spirit and values underlying the Convention and (b) to defame the dignity of Jewish persons persecuted by the Nazis during the Holocaust.[29] The European Court of Human Rights further opined that given Germany's historical links to Nazi atrocities, the German State had a special duty to disavow any denial or other whitewashing of that painful and horrendous historical truth.[30] The European Court of Human Rights found that Mr. Pastors complaint was 'manifestly ill-founded' and did *not* constitute a violation of Article 10 of the European Convention. This given that Article 10(2) of the Convention permits interference with the freedom of expression prescribed by law if and when necessary in a democratic society as, for instance, for "the protection of the reputation or rights of others."[31] It is apparent then that revisionist history is something that the European Court of Human Rights is quite sensitive to and considers inherently anti-democratic, particularly where that revisionism seeks to denigrate any particular ethnic, religious or other protected group in the process.

---

[28] *European Convention on Human Rights* Article 17 https://www.echr.coe.int/documents/convention_eng.pdf (Accessed August 20, 2024).

[29] Pastors v Germany European Court of Human Rights (Application No. 5525/14) Judgment 3 October 2019 para 46 https://hudoc.echr.coe.int/fre#{%22documentcollectionid2%22:[%22GRANDCHAMBER%22,%22CHAMBER%22],%22itemid%22:[%22001-196148%22]} (Accessed August 20, 2024).

[30] Pastors v Germany European Court of Human Rights (Application No. 5525/14) Judgment 3 October 2019 para 46 https://hudoc.echr.coe.int/fre#{%22documentcollectionid2%22:[%22GRANDCHAMBER%22,%22CHAMBER%22],%22itemid%22:[%22001-196148%22]} (Accessed August 20, 2024).

[31] *European Convention on Human Rights* Article 10(2) https://www.echr.coe.int/documents/convention_eng.pdf (Accessed August 20, 2024).

3.2.3 Kaboglu and Oran v Turkey (European Court of Human Rights) (Application Nos. 1759/08, 50766/10 and 50782/10) Judgment 30 October 2018

Kaboglu and Oran are university professors specializing in human rights. They were authors of an advisory report on minority and cultural rights for a Human Rights Council in which Council they held high office. Subsequent to the issuance and public disclosure of their report; they were the targets of verbal assaults and threats of physical violence, some appearing in press coverage.[32] The applicant professors had in that report advocated (in a respectful fashion that did not denigrate their ultra-nationalist opponents) for a more democratic Turkish culture that values diversity, minority rights and inclusion. The latter view being in opposition thus to the prevailing Turkish ethos that stressed a more homogenous monocultural society and ethic as a means to national strength and cohesion. The domestic courts had dismissed the complainants' request for damages relating to alleged stigmatization and fear for personal safety resulting from the press coverage at issue. The domestic courts maintained that (a) the press coverage was fair and did not exceed the bounds of what was acceptable in the debate of the contentious issues and that (b) the authors of the press articles enjoyed freedom of expression to have, as they did, stated their opposing views. The case raises then freedom of the press issues and specifically the matter of academic freedom of university professors.

The European Court of Human Rights held that the complainant professors were not political figures who could be expected to tolerate more virulent attacks on their views. The professors had been accused in the press of undermining the cohesiveness of the Turkish State and allegedly being pawns of foreign powers in this regard which wished to weaken the Turkish State. Certain aspects of the press coverage were held by the European Court of Human Rights, in contrast to the findings of the domestic courts, to be such as to incite violence against the professor complainants. The European Court of Human Rights found that there had been a violation of Article 8 (right to private life) of the European Convention and ordered compensatory damages. This due to the European Court of Human Rights finding that "passages [in the press report] that constituted hate speech and incitement to violence, [were] thus ... likely to expose them [the complainants] to public contempt."[33]

In the final analysis then the European Court of Human Rights affirmed in *Kaboglu and Oran v Turkey* that the State has an obligation to protect from vilification, and its often violent sequelae, also those who advocate for cultural diversity and minority rights. Attacks on those who agitate for a more democratic, inclusive and pluralistic society, when those attacks reach to a certain extreme, the

[32] Kaboglu and Oran v Turkey LawEuro information Note on the Court's case-law 22 October 2018 https://laweuro.com/?p=4766 (Accessed August 20, 2024).

[33] Kaboglu and Oran v. Turkey (European Court of Human Rights) judgment 30.10.2018 [Section II] Law Euro https://laweuro.com/?p=4766 (Accessed August 20, 2024).

European Court of Human Rights judgment instructs in this case, are not properly to be considered shielded by the freedom of the press guarantee. This since the Convention stipulates limits on freedom of expression when it significantly adversely affects the lawful rights of others. The State has a positive obligation to ensure that the rights of others are not compromised using freedom of expression as a shield.

Unfortunately, in *Kaboglu and Oran v Turkey*, the European Court of Human Rights did *not* address the violation of *the professors'* Convention Article 10 right to freedom of expression/academic freedom. That violation arguably resulted from the untoward hateful attacks published in the press which attacks were intended to 'chill' the scholarly speech of these academics.[34] In not addressing the Article 10 rights of the professors in *Kaboglu and Oran v Turkey*; the European Court of Human Rights missed a valuable opportunity.[35] That is, in part, the opportunity, on the view here, to have *delegitimized* the bolstering (through the domestic courts) of the attempt by a select Turkish press outlet(s) to quash the academic freedom of university educators advocating for a new democratic ethic of diversity, pluralism and equity in Turkey. Further, there was a missed opportunity, as Sophia Sideridou (of the Human Rights Centre of Ghent University) highlights, to affirm the State's *positive obligation* to create a climate in which academics can freely engage in their scholarly work and express their considered academic views free from "third party interference."[36]

---

[34] See Strasbourg Observers (26 November 2018) *Kaboglu and Oran v Turkey*: Protecting the private life of scholars, yet failing to recognize the academic freedom dimension at issue. Commentary of Sophia Sideridou (intern at the Human Rights Centre of Ghent University) https://strasbourgobservers.com/2018/11/26/kaboglu-and-oran-v-turkey-protecting-the-private-life-of-scholars-yet-failing-to-recognize-the-academic-fre (Accessed August 20, 2024).

[35] See Strasbourg Observers (26 November 2018) *Kaboglu and Oran v Turkey*: Protecting the private life of scholars, yet failing to recognize the academic freedom dimension at issue. Commentary of Sophia Sideridou (intern at the Human Rights Centre of Ghent University) https://strasbourgobservers.com/2018/11/26/kaboglu-and-oran-v-turkey-protecting-the-private-life-of-scholars-yet-failing-to-recognize-the-academic-fre (Accessed August 20, 2024).

[36] For discussion of this point see Strasbourg Observers (26 November, 2018) *Kaboglu and Oran v Turkey*: Protecting the private life of scholars, yet failing to recognize the academic freedom dimension at issue. Commentary of Sophia Sideridou https://strasbourgobservers.com/2018/11/26/kaboglu-and-oran-v-turkey-protecting-the-private-life-of-scholars-yet-failing-to-recognize-the-academic-freedom-dimension-at-issue/ (Accessed August 20, 2024).

3.3 Revisionist History as Reflected in the Struggle to Eliminate Affirmative Action in US University Admissions

3.3.1 Introduction

Next, we consider *Students for Fair Admissions, Inc. v President and Fellows of Harvard University*[37] which addresses the question of affirmative action in Harvard University admissions. This involving consideration of race or ethnicity as one potential factor in the Harvard admissions eligibility assessment. Affirmative action regarding university admissions is touted by proponents as an indicium of a recognition of historical systemic inequities imposed on certain marginalized ethnic/racial groups and the effort to correct these at the institutional level. The latter not through a quota system or a target percentage of minority ethnic students to be achieved, but rather indirectly through the attempt to increase the numbers of underrepresented students (underrepresented along various dimensions such as social class, ethnicity etc.). The objective being to create a more inclusive and diverse university student body and a more stimulating university environment for students. That objective of a diverse student body, Harvard argues, is a compelling interest for the university and for the State as it reflects and reinforces democratic values. However, there are significant issues being highlighted through litigation regarding the fairness of the application *in practice* of affirmative action at Harvard University and certain other schools. Certain admissions strategies, such as those at Harvard, complainants argue, are (a) systemically disproportionately adversely impacting American students of Asian heritage and (b) hence are allegedly not consistent with democratic principles. At the same time, students of African American ancestry and certain other historically disadvantaged minorities are still marginalized in US society also educationally and may benefit to a degree from affirmative action in US university admissions. The issue arises then also as to whether elimination of affirmative action in US university admissions at this time (rather than attempts to achieve its fair and individualistic application) is, in the final analysis, tantamount to a denial of past and current social injustices in education relating to ethnicity, particularly but not exclusively as against Afro -Americans. If the latter be the case, then elimination of affirmative action in US university admissions at present would arguably represent yet another iteration of 'revisionist history.'

It should be noted that US universities that consider race in the admissions process for an individual student from a particular ethnic minority do *not* do so, they assert, to rectify historical inequity and injustice in university admissions. Rather the universities assert a rationale based on the educational and other benefits of increasing student diversity. This is in line with the adoption of the opinion of the

[37] *Students for Fair Admissions, Inc. v President and Fellows of Harvard University* SCOTUSblog https://www.scotusblog.com/case-files/cases/students-for-fair-admissions-inc-v-president-fellows-of-harvard-college/ (Accessed August 20, 2024).

United States Supreme Court (Justice Powell writing for the majority) in *Bakke*[38] That opinion held that no one university can correct historical injustices and hence race considerations in university admissions as remedial are, according to the Bakke opinion, unconstitutional.[39] Yet one might consider that Harvard's preference for legacy student candidates,[40] the children of Harvard faculty and the children of donors to Harvard (that results in a Harvard student body that is statistically significantly more white and wealthy than diverse) is itself, as several commentators have noted, an anomalous affirmative action program.[41] This in that it favors privileged students who in many cases have families that have for generations been privileged. Hence the legacy system, for instance, arguably serves to maintain a certain *status quo* when it comes to the level of diversity and ethnic representation in the Harvard student body.

Questions arise as to (a) whether affirmative action in US university admissions can be more fairly and individualistically implemented and (b) whether resistance to a more inclusive society in which all can thrive can be largely overcome. Ending race-based affirmative action[42] despite the gross underrepresentation of African Americans and certain other minorities generally at most US universities, especially at the elite schools, is to risk suffering under and perpetuating the destructive illusion that US society functions as a quintessential meritocracy that is operating smoothly. In fact, however, a significant level of diversity is still not achieved at the US elite universities in particular and minorities are underrepresented as mentioned for reasons unrelated to merit.

Recall the Oklahoma House Bill 1775 discussed in *Black Emergency Response Team et al. v O-Connor et al.*[43] in the context of perpetuating the illusion of the US as a society grounded not just on constitutional theory but also, *fully in practice*, on equity That Bill *prohibited* the teaching of or classroom discussion of (a) challenges to the notion of the operational reality of the meritocratic society in the students' personal actual societal context and (b) the notion that ethnicity/race *must not be*

---

[38] United States Supreme Court Regents of University of California v Bakke 438 U.S. 265 (1978) https://supreme.justia.com/cases/federal/us/438/265/#tab-opinion-1952756 (Accessed August 20, 2024).

[39] Ginsburg, RB and Merritt, DJ *Affirmative action: An international human rights dialogue*, Benjamin N. Cardozo Lecture, Cardozo Lecture given by Justice Ginsburg at the Association of the Bar of the City of New York on 11 February 1999 at pp. 19–20 https://constcourt.ge/files/7/JCL-ENG-Vol-2-(2020)/JCL-2020-Vol.2-ENG-9-32.pdf (Accessed August 20, 2024).

[40] Legacy students are those who have relatives who attended the same university.

[41] Inside Higher Education (26 July 2023) Affirmative Action for the Rich: The ban on affirmative action has put pressure on selective colleges to end legacy preferences in admissions. But the advantages of familial wealth go beyond alumni status https://www.insidehighered.com/news/admissions/traditional-age/2023/07/26/would-ending-legacy-admissions-improve-elite-college (Accessed August 20, 2024).

[42] *Students for Fair Admission*, as will be here discussed, in fact did end race-based affirmative action in US university admissions.

[43] Black Emergency Response Team et al. v John O'Connor, Attorney General of Oklahoma et al. https://www.aclu.org/legal-document/amended-complaint-6 (Accessed August 20, 2024).

ignored when assessing fairness in institutional operations in US society and in evaluating the treatment accorded minority groups, in particular persons of African descent. That is, there is a *prohibition* in the Oklahoma House Bill 1775 that seeks to *discount* the notion that the country's racialized history makes alleged 'colour blindness' both misguided and bigoted in considering institutionalized and systemic practices that impact Afro-Americans and other minorities. We will consider whether the majority opinion in the Harvard and North Carolina university[44] fair admissions cases harken to the same illogic as in the *Black Emergency Response Team et al. v O-Connor et al.* case.[45] That is an illogic *professing* colour blindness and individualized assessment while in fact, through various measures, *in effect* reinforcing racism, race consciousness and inequity.

3.3.2 (United States Supreme Court) Students for Fair Admissions, Inc. v President and Fellows of Harvard University: On Whether 'Colour Blind' University Admissions Is Possible or Equitable

The US Supreme Court majority in the fair admissions case *Students for Fair Admissions, Inc. v President and Fellows of Harvard University*[46] ruled to end affirmative action for ethnic minorities in university admissions. This the Court's Majority did based on a rationale that doing so was necessary to achieve compliance in the university admissions process with the US constitutional equality guarantee. The majority in the Fair Admissions case at the US Supreme Court concerning Harvard (together with the University of North Carolina) hence eliminated race *per se* as a possible 'positive tip' (a boost in the admissions score) in the university admissions process pursuant to a holistic assessment of the applicant. Instead, the *Fair Admissions* Majority of the Court in that case held that the only permissible consideration of race/ethnicity would be in the context of evaluating a student's admissions essay where the student may have chosen to discuss the impact of race/ethnicity in their individual experience (as inspiration, disadvantage or both).

A key question in regard to *professed* 'colour blindness' in the context of the Harvard fair university admission case and other like cases is whether *the*

[44] Students for Fair Admissions, Inc. v. University of North Carolina Trial Findings of Fact and Law, District Judge Loretta C. Biggs App. 1 Appendix A In the United States District Court for the Middle District of North Carolina 1:14CV954 Filed October 18, 2021 https://www.scotusblog.com/wp-content/uploads/2021/11/20211111164136730_SFFA-Appendix.pdf (Accessed August 20, 2024).

[45] Black Emergency Response Team et al. v John O'Connor, Attorney General of Oklahoma et al. https://www.aclu.org/legal-document/amended-complaint-6 (Accessed August 20, 2024).

[46] *Students for Fair Admissions, Inc. v President and Fellows of Harvard University* (Supreme Court of the United States) (SCOTUSblog) https://www.scotusblog.com/case-files/cases/students-for-fair-admissions-inc-v-president-fellows-of-harvard-college/ (Accessed August 20, 2024).

elimination of the self-identification as to race/ethnicity (by the student no longer checking the relevant box on the application form) accomplishes the objective of equity. That is, for instance, the issue arises as to whether racial/ethnic minorities are in practice, by design or otherwise, kept to a certain lower limit in the Harvard student population. The latter, for example, because of Harvard's preference for legacy applicants (the children of Harvard alumni), for the children of wealthy donors to Harvard and for the children of Harvard faculty. Is socioeconomic status then (highly correlated as it is with legacy admissions, admissions of students with donor parents and students of faculty parents) here a strong proxy for race/ethnicity in the Harvard admission practice? Arguably socioeconomic considerations (through providing a positive tip to legacy students, and students of donor and faculty parents) are having the effect of reducing racial/ethnic minority diversity and representation in the student body. Note in the latter regard that Harvard's 2019 class admissions were constituted of 40% Caucasian while 82% of the admitted students were wealthy.[47]

It would appear that a reasonable argument can be made that the existing bias in favor of high socioeconomic students (relating to the preference for student applicants who are the children of donors, legacy applicants and applicants who are the children of faculty) *in effect* mitigated, to a significant extent, the positive impacts of affirmative action. The latter in terms of (a) mitigating the potential greater minority ethnic diversity in the student body resulting from affirmative action and, it would appear, also (b) weakening the possibility for increased representation from lower socioeconomic groups in the Harvard student body. To the latter point consider that the complainants in the Harvard case provide evidence that the percentage of minority ethnic students in various ethnic categories stayed quite remarkably stable for Harvard over the several years studied (2009–2018).[48] For Asian-Americans that admittance rate was 17–20% from 2009–2018. In 2019, however, after the Fair admissions lawsuit against Harvard; Asian-Americans were (it appears uncontested) admitted at a statistically significantly higher rate than Caucasians for the first time.[49] If the foregoing statistics are correct, and there is no other mediating factor; then it is difficult not to consider that systemic institutional biasing factors relating to the admissions process may have played a role in producing such results regarding minority student admittance rates.

[47] Students for Fair Admissions, Inc. v President and Fellows of Harvard University, United States Supreme Court Complaint at p. 17 https://www.supremecourt.gov/DocketPDF/20/20-1199/169941/20210225095525027_Harvard%20Cert%20Petn%20Feb%2025.pdf (Accessed August 20, 2024).

[48] Students for Fair Admissions, Inc. v President and Fellows of Harvard University (United States Supreme Court) Oral argument audio Docket Number: 20-1199, Date Argued: 10/31/22 https://www.supremecourt.gov/oral_arguments/audio/2022/20-1199 (Accessed August 20, 2024).

[49] Students for Fair Admissions, Inc. v President and Fellows of Harvard University, United States Supreme Court, Oral Argument audio Docket Number: 20-1199, Date Argued: 10/31/22 https://www.supremecourt.gov/oral_arguments/audio/2022/20-1199 (Accessed August 20, 2024).

In oral argument, counsel for the complainants maintained that Harvard declined even after the fair admissions lawsuit against the university was filed (a) to end its preference for legacy student candidates or (b) to adopt methods that would better enhance admissions opportunities for lower socioeconomic student candidates.[50] Counsel for the complainants argued that both such measures would greatly enhance student diversity and assist in moving the Harvard student representation *away* from one that is predominantly Caucasian, linked to generational wealth and to a societally privileged class.[51] Opposing counsel maintained that the evidence did *not* support the view that eliminating the aforementioned preferences linked to privilege would be a race-neutral alternative admissions strategy that would significantly enhance student diversity and hence help foster a stimulating educational environment.[52] At the same time; counsel for the United States amicus curiae supporting the Respondent (counsel Gen. Elizabeth Prelogar, Solicitor General, Department of Justice Washington, D.C.) *conceded* that if evidence did exist that university diversity objectives could be much better obtained if universities were to end preferences for legacy applicants and children of donors; then it would be incumbent on the universities like Harvard (that consider such applicant characteristics) to do so. Yet, at the same time, the discussion of counsel Prelogar with certain of the United States Supreme Court Justices in this case reverted, respectfully, on the view here, to racial tropes and stereotype. The suggestion was advanced, for instance, that if there was a significant move away from usual Harvard admissions practice (which includes preferences for the privileged legacy students and other groups characterized by an over-representation of more affluent Caucasian students as well as affirmative action considering 'race') to a more race-neutral alternative, there would be a purported risk of (a) compromising the academic quality of the incoming student body and (b) perhaps even exacerbating the comparatively lower percentage of minorities in the Harvard student body.[53] This perspective, absent uncontested actual real world data regarding the actual university performance of students from lower socioeconomic and less privileged backgrounds (especially from year two on after a period of adjustment to Harvard in particular and university in general and with the university offering the proper support) is on the author's view unnecessarily pessimistic. Furthermore, respectfully, on the current author's view, the anxiety reflected *in*

[50] Students for Fair Admissions, Inc. v President and Fellows of Harvard University, United States Supreme Court, Oral Argument audio Docket Number: 20-1199, Date Argued: 10/31/22 https://www.supremecourt.gov/oral_arguments/audio/2022/20-1199 (Accessed August 20, 2024).

[51] Students for Fair Admissions, Inc. v President and Fellows of Harvard University, United States Supreme Court, Oral Argument audio Docket Number: 20-1199, Date Argued: 10/31/22 https://www.supremecourt.gov/oral_arguments/audio/2022/20-1199 (Accessed August 20, 2024).

[52] Students for Fair Admissions, Inc. v President and Fellows of Harvard University, United States Supreme Court, Oral Argument audio Docket Number: 20-1199, Date Argued: 10/31/22 https://www.supremecourt.gov/oral_arguments/audio/2022/20-1199 (Accessed August 20, 2024).

[53] Students for Fair Admissions, Inc. v President and Fellows of Harvard University, United States Supreme Court, Oral Argument audio Docket Number: 20-1199, Date Argued: 10/31/22 https://www.supremecourt.gov/oral_arguments/audio/2022/20-1199 (Accessed August 20, 2024).

practice about, in particular, ending legacy preferences and preferences for other select privileged student candidates reflects an implicit endorsement of an *alleged* pure untainted meritocratic system. That system is premised on the *assumption* that privileged students (those who are legacy candidates or the children of donors, for instance, with comparable high Scholastic Aptitude test scores and excellent high school records as have student candidates from less privileged groups) are somehow a surer route to maintaining Harvard's touted academic excellence. There is no inherent reason, however, why students from less privileged backgrounds, often who are minority group students of colour, would not succeed at the elite schools. The latter given that they meet all the entrance qualifications but are merely given a 'positive tip' at the final selection stage when candidates have to be selected from a large pool of *qualified applicants*. The potential tips (bonus admission points) at this final selection stage (impacting selection from amongst *qualified applicants*) applies only to student applicants who fall into one or more of four categories eligible for the tip: (a) legacy applicants, (b) recruited athlete applicants, (c) applicants eligible for financial aid and (d) applicants belonging to a minority ethnic/racial group. One wonders, furthermore, how much content-based viewpoint diversity can be achieved in the Harvard student body when the majority of the students share the same social class, ethnic and privileged background experience. While the latter are not necessarily indicators of shared political and social issue viewpoint, in many instances these characteristics are correlates of the same.

In the current author's view, there is a substantial difference between academic quality based on actual performance in university versus academic quality inferred from the indicators that Harvard uses to try and 'crystal ball' who will make the best contribution to and benefit most from Harvard educationally and otherwise. University is a categorically different type of learning environment than the pre-university educational experience. Attributes that are heavily valued in university such as independent and critical thinking; originality and creativity are not necessarily reflected in the student's pre-university experience and recommendation letters. This particularly *may* be the case if the student is from an ethnic minority and/or lower socioeconomic group where one often learns that *invisibility* at school is often the expected and safest option for most in the latter groups. In this respect it is noteworthy that *high achieving Asian Americans student applicants to Harvard* are, the complainants allege, systematically assigned personal ratings (through admissions interviews and assessment of other admissions material) that reflect purportedly being more abrasive with less leadership qualities than members of other ethnic groups. Perhaps these typical negative personal ratings (in the admissions process) for Asian American student applicants to Harvard reflect the dissonance experienced by some raters when minority students of this ethnic group defy the speculated unconscious stereotype as to the unassuming Asian-American student (someone who does not attract much of the limelight). The stereotype of the quiet non-assertive Asian-American student is perhaps the normative more expected prototypical model for consideration regarding admission to Harvard for students applicants from this ethnic group. Another key question then is whether certain ethnic groups, such as Americans of Asian heritage, have been discriminated against in the Harvard admissions practice. This in the latter case through personal ratings which Harvard relies on despite this rating being comprised of subjective data easily corrupted by conscious or unconscious biases and misperceptions. Harvard maintains that (a) the personal ratings are part of a very preliminary screening of applicants by an initial reader *who does not take race into account* and that (b) these ratings are not determinative as to admission or non-admission.[54] However, race considerations may, at least unintentionally and unconsciously, yet be factoring into the personal rating itself in regards to Asian-American applicants to Harvard.

It is noteworthy that minorities, according to Harvard, have benefited to some extent from the consideration of race in university admissions. For instance, Harvard asserted in its reply brief that Asian-American students make up 20% of the Harvard student body in contemporary times compared to the 3.4% of the student body in 1980.[55] The question before the Court however in the Fair Admissions case was in part whether so-called *race neutral* admission practices are both a constitutionally and practically viable path to equity in university admissions. Let us explore further then the issue of so-called race as a factor in university admissions and the United States Supreme Court analysis in this regard in the Harvard Fair Admissions case.

3.3.3 (United States Supreme Court) Students for Fair Admissions, Inc. v President and Fellows of Harvard University: Overturning Precedent

In *Students for Fair Admission* (Harvard)[56] the central issue was whether Harvard's use of race as a factor in Harvard admissions violates Title VI of the Civil Rights Act of 1964 which stipulates that:

> No person in the United States shall, on the ground of race, color, or national origin, be excluded from participation in, be denied the benefits of, or be subjected to discrimination under any program or activity receiving Federal financial assistance.[57]

Harvard University, though a private school, does build part of its financial resources through federal funding such as the monies it receives from federal research grants and hence is bound by Title VI of the Civil Rights Act.

Specifically, *Students for Fair Admissions, Inc. v President and Fellows of Harvard University* addresses whether (a) Harvard uses race to discriminate against

---

[54] Students for Fair Admissions, Inc. v President and Fellows of Harvard University, United States Supreme Court Respondent Brief at p. 8 July 2022.

[55] Students for Fair Admissions, Inc. v President and Fellows of Harvard University, United States Supreme Court Respondent Brief at p. 8 July 2022 at p. 11.

[56] *Students for Fair Admissions, Inc. v President and Fellows of Harvard University* SCOTUSblog https://www.scotusblog.com/case-files/cases/students-for-fair-admissions-inc-v-president-fellows-of-harvard-college/ (Accessed August 20, 2024).

[57] Section 601 Civil Rights Act (1964) statute 42 U.S.C. §2000d.

American students of Asian ethnic heritage and (b) discriminates also by disavowing race-neutral alternatives that would purportedly ensure a fairer admissions practice. Harvard argues in opposition that no viable race-neutral alternatives exist at present for admissions and that the university does not discriminate against Asian-Americans. Harvard also claims it does *not* attempt to achieve a "critical mass" of underrepresented students defined by race and/or other factors. Eliminating tips for race, for legacy applicants, for student applicant children of donors and for student applicant children of faculty[58] would be, in theory, a move in the direction at least of a more race neutral admissions strategy. Questions have been raised, however, as to whether eliminating the positive tip for race would lead to an exacerbated under-representation of minorities, particularly African Americans, in the Harvard student body. Note that though socioeconomic status is correlated to a significant degree with race/ethnicity, that the tip that considers socioeconomic status does *not* exclude or disfavor from a positive weighting also poor white applicants eligible for financial aid.

The student complainants in this Harvard admissions case did prevail at the United States Supreme Court. That decision overturns United States Supreme Court precedent in *Grutter v. Bollinger*[59] which allowed for the consideration of race as *a* potential factor for consideration in university admissions but with certain strict guardrails in place. *Grutter* concerned the admissions policy and practice of the University of Michigan law school. The United States Supreme Court ruled in *Grutter* that (a) using race as but *one factor* in assessing student admissibility and (b) using an individualized approach does *not* violate the Fourteenth Amendment equality provision or the 1964 Civil Rights Act *if* (c) it serves a compelling State interest in fostering University of Michigan law school student population diversity. That diversity consideration by the Michigan University Law School, the university argued, was along several dimensions (viewpoints, cultures etc.) and not just race. This though the university maintained that, at the same time, it had an interest in addressing the underrepresentation of African American, Hispanic American and Native Americans[60] (indigenous) students in its student body and so was especially interested (though not exclusively) in racial/ethnic diversity.

The Grutter United States Supreme Court held that the consideration of race in university admissions must be "narrowly tailored." That is, each applicant must be considered in comparison to all others with the requisite qualifications and their file considered holistically. Race, if considered as *a* factor, may be considered with respect to a particular applicant as a positive tip or weighting plus. Quotas based on race or ethnicity were deemed by the Court to be unconstitutional consistent with the

---

[58] Recall that legacy applicants, student applicant children of donors and student applicant children of faculty are disproportionately Caucasian and privileged economically.

[59] *Grutter v. Bollinger* 539 U.S. 306 (2003) https://supreme.justia.com/cases/federal/us/539/306/#tab-opinion-1961290 (Accessed August 20, 2024).

[60] "Native Americans" is the term used in the *Grutter v. Bollinger* case to describe indigenous students.

decision in *Bakke*.[61] The Court held further that all applicants must be considered based on the same admissions policy and practice and the same criteria applied. Hence separate admission processes or tracks defined by race or ethnicity, or any other diversity factor were held to be unlawful and to constitute violations of Title VI of the 1964 Civil Rights Act. No student then is to be admitted or rejected based on a single or a combined diversity dimension score. Rather the whole of the applicant's file is to be considered with both objective measures and soft measures (i.e., letters of recommendation etc.) taken into account in the admissions decision with race merely being a potential plus factor. Inflexible automatic scoring systems that do not actually consider the student holistically were rejected as not serving the diversity interest.

The Grutter United States Supreme Court also determined that race conscious admissions should be time-limited and that universities should work to achieve their reasonable objectives with regard to student body diversity. The University of Michigan argued that it sought to attain a "critical mass" (undefined) of underrepresented minorities in its student population *without* reaching for a specified percentage to achieve some sort of racial or other balancing or target quota. The university contended it sought to achieve a critical mass of underrepresented minority students in its student body in that such diversity in ethnicity and along other dimensions would contribute to the good functioning of the school and ultimately to the legal profession when these students took up positions in the profession. Universities were guided by the Grutter United States Supreme Court decision not to prolong such race conscious admissions practices beyond a point where they are still needed to serve the university's diversity interest.[62]

3.3.4 The Purported 'Separate but Unequal' Issue in the University Fair Admission Cases

In the final selection process, Harvard and University North Carolina, like many other US universities at the time of the Fair Admissions case,[63] considered race

[61] In *Bakke* the United States Supreme Court held that a racial imbalance in a university student body must be traceable by provable evidence to discrimination to justify a more direct use of race to correct such imbalance. Justice Powell in *Bakke* held that general societal discrimination based on race with no determined effects on the make-up of the university student body is *not* adequate to justify reliance on race classification in university admissions. Impermissible university admissions practice then involves using race not simply as part of a more holistic consideration but rather as a heavily weighted factor through a quota or some other system. Justice Powell in *Bakke* held that only the compelling interest in student diversity could justify any consideration of race in university admissions. Powell held that the State and university interest in student diversity (along many dimensions not just race) was encompassed by the First Amendment right. See *Regents of the University of California v. Bakke* 26 June 1978 438 U.S. 265 (1978).

[62] See Syllabus *Grutter v. Bollinger* 539 U.S. 306 (2003) https://supreme.justia.com/cases/federal/us/539/306/#tab-opinion-1961290 (Accessed August 20, 2024).

[63] Students for Fair Admission Inc v President and Fellows of Harvard University No. 20-1199. (United States Supreme Court) Argued October 31, 2022—Decided June 29, 2023 (Together with

along with one or more certain other factors (such as legacy status, recruited athlete status and financial aid eligibility) for a positive tip. The objective, Harvard maintained, in considering race was to ensure that there was no dramatic reduction in the representation of minority students in the incoming freshman class. The data reported indicated that race was a significant determinative 'positive tip' in admissions scoring for a considerable percentage of African American and Hispanic students admitted to Harvard.

The majority of the United States Supreme Court in *Fair Admissions*[64] found that the Harvard and the University of North Carolina admissions policy considering race *violated* the equal protection clause of the Fourteenth Amendment. Part of the majority's reasoning relied on the notion that "separate cannot be equal."[65] Arguably, however, this was *not* a case that could be reduced to or framed as 'separate but unequal.' This in that, as discussed, African American and Hispanic and other students of colour had to *meet the same entrance qualifications to Harvard and University of North Carolina as do all other students.* The positive tip for race was being applied exclusively in the final selection stage in considering only *qualified candidates.* Furthermore, that positive tip for race arguably promoted *equity* in recognition of historical and current barriers to higher education for minorities in the United States.[66]

In addition, it is to be noted that at the time of the United Sates Supreme Court decision in the Harvard and North Carolina Fair Admissions cases (a) Harvard and University of North Carolina *in effect* provided a positive tip to majority Caucasian students through *legacy admissions* in the final selection process and (b) that the positive tip for legacy student applicants was *not* deemed by the United States Supreme Court majority in these cases to be unconstitutional 'separate but unequal' treatment. Further, since Caucasian students are *not* underrepresented at Harvard or

No. 21-707, Students for Fair Admissions, Inc. v. University of North Carolina et al.) https://www.scotusblog.com/case-files/cases/students-for-fair-admissions-inc-v-president-fellows-of-harvard-college/ (Accessed August 20, 2024).

[64]Students for Fair Admission Inc v President and Fellows of Harvard University No. 20-1199. (United States Supreme Court) Argued October 31, 2022—Decided June 29, 2023 (Together with No. 21-707, Students for Fair Admissions, Inc. v. University of North Carolina et al.) https://www.scotusblog.com/case-files/cases/students-for-fair-admissions-inc-v-president-fellows-of-harvard-college/ (Accessed August 20, 2024).

[65]Students for Fair Admission Inc v President and Fellows of Harvard University No. 20-1199. (United States Supreme Court) Argued October 31, 2022—Decided June 29, 2023 (Together with No. 21-707, Students for Fair Admissions, Inc. v. University of North Carolina et al.) Syllabus at p. 4 https://www.scotusblog.com/case-files/cases/students-for-fair-admissions-inc-v-president-fellows-of-harvard-college/ (Accessed August 20, 2024).

[66]To ignore both historical barriers to higher education for minorities in the United States as well as the current legacy of those barriers with respect to today's underrepresentation of minorities in US university admissions is arguably itself a means to perpetuate an implicit 'separate but unequal' admissions system.

the University of North Carolina,[67] it is difficult to justify a positive tip for legacy students (who the data reveals are predominantly Caucasian) based on the professed university objective of student diversity. Student diversity, it will be recalled, is the rationale for 'positive tips' (in admissions scoring) promulgated by some universities and found by the Courts, *prior to* the Fair Admissions Harvard (together with N Carolina) case, to be also a compelling State interest justifying university admission positive tips relating to race. The universities had in fact somewhat of a shield in their diversity argument as a rationale for considering race in admissions (without setting a quota or any target on what would constitute a critical mass of minority students). This on the assumption that (a) seeking diversity in the student body allows for enhanced student exposure to challenging and different viewpoints[68] and that (b) providing such experiences is part of the university's prerogative under the First Amendment and an aspect of university autonomy.[69] Yet in practice the student population at Harvard and at University North Carolina was and is predominately Caucasian.

It seems highly ironic from this author's perspective; with respect, that the majority in the Harvard Fair Admissions case should cite *Brown v Board of Education*[70] in support of their ruling. This since *Brown* was directed to opening up equal access to African American schoolchildren to publicly funded schools. The latter in full recognition and acknowledgement of (a) an historical systemic racial injustice in basic schooling in the United States and (b) the substandard state in various respects (including teaching quality) of many of those public schools attended by African Americans at the time of the Brown case. It is furthermore clear that elite universities like Harvard, as well as other universities, through their boosts in admission points for legacy applicants and favoritism toward the children of donors,[71] for instance, are indirectly arguably advantaging mostly Caucasian students (an affirmative action program, some have suggested, then for Caucasians but without an equity objective).

---

[67] A Jackson (2023) Legacy preferences should join racial preferences in dustbin *The Carolina Journal* 2 August 2023 https://www.carolinajournal.com/opinion/legacy-preferences-should-join-racial-preferences-in-dustbin/ (Accessed August 20, 2024).

[68] Whether ethnicity is a proxy for viewpoint is of course an open question and certainly it would seem safe to say that ethnicity is *not* always a proxy for content viewpoint. As the latter may be influenced by a host of intersecting factors.

[69] Terrell (2011), p. 239. See commentary on Justice Powell's reliance in *Bakke* (Regents of Univ. of California v. Bakke, 438 U.S. 265 (1978)) on the First Amendment to justify the university's consideration of race in an effort to achieve diversity.

[70] Brown v. Board of Education, 347 U.S. 483 (1954) Argued December 9, 1952 Reargued December 8, 1953 Decided May 17, 1954 https://www.archives.gov/milestone-documents/brown-v-board-of-education (Accessed August 20, 2024).

[71] DR Franklin and SW Zwickel (Harvard Crimson) *In Admissions, Harvard Favors Those Who Fund It, Internal Emails Show* https://www.thecrimson.com/article/2018/10/18/day-three-harvard-admissions-trial/ (Accessed August 20, 2024).

3.4 Comparative Law Perspective on Affirmative Action

3.4.1 Judgment of the European Court of Justice 11 November 1997 Case C-409/95: Hellmut Marschall v Land Nordrhein-Westfalen (Germany) Reference for a Preliminary Ruling Regarding Affirmative Action for Women

In this section we consider the case *Hellmut Marschall v Land Nordrhein-Westfalen*,[72] a Reference case from Germany to the European Court of Justice requesting its guidance in interpretation of European Union employment law and on equity under that law. The European Court of Justice is a court of the European Union intended, among other things, to (a) ensure universality of application and interpretation of European Union law across member States; (b) consider applications to the European Court of Justice from individuals or entities that allege a violation of their rights by an European Union institution and (c) offer relief that rectifies instances of misinterpretation of European Union law and consequent rights violations.[73]

In *Hellmut Marschall v Land Nordrhein-Westfalen* (hereafter *Land*) an issue arose concerning European Union law affecting public servants. The particular law in question stipulated that where there was a disproportionately lower female representation in a certain high career post, those authorities responsible for promotion could consider gender in making promotion decisions. Specifically, the law at issue authorized affirmative action favoring women in the aforementioned situation *if* the women candidates for the higher position were found to be equally competent and suitable with a comparable performance record to that of the male candidates. This was set out as the rule except where there were individual factors relating to the male candidate that augured in his favor.

The *Land* argued that the affirmative action plan allowing consideration of gender was intended to correct historical inequities that worked against women being hired for the more senior public service positions, The historical inequities resulting in disproportionately lower numbers of women in senior public service positions were due in part to the traditional view that (a) the male is the head of the household and most typically the sole income earner and (b) to concerns over the women interrupting their careers to have children. The *Land* maintained that as the affirmative action plan was administered with attention to the individual case; the affirmative action plan was valid under European Union law. The German law in question

[72] Judgment of the European Court of Justice 11 November 1997. *Hellmut Marschall v Land Nordrhein-Westfalen* (Germany) Reference for a preliminary ruling https://eur-lex.europa.eu/legal-content/EN/TXT/?uri=CELEX%3A61995CJ0409 (Accessed August 20, 2024).

[73] Court of Justice of the European Union https://european-union.europa.eu/institutions-law-budget/institutions-and-bodies/institutions-and-bodies-profiles/court-justice-european-union-cjeu_en (Accessed August 20, 2024).

stipulated that where there were factors unique to a particular male candidate that tipped the balance in his favor concerning i.e., fair employment and promotion practice,[74] such factors would need to be taken into account and the male would be offered the job promotion (that provision is what the courts referred to as the 'saving clause' in the German law at issue).

Mr. Marschall is a teacher working for *The Land* earning the basic salary for his job category. He applied for a promotion for which he was qualified but was told that the position would be offered to a female candidate. His appeal to domestic authorities failed as they determined that relevant German national law required that (a) since at the time there was lower female representation at that level and (b) both candidates were equally qualified; the position must be offered to a female. The European Court of Justice thus in this case needed to consider whether the national law at issue did in fact, through considering gender, serve to promote equity for males and females in employment and employment related opportunities such as promotion in such a manner as not to be unlawfully discriminatory.

The European Court of Justice had in a previous case held that (a) the State must institute strategies for overcoming gender bias in employment that creates barriers for women and that (b) affirmative action properly drafted and instituted could be one such strategy. However, at the same time, the European Court of Justice ruled that application of affirmative action favoring equally qualified women candidates over male candidates (in situations where women were disproportionately underrepresented) must *not* be rigidly applied. Rigid application involves ignoring relevant individual aspects of the male candidate's application and circumstance, objectively assessed, that may bode in his favor notwithstanding gender-based affirmative action giving preference to females. Where rigid application has occurred; the affirmative action plan (without a 'saving clause') has exceeded its legitimate scope and is improperly discriminatory based on gender.[75]

The European Court of Justice then in *Marschall* affirmed that the State may, under certain schemes, lawfully engage in positive initiatives through affirmative action to equalize the playing field i.e., in employment for similarly highly qualified candidates from a protected group defined by gender. This the European Court of Justice ruled as acceptable as long as (a) those not given the advantage in being a member of a historically underrepresented group do not have unique factors that should weigh rather in *their* favor in the competition,: and (b) the scheme is temporary and applied flexibly such that it does not undermine the "merit principle."[76]

---

[74] These would be factors that did *not* discriminate against females but rather weighed in favor of the particular male in the specific case.

[75] See Case C-450/93 Kalanke v Freie Hansestadt Bremen [1995] ECR 1-3051. Communication from the Commission to the European Parliament and the Council on its Interpretation of the judgment in Case C-450/93, *Kalanke v Freie Hansestadt Bremen*, COM (96) 88 (final); Opinion of the UN Economic and Social Council (ECOSOC) on the 'Proposal for a Council Directive amending Directive (97/C 30/19) OJ C.30/57 30.1.97761207.'

[76] O'Hare (2000), pp. 6–7.

International human rights law in fact does *not* prohibit affirmative action, properly implemented, in the effort to establish *de facto* equality of opportunity.[77] Further, the European Court of Human Rights has interpreted the *European Convention on Human Rights and Fundamental Freedoms* and certain other international human rights law to, in the proper circumstances, require such *positive action* applied fairly in order to practically achieve equity.[78] Such positive action is held by the European Court of Human Rights to (a) protect in practice, and not just theory, Convention fundamental rights and freedoms, and (b) to perpetuate plurality and inclusion and hence democratic values.[79] The latter view arguably well echoes at least the 'diversity' (plurality) justification for affirmative action (a) reflected also in rationales for affirmative action relating to attempts to enhance racial/ethnic diversity in US university admissions and (b) accepted as constitutional by the United States Supreme Court *prior to* the Harvard Fair admissions case.[80] However, in regards to race-based affirmative action in US university admissions, neither (a) equity objectives (correcting historical and continuing barriers for minority students of colour in US university admissions) nor (b) student diversity in race/ethnicity *achieved through race-based* 'positive tips' in final selection university admissions scoring were found to be constitutionally sound rationales in the view of the United States Supreme Court majority in *Fair* Admissions.[81] In contrast, the European Court of Human Rights in commenting on discrimination specifically in access to education states:

> ...Article 14 of the Convention does not prohibit a member State from treating groups differently in order to correct "factual inequalities" between them; indeed in certain circumstances a failure to attempt to correct inequality through different treatment may in itself give

[77] O'Hare (2000), pp. 12–16.

[78] Jean-François Akandji-Kombe (2007) *Positive Obligations under the European Convention of Human Rights: A guide to the implementation of the European Convention on Human Rights* Human rights handbooks, No. 7 Directorate General of Human Rights Strasbourg.

[79] Jean-François Akandji-Kombe (2007) *Positive Obligations under the European Convention of Human Rights: A guide to the implementation of the European Convention on Human Rights* Human rights handbooks, No. 7 Directorate General of Human Rights Strasbourg.

[80] Students for Fair Admission Inc v President and Fellows of Harvard University No. 20-1199. (United States Supreme Court) Argued October 31, 2022—Decided June 29, 2023 (Together with No. 21-707, Students for Fair Admissions, Inc. v. University of North Carolina et al.) https://www.scotusblog.com/case-files/cases/students-for-fair-admissions-inc-v-president-fellows-of-harvard-college/ (Accessed August 20, 2024).

[81] Students for Fair Admission Inc v President and Fellows of Harvard University No. 20-1199. (United States Supreme Court) Argued October 31, 2022—Decided June 29, 2023 (Together with No. 21-707, Students for Fair Admissions, Inc. v. University of North Carolina et al.) https://www.scotusblog.com/case-files/cases/students-for-fair-admissions-inc-v-president-fellows-of-harvard-college/ (Accessed August 20, 2024).

> rise to a breach of the Article.[82](European Convention article 14 is a prohibition on discrimination).[83]

In the US university admission cases we considered in this chapter; we were discussing access to particular universities (those that were using a race/ethnicity-based affirmative action admissions strategy) and not addressing access to education generally. Nevertheless, it is noteworthy that the European Court of Human Rights considers that *affirmative action* in the educational access space may, in certain contexts, be required to fulfill the Article 14 *non-discrimination* European Convention rights guarantee.

The European Court of Human Rights, in addition, has interpreted the right to education set out at Article 2 of Protocol No. 1[84] to the *European Convention on Human Rights* as applying to higher education and as *obligating* the State to ensure access to particular post-secondary institutions on an equitable basis:

> Since Article 2 of Protocol No. 1 to the Convention applies to higher education, any State setting up such institutions will be under an obligation to afford an effective right of access to them (Leyla Şahin v. Turkey [GC], §§ 136–137). In other words, any access to institutions of higher education that may exist at a given time will form an integral part of the right stated in the first sentence of that Article (Mürsel Eren v. Turkey, § 41; Irfan Temel and Others v. Turkey, § 39).[85]

In summary then it appears that both (a) European State law (as interpreted by the European Court of Justice regarding the required consistency with European Union law) and (b) European human rights law (the Convention as interpreted by the European Court of Human Rights) are more amenable to the notion of *affirmative action as remedial* (in rectifying, insofar as possible, historical injustices and ongoing systemic institutionalized inequity for certain protected groups in access to education generally and in access to post-secondary education) than is US case law. In this regard, recall US Supreme Court constitutional case law on the issue of race-based affirmative action in university admissions since *Bakke*.[86] Consider

---

[82] European Court of Human Rights Key Theme Article 2 Protocol No. 1 Discrimination in access to education (Last updated: 01/09/2022) at p. 1 https://ks.echr.coe.int/documents/d/echr-ks/discrimination-in-access-to-education (Accessed August 20, 2024).

[83] European Convention of Rights and Freedoms "Article 14: Prohibition of discrimination: The enjoyment of the rights and freedoms set forth in this Convention shall be secured without discrimination on any ground such as sex, race, colour, language, religion, political or other opinion, national or social origin, association with a national minority, property, birth or other status." https://www.echr.coe.int/documents/convention_eng.pdf (Accessed August 20, 2024).

[84] European Court of Human Rights, Right to Education, Guide on Article 2 of Protocol No. 1 to the European Convention on Human Rights, Article 2 of Protocol No. 1—Right to education: "No person shall be denied the right to education. In the exercise of any functions which it assumes in relation to education and to teaching," at p. 1 https://www.echr.coe.int/documents/guide_art_2_protocol_1_eng.pdf (Accessed August 20, 2024).

[85] European Court of Human Rights, Right to Education, Guide on Article 2 of Protocol No. 1 to the European Convention on Human Rights point 13 at p. 7 https://www.echr.coe.int/documents/guide_art_2_protocol_1_eng.pdf (Accessed August 20, 2024).

[86] Regents of University of California v. Bakke 438 U.S. 265 (1978).

particularly the challenge of addressing the underrepresentation of certain ethnic/racial groups in US university student populations when the remedial model has been abandoned, as it has, along now also with race-based affirmative action in the university admission selection process. The Fair Admissions majority United States Supreme Court ruling[87] further seriously undercut realistic attempts to achieve student diversity in terms of adequate representation of minority students of colour while the opinion, at the same time, retained significant advantages in admissions scoring for legacy and other student groups (i.e. applicant children of donors and of faculty) who are predominately Caucasian and wealthy. The latter is *contrary* to the university stated mission of achieving *student diversity* also ethnically and thereby promoting tolerance and understanding across ethnic groups. Consider then that the Fair Admissions United States Supreme Court majority ruling is somewhat ironic. This in that rather than promoting a so-called 'colour blind' admissions strategy as the Court majority claimed, it instead demands, in practice, an *assiduous disregard* of the legacy of historical injustice against certain ethnic minorities of colour -hence a tacit but concerted *in effect* adverse consideration of race when it comes to disadvantaged students. At the same time, the decision permits preferential racial biases in admissions for Caucasian students that flow from positive tips assigned to i.e. legacy students.

Not surprisingly race-based affirmative action for underrepresented ethnic minorities in US university admissions, counterbalanced by admission biases in favor of other groups, has been woefully inadequate in levelling the playing field for minorities of colour. This is evidenced by the ethnic composition of the student body; especially at elite schools such as Harvard University. Yet, despite the significant *overrepresentation* of Caucasian wealthy student families in the preferred student applicant groups for US university admission, remedial affirmative action strategies designed to better foster student diversity in race/ethnicity (and to some degree its correlates such as socioeconomic status) have been abandoned pursuant to the *Students for Fair Admissions* court directive.

3.4.2 Affirmative Action as Remedial to Address Historical Injustice: A Notion Incorporated into the Canadian Charter of Rights and Freedoms

It is an interesting point of comparative law to note that Canada considers it *constitutional* for government to employ affirmative action to *remedy* historical

[87] Students for Fair Admission Inc v President and Fellows of Harvard University No. 20-1199. (United States Supreme Court) Argued October 31, 2022—Decided June 29, 2023 (Together with No. 21-707, Students for Fair Admissions, Inc. v. University of North Carolina et al.) https://www.scotusblog.com/case-files/cases/students-for-fair-admissions-inc-v-president-fellows-of-harvard-college/ (Accessed August 20, 2024).

injustice.[88] In fact, *the constitutionality of affirmative action as remedial* is explicitly addressed at s. 15 (2) of the *Canadian Charter of Rights and Freedoms*[89] as follows:

> 15. (1) Every individual is equal before and under the law and has the right to the equal protection and equal benefit of the law without discrimination and, in particular, without discrimination based on race, national or ethnic origin, colour, religion, sex, age or mental or physical disability.
>
> (2) *Section (1) does not preclude any law, program or activity that has as its object the amelioration of conditions of disadvantaged individuals or groups* including those that are disadvantaged because of race, national or ethnic origin, colour, religion, sex, age or mental or physical disability (emphasis added).[90]

It is arguably still, to some degree however, an open and complex question as to precisely the full range of contexts in which Canadian universities receiving federal funds are subject to *Canadian Charter* obligations and constraints.[91] That depends (for the purposes of a lawsuit, for instance, under s 15(2) of the Charter) in part on whether and to what extent universities are considered part of government or regarded as implementing "a specific government policy or program."[92] Even if Canadian universities in more current cases are found not to be part of government; legally in Canada, for the purpose of considering affirmative action and university admissions; a university admissions policy might arguably still be subject to judicial review in Canada under provincial or territorial human rights legal frameworks.[93] The latter if, for instance, the affirmative action university admissions policy (a) *discriminates* on the basis of a protected ground in the *absence* of a demonstrable remedial intent relating to historical and continuing injustice and (b) the complainant is *not* part of a group which has suffered alleged historical systemic injustice leading to current inequities in Canadian university admission.

[88] The Fourteenth Amendment of the US Constitution arguably itself reflects an affirmative step in attempting to redress historical injustices perpetrated against formerly enslaved persons of African descent forcibly brought to America. This by ensuring to them constitutionally (if not necessarily consistently in practice) their rights and privileges as US citizens and likewise to their descendants.

[89] Canadian Charter of Rights and Freedoms Available for download from https://www.justice.gc.ca/eng/csj-sjc/rfc-dlc/ccrf-ccdl/ (Accessed August 20, 2024).

[90] Canadian Charter of Rights and Freedoms Available for download from https://www.justice.gc.ca/eng/csj-sjc/rfc-dlc/ccrf-ccdl/ (Accessed August 20, 2024).

[91] Cook (2021), pp. 957–971.

[92] Centre for Constitutional Studies *Charter Rights on Campus? It Depends Where You Live* Case Littlewood, Student Researcher https://www.constitutionalstudies.ca/2020/08/charter-rights-on-campus-it-depends-where-you-live/ (Accessed August 20, 2024).

[93] See for a discussion of human rights legislation in Ontario, Canada and the issue of remedies for historical injustice and their legacy: Gall, G (2004) *Human Rights legislation and redress for past wrongs* https://www.ohrc.on.ca/en/race-policy-dialogue-papers/human-rights-legislation-and-redress-past-wrongs (Accessed August 20, 2024).

3.5 Concluding Comment on the Harvard Students for Fair Admissions Case

The Harvard *Students for Fair Admission* case[94] is, on the analysis here, replete with contradictions. This in that on the one hand the universities argue that the Fourteenth Amendment does *not* require colour blindness since race is one factor to consider when creating a diverse student body as is consistent with democratic values. Yet the universities, according to United States Supreme Court *Students for Fair Admission* case law, are now required to be colour blind and blind to history. This being reflected in the judicial directive to abandon race-based affirmative action as (a) a remedial strategy for past and current ethnically based systemic inequities and (b) in the effort to achieve student diversity. At the same time, the universities are permitted to be *in effect* colour conscious by acting on their preference for privileged students with certain characteristics (i.e., being a legacy candidate or child of a donor to the university or the child of a faculty member) that are strongly correlated with being Caucasian. Further, the Asian-American minority complainants in the Students for Fair Admission university case, however, themselves argue *for* colour blindness in the university admission process (that is, elimination of race as a consideration in admissions) adding even further complexity to the case. The latter even if it might lead to exacerbation of underrepresentation for certain disadvantaged ethnic minorities such as Afro-Americans (Asian Americans are generally *disadvantaged* on the personal rating by admission officers at Harvard (based on alleged racial/ethnic stereotyping) and Afro-Americans generally are *advantaged* by the' positive tip' related to race in the final university admissions selection process amongst *qualified students*).

In short then the current US university admission system post *Students for Fair Admission*[95] is, on the respectful view here, (a) disingenuous in its treatment of race/ethnicity and is (b) not designed to substantively address complex human rights issues that have plagued US university admissions practice both historically and currently. As discussed, the Students for Fair Admissions case,[96] while it ended race-based affirmative action for *racial/ethnic minority students*, did *not* in practice

[94] Students for Fair Admission Inc v President and Fellows of Harvard University No. 20-1199. (United States Supreme Court) Argued October 31, 2022—Decided June 29, 2023 (Together with No. 21-707, Students for Fair Admissions, Inc. v. University of North Carolina et al.) https://www.scotusblog.com/case-files/cases/students-for-fair-admissions-inc-v-president-fellows-of-harvard-college/ (Accessed August 20, 2024).

[95] Students for Fair Admission Inc v President and Fellows of Harvard University No. 20-1199. (United States Supreme Court) Argued October 31, 2022—Decided June 29, 2023 (Together with No. 21-707, Students for Fair Admissions, Inc. v. University of North Carolina et al.) https://www.scotusblog.com/case-files/cases/students-for-fair-admissions-inc-v-president-fellows-of-harvard-college/ (Accessed August 20, 2024).

[96] Students for Fair Admission Inc v President and Fellows of Harvard University No. 20-1199. (United States Supreme Court) Argued October 31, 2022—Decided June 29, 2023 (Together with No. 21-707, Students for Fair Admissions, Inc. v. University of North Carolina et al.) https://www.

eliminate the possibility for indirect considerations of race in university admissions for other more privileged groups (i.e., legacy applicants who are predominantly Caucasian). Nor did the United States Supreme Court majority in the Students Fair Admissions case hold such indirect considerations of race in university admissions for other more privileged groups to be unconstitutional.

3.6 Lawyers for Civil Rights' Complaint Concerning Harvard's Legacy Admissions

It is to be noted that just days following the release of the US Supreme Court ruling on the Harvard and N Carolina University[97] students for fair admissions cases, the US NGO 'Lawyers for Civil Rights' filed a complaint with the US Department of Education.[98] That complaint claimed that Harvard's preference in the final selection in admissions with regard to legacy students (providing a positive tip for legacy applicants) violates the US Civil Rights Act. The legacy system, the complainants argue, disadvantages African American and Latino communities which are disproportionately less wealthy than Caucasian communities, especially when considering Caucasian communities from which legacies and children of donors are generally drawn. The legacy system and giving preference to children of donors and of faculty, the complainants contend, does *not* reflect merit but rather a system designed to ensure a preponderance of white wealthy students at elite schools. Many elite universities, however, like Harvard, wish to retain such a system of legacy (as well as preference for the children of donors and faculty) in that it is thought to foster donations and purportedly build community. Build community *amongst whom*, however, might be the appropriate question to ask then.

Materials

A Jackson (2023) Legacy preferences should join racial preferences in dustbin *The Carolina Journal* 2 August 2023 https://www.carolinajournal.com/opinion/legacy-preferences-should-join-racial-preferences-in-dustbin/ (Accessed August 20, 2024)

scotusblog.com/case-files/cases/students-for-fair-admissions-inc-v-president-fellows-of-harvard-college/ (Accessed August 20, 2024).

[97] Scotus Blog Students for Fair Admissions, Inc. v. University of North Carolina https://www.scotusblog.com/case-files/cases/students-for-fair-admissions-inc-v-university-of-north-carolina/ (Accessed 26 December 2023).

[98] The complaint was filed on behalf of Chica Project, African Community Economic Development of New England, and the Greater Boston Latino Network Associated Press 'Nonprofit files civil rights complaint challenging legacy admissions at Harvard'. Jul 3, 2023 12:42 PM EDT.

Akandji-Kombe, Jean-François (2007) *Positive Obligations under the European Convention of Human Rights: A guide to the implementation of the European Convention on Human Rights.* Human rights handbooks, No. 7 Directorate General of Human Rights Strasbourg https://rm.coe.int/168007ff4d (Accessed August 20, 2024)

Canadian Charter of Rights and Freedoms Available for download from https://www.justice.gc.ca/eng/csj-sjc/rfc-dlc/ccrf-ccdl/ (Accessed August 20, 2024)

Centre for Constitutional Studies *Charter Rights on Campus? It Depends Where You Live* Case Littlewood, Student Researcher https://www.constitutionalstudies.ca/2020/08/charter-rights-on-campus-it-depends-where-you-live/ (Accessed August 20, 2024)

Civil Rights Act (1964) statute 42 U.S.C. §2000d Prohibition against exclusion from participation in, denial of benefits of, and discrimination under federally assisted programs on ground of race, color, or national origin Cornell Law School, Legal Information Institute https://www.law.cornell.edu/uscode/text/42/2000d (Accessed August 20, 2024)

Communication from the Commission to the European Parliament and the Council on its Interpretation of the judgment in Case C-450/93, *Kalanke v Freie Hansestadt Bremen* https://eur-lex.europa.eu/legal-content/EN/TXT/?uri=CELEX%3A51996DC0088 (Accessed August 20, 2024)

Court of Justice of the European Union Overview https://european-union.europa.eu/institutions-law-budget/institutions-and-bodies/institutions-and-bodies-profiles/court-justice-european-union-cjeu_en (Accessed August 20, 2024)

DR Franklin and SW Zwickel (Harvard Crimson) *In Admissions, Harvard Favors Those Who Fund It, Internal Emails Show* https://www.thecrimson.com/article/2018/10/18/day-three-harvard-admissions-trial/ (Accessed August 20, 2024)

European Convention on Human Rights https://www.echr.coe.int/documents/convention_eng.pdf (Accessed August 20, 2024)

European Court of Human Rights Key Theme Article 2 Protocol No. 1 Discrimination on access to education (Last updated: 01/09/2022) https://ks.echr.coe.int/documents/d/echr-ks/discrimination-in-access-to-education (Accessed August 20, 2024)

European Court of Human Rights, Right to Education, Guide on Article 2 of Protocol No. 1 to the European Convention on Human Rights https://www.echr.coe.int/documents/d/echr/guide_art_2_protocol_1_eng#:~:text=%E2%80%9CNo%20person%20shall%20be%20denied,own%20religious%20and%20philosophical%20convictions.%E2%80%9D&text=1.,-The%20first%20sentence (Accessed August 20, 2024)

Federal Government https://www.federalregister.gov/documents/2021/01/25/2021-01753/advancing-racial-equity-and-support-for-underserved-communities-through-the-federal-government (Accessed August 20, 2024)

Gall, G (2004) Human Rights legislation and redress for past wrongs https://www.ohrc.on.ca/en/race-policy-dialogue-papers/human-rights-legislation-and-redress-past-wrongs (Accessed August 20, 2024)

Ginsburg, RB and Merritt, DJ Affirmative action: An international human rights dialogue, Benjamin N. Cardozo Lecture, Cardozo Lecture given by Justice Ginsburg at the Association of the Bar of the City of New York on 11 February 1999 https://constcourt.ge/files/7/JCL-ENG-Vol-2-(2020)/JCL-2020-Vol.2-ENG-9-32.pdf (Accessed August 20, 2024)

H.B. 1775 70 OK Stat § 70-24-157 (2021) Education; prohibiting certain training for students; prohibiting courses from including certain concept https://legiscan.com/OK/text/HB1775/id/2387002 (Accessed August 20, 2024)

Inside Higher Education (26 July 2023) Affirmative Action for the Rich: The ban on affirmative action has put pressure on selective colleges to end legacy preferences in admissions. But the advantages of familial wealth go beyond alumni status https://www.insidehighered.com/news/admissions/traditional-age/2023/07/26/would-ending-legacy-admissions-improve-elite-college (Accessed August 20, 2024)

President Biden Revokes Trump Executive Order 13950 and Issues "Advancing Racial Equity and Support for Underserved Communities Through the Federal Government," https://www.dol.gov/agencies/ofccp/executive-order-13950 (Accessed August 20, 2024)

Scotus Blog: Students for Fair Admissions, Inc. v. University of North Carolina https://www.scotusblog.com/case-files/cases/students-for-fair-admissions-inc-v-university-of-north-carolina/ (Accessed August 20, 2024)

Strasbourg Observers (26 November 2018) Kaboglu and Oran v Turkey: Protecting the private life of scholars, yet failing to recognize the academic freedom dimension at issue. Commentary of Sophia Sideridou https://strasbourgobservers.com/2018/11/26/kaboglu-and-oran-v-turkey-protecting-the-private-life-of-scholars-yet-failing-to-recognize-the-academic-freedom-dimension-at-issue/ (Accessed August 20, 2024)

Trump Executive Order 13950 of September 22, 2020 Combating Race and Sex Stereotyping https://www.federalregister.gov/documents/2020/09/28/2020-21534/combating-race-and-sex-stereotyping (Accessed August 20, 2024)

United States Supreme Court Cases

Brown v. Board of Education, 347 U.S. 483 (1954) Argued December 9, 1952 Reargued December 8, 1953 Decided May 17, 1954 https://www.archives.gov/milestone-documents/brown-v-board-of-education (Accessed August 20, 2024)

Grutter v. Bollinger 539 U.S. 306 (2003) (United States Supreme Court) https://supreme.justia.com/cases/federal/us/539/306/#tab-opinion-1961290 (Accessed August 20, 2024)

Regents of University of California v Bakke 438 U.S. 265 (1978) (United States Supreme Court) https://supreme.justia.com/cases/federal/us/438/265/#tab-opinion-1952756 (Accessed August 20, 2024)

Students for Fair Admissions, Inc. v President and Fellows of Harvard University (United States Supreme Court) Complaint https://www.supremecourt.gov/DocketPDF/20/20-1199/169941/20210225095525027_Harvard%20Cert%20Petn%20Feb%2025.pdf (Accessed August 20, 2024)

Students for Fair Admissions, Inc. v President and Fellows of Harvard University (United States Supreme Court) (Docket All Case Documents filed) https://www.scotusblog.com/case-files/cases/students-for-fair-admissions-inc-v-president-fellows-of-harvard-college/ (Accessed August 20, 2024)

Students for Fair Admissions, Inc. v President and Fellows of Harvard University (United States Supreme Court) Oral Argument (Available under Media Oral Argument October 31, 2022) OYEZ Cornell Legal Information Institute https://www.oyez.org/cases/2022/20-1199 (Accessed August 20, 2024)

Students for Fair Admissions, Inc. v President and Fellows of Harvard University, United States Supreme Court Respondent Brief https://www.supremecourt.gov/DocketPDF/20/20-1199/230739/20220725122633156_20-1199%20bs.pdf (Accessed August 20, 2024)

Students for Fair Admissions, Inc. v. University of North Carolina (heard by the United States Supreme Court together with Students for Fair Admissions, Inc. v President and Fellows of Harvard University) Trial Findings of Fact and Law, District Judge Loretta C. Biggs App. 1 Appendix A In the United States District Court for the Middle District of North Carolina 1:14CV954. Filed October 18, 2021 https://www.scotusblog.com/wp-content/uploads/2021/11/20211111164136730_SFFA-Appendix.pdf (Accessed August 20, 2024)

United States Lower Court Cases

Black Emergency Response Team et al. v John O'Connor, Attorney General of Oklahoma et al. Amended Complaint (United States District Court for the Western District of Oklahoma) https://www.aclu.org/legal-document/amended-complaint-6 (Accessed August 20, 2024)

Black Emergency Response Team et al. v John O'Connor, Attorney General of Oklahoma et al. Plaintiffs' Memorandum of Law in Opposition to Edmond Public School's Motion to Dismiss (United States District Court for the Western District of Oklahoma) https://www.aclu.org/legal-document/plaintiffs-response-opposition-eps-defendants-motion-dismiss (Accessed August 20, 2024)

Black Emergency Response Team et al. v John O'Connor, Attorney General of Oklahoma et al. Plaintiffs' Memorandum of Law in Opposition to Oklahoma University Regent's Motion to Dismiss (United States District Court for the Western District of Oklahoma) https://www.aclu.org/legal-document/plaintiffs-response-opposition-ou-regents-motion-dismiss (Accessed August 20, 2024)

Santa Cruz Lesbian & Gay Cmty. Ctr. v Trump (United States District Court Northern District of California), San Jose Division 508 F. Supp. 3d at 543.

European Court of Human Rights Cases

Kaboglu and Oran v Turkey (European Court of Human Rights) LawEuro information Note on the Court's case-law 222 October 2018 https://laweuro.com/?p=4766 (Accessed August 20, 2024)

Pastors v Germany (European Court of Human Rights) (Application No. 5525/14) Judgment 3 October 2019 https://hudoc.echr.coe.int/fre#{%22documentcollectionid2%22:[%22GRANDCHAMBER%22,%22CHAMBER%22],%22itemid%22:[%22001-196148%22]} (Accessed August 20, 2024)

European Court of Justice Cases

Hellmut Marschall v Land Nordrhein-Westfalen (Germany) Reference for a preliminary ruling Judgment of the European Court of Justice 11 November 1997. https://eur-lex.europa.eu/legal-content/EN/TXT/?uri=CELEX%3A61995CJ0409 (Accessed August 20, 2024)

Kalanke v Freie Hansestadt Bremen [1995] ECJ (European Court of Justice) Case C-450/93 https://www.equalrightstrust.org/ertdocumentbank/Kalanke.pdf (Accessed August 20, 2024)

References

Cook H (2021) Charter applicability to universities and the regulation of on-campus expression. Alberta Law Rev 58(4):957–971. https://albertalawreview.com/index.php/ALR/article/view/2658/2612. Accessed 20 Aug 2024

O'Hare U (2000) Equality and affirmative action in international human rights law and its relevance to the European Union. Int J Discrimination Law 4:3–45

Terrell MT (2011) Bucking Grutter: why critical mass should be thrown off the affirmative-action horse. Tex J Civil Liberties Civil Rights 16:233. https://heinonline.org/HOL/LandingPage?handle=hein.journals/tfcl16&div=13&id=&page=. Accessed 20 Aug 2024

Chapter 4
The Abortion Culture War and De-Democratization: States as Final Arbiters of Fundamental Human Rights and the Privatization of Abortion Restriction Enforcement

Abstract This chapter examines the abortion 'culture war' in the context of the United States Supreme Court Dobbs decision. *Dobbs* overturned *Roe v Wade* and delegated to the States the determination as to when, if ever, abortion is legal in the particular State. The decision thus equated to an abandonment of any federal constitutionally based principled guidelines in regard to the legal status of abortion in any State. In addition, the issue is addressed as to whether the United States Supreme Court properly decided *Dobbs* in part since the Court did not determine the fetal personhood question, even going so far as to decline to hear a subsequent fetal personhood case. Also explored is the delegation of State authority to private citizens to enforce State abortion policy thus invading the individual's privacy, family life and also compromising their personal autonomy and bodily integrity in the process. The implications of the latter for democracy (i.e., untoward State intrusions into private life) and constitutional due process are considered as an issue that cuts across both sides of the abortion controversy.

4.1 Thomas E. Dobbs, State Health Officer of the Mississippi Department of Health et al. v Jackson Women's Health Organization et al. United States Supreme Court 597 U. S. ____ (2022)

Thomas E. Dobbs, State Health Officer of the Mississippi Department of Health et al. v Jackson Women's Health Organization et *al.* 597 U. S. ____ (2022) addresses the abortion issue.[1] The *Dobbs* United States Supreme Court majority opinion holds that "It is time to heed the Constitution and return the issue of abortion to the people's elected representatives."[2] Justice Alito maintains in *Dobbs* that the people

[1]Thomas E. Dobbs, State Health Officer of the Mississippi Department of Health et al. v Jackson Women's Health Organization et al. 597 U. S. ____ (2022) Justice Alito majority opinion.

[2]Thomas E. Dobbs, State Health Officer of the Mississippi Department of Health et al. v Jackson Women's Health Organization et al. 597 U. S. ____ (2022) Justice Alito majority opinion at p. 6.

S. C. Grover, *Litigating the Politics of Human Rights*, Ius Gentium: Comparative Perspectives on Law and Justice 121, https://doi.org/10.1007/978-3-031-82463-0_4

should debate the abortion issue and vote on what they consider the appropriate resolution. In the latter regard, Justice Alito contended that "That is what the Constitution and the rule of law demand."[3] It will be argued here, in contrast, that such fundamental human rights questions are *not* a matter for a majoritarian voting resolution in the legislature but rather reference to the values underpinning democracy itself and constitutional principle. Hence, on the view here, especially when a fundamental human rights matter is so divisive, the Supreme Court of the United States cannot properly shirk its duty to offer a principled humane resolution.

The Dobbs case involved a Mississippi statute; the Mississippi's Gestational Age Act, Miss. Code Ann. §41-41-191 (2018), which stipulated the following:

> Except in a medical emergency or in the case of a severe fetal abnormality, a person shall not intentionally or knowingly perform . . . or induce an abortion of an unborn human being if the probable gestational age of the unborn human being has been determined to be greater than fifteen (15) weeks.[4]

The Dobbs majority opinion cited various factual findings that the Mississippi legislature made in supporting the aforesaid statute; namely that: "… at 5 or 6 weeks' gestational age an "unborn human being's heart begins beating"; at 8 weeks the "unborn human being begins to move about in the womb"; at 9 weeks "all basic physiological functions are present"; at 10 weeks "vital organs begin to function," and "[h]air, fingernails, and toenails . . . begin to form"; at 11 weeks "an unborn human being's diaphragm is developing," and he or she may "move about freely in the womb"; and at 12 weeks the "unborn human being" has "taken on 'the human form' in all relevant respects."[5]

The Jackson Women's Health Organization, an abortion clinic, and one of the doctors from the clinic challenged the Mississippi's Gestational Age Act as unconstitutional arguing that the statute violated the constitutional right to abortion. The District Court ruled in favor of the clinic holding that only at point of viability could non-therapeutic abortions be held unlawful and unconstitutional. The District Court permanently blocked enforcement of the said Mississippi statute finding that 15 weeks gestation of the fetus is *prior to* viability. The Appeals Court affirmed (Fifth Circuit 945 F. 3d 265 (2019)). The abortion clinic had argued that banning *pre-viability abortions* would be tantamount to overruling the landmark United States Supreme Court abortion decisions of *Roe*[6] and *Casey*[7] which provided a

---

[3]Thomas E. Dobbs, State Health Officer of the Mississippi Department of Health et al. v Jackson Women's Health Organization et al. 597 U. S. ____ (2022) Justice Alito majority opinion at p. 6.

[4]In Thomas E. Dobbs, State Health Officer of the Mississippi Department of Health et al. v Jackson Women's Health Organization et al. 597 U. S. ____ (2022) Justice Alito majority opinion at p. 6 the Miss. Code Ann. §41-41-191 (2018) is cited. Fifteen weeks is held by the medical community to be a *pre-viability* stage of fetal development.

[5]Thomas E. Dobbs, State Health Officer of the Mississippi Department of Health et al. v Jackson Women's Health Organization et al. 597 U. S. ____ (2022) Justice Alito majority opinion at p. 7.

[6]Roe v. Wade 410 U. S. 113.

[7]Planned Parenthood of Southeastern Pa. v. Casey, 505 U. S. 833.

constitutional basis for abortion within certain parameters. The Mississippi Department of Health appealed to the United States Supreme Court arguing that *Roe* and *Casey* precedents had been "wrongly decided" and that the Mississippi Act in question is constitutional and can withstand rational basis review scrutiny by the courts.[8]

The majority United States Supreme Court opinion in *Dobbs* holds that there is no constitutional right to abortion set out either explicitly or implicitly in the US Constitution. The Dobbs United States Supreme Court opinion rejected the notion that a constitutional right to abortion flowed from a constitutional right to privacy understood as the right to autonomous decision-making. Instead, the Dobbs United States Supreme Court majority held that there was in fact no constitutional right to privacy (understood in terms of personal autonomy) upon which a subsidiary right to abortion could be grounded. The Dobbs majority also rejected the notion that a right to abortion was subsumed under the liberty right protected under the Fourteenth Amendment due process clause. *Dobbs* further held that constitutionally based equal protection under the law was not implicated by the State's regulation of abortion which the Court's majority maintained does *not* involve sex-based classification. As to the latter, the United States Supreme Court precedent set out that the "goal of preventing abortion" does not constitute "invidiously discriminatory animus" against women."[9]

A question may be raised as to whether a right that is understood to be fundamental but not enumerated in the Constitution must, to be counted, be deeply rooted in the country's history and tradition as is the test suggested by the Dobbs majority. One wonders what consideration is given then to developing understandings of central issues and changes in society that shed new light on issues. It has been pointed out that women's status in Western society has changed over the decades with their enjoying more personal autonomy and there have been, at the same time, as a result of medical technological advances, new understandings of the developing unborn.[10] These aspects of modernization then can and should, on the view here, be expected to impact the formulation of the abortion issue. Aside from the core issue of a purported right to abortion then, but speaking generally, fundamental rights denied based on misapprehensions and/or contentious social norms (where such exist) must not be continued to be denied and then that block rationalized simply on historical practice and tradition. Yet, as the Dissenting United States Supreme Court justices in *Dobbs* noted, the majority in *Dobbs* articulated a new arguably erroneous standard for claimed fundamental rights meeting constitutional muster such that "all rights that have no history stretching back to the mid-19th century are insecure. If the

[8]Thomas E. Dobbs, State Health Officer of the Mississippi Department of Health et al. v Jackson Women's Health Organization et al. 597 U. S. ____ (2022) Syllabus at p. 1.

[9]Bray v. Alexandria Women's Health Clinic, 506 U. S. 263, 273–274 (1993) Cited in Thomas E. Dobbs, State Health Officer of the Mississippi Department of Health et al. v Jackson Women's Health Organization et al. 597 U. S. ____ (2022) Justice Alito majority opinion at p 11.

[10]See Ziegler (2018), pp. 15–40.

ratifiers did not understand something as central to freedom, then neither can we. Or said more particularly: If those people did not understand reproductive rights as part of the guarantee of liberty conferred in the Fourteenth Amendment, then those rights do not exist,"[11] The United States Supreme Court dissenters in *Dobbs* argued in contrast, relying on Justice Harlan, that the "constitutional "tradition" of this country is not captured whole at a single moment…Rather, its meaning gains content from the long sweep of our history and from successive judicial precedents—each looking to the last and each seeking to apply the Constitution's most fundamental commitments to new conditions."[12]

The Dissenting Justices in *Dobbs* further highlighted that the ratifiers of the Fourteenth Amendment[13] were, in any case, all men and in fact men who "did not perceive women as equals, and did not recognize women's rights."[14] It would appear then that, to some extent, the debate between the majority versus dissenting United States Supreme Court justices in *Dobbs* morphed into a dispute between (a) those who interpret the Constitution as strict 'originalists' and (b) those who view it as a 'living document' that must largely be interpreted in the context of the contemporary times. Thus, the Dissenting Justices in *Dobbs* held that "The Framers defined rights in general terms, to permit future evolution in their scope and meaning. And over the course of our history, this Court has taken up the Framers' invitation"[15] while still taking account of "constitutional principles, constitutional history, and constitutional precedent."[16] The rather entrenched chasm in legal philosophical perspective then between (a) the 'originalist' justices and (b) the 'living document' justices seems to have distracted from the possibility for an analysis and focus that might have bridged the gap between the two views in *Dobbs*.

Justice Alito, in rendering the majority United States Supreme Court opinion in *Dobbs*, expressed the concern that the liberty right articulated in the due process clause of the Constitution not be "subtly transformed into the policy preferences of

---

[11]Thomas E. Dobbs, State Health Officer of the Mississippi Department of Health et al. v Jackson Women's Health Organization et al. 597 U. S. ____ (2022) Dissenting Opinion at p. 14 (Breyer, Sotomayor, and Kagan JJ., dissenting).

[12]See Poe v. Ullman, 367 U. S. 497, 542 (1961) (dissenting opinion) Referenced in Thomas E. Dobbs, State Health Officer of the Mississippi Department of Health et al. v Jackson Women's Health Organization et al. 597 U. S. ____ (2022) Dissenting Opinion at p. 18.

[13]Both *Roe* and *Casey* based the right to abortion on the Fourteen Amendment.

[14]Thomas E. Dobbs, State Health Officer of the Mississippi Department of Health et al. v Jackson Women's Health Organization et al. 597 U. S. ____ (2022) Dissenting Opinion at p. 15 (Breyer, Sotomayor, and Kagan JJ., dissenting).

[15]Thomas E. Dobbs, State Health Officer of the Mississippi Department of Health et al. v Jackson Women's Health Organization et al. 597 U. S. ____ (2022) Dissenting Opinion at p. 16 (Breyer, Sotomayor, and Kagan JJ., dissenting).

[16]Thomas E. Dobbs, State Health Officer of the Mississippi Department of Health et al. v Jackson Women's Health Organization et al. 597 U. S. ____ (2022) Dissenting Opinion at p. 18 (Breyer, Sotomayor, and Kagan JJ., dissenting).

the Members of this Court."[17] On the current author's view, however, equally inappropriate and detrimental to democracy is a judiciary that ostensibly transforms a fundamental human rights matter or question such as is abortion (whether involving a constitutionally based right or not) into a policy issue in the first instance. The latter, it is here argued, occurred with the majority United States Supreme Court opinion in *Dobbs*. The Dobbs United States Supreme Court sent the abortion question, a basic human rights matter, back to the States for *discretionary* policy decision-making by each particular State. The latter is, on the view here, antithetical to (a) a just resolution of a fundamental human rights matter and to (b) honoring of the democratic values underpinning the Constitution which entail first and foremost respect for basic human rights. In this regard consider also that the United States Supreme Court majority in *Dobbs* rejected the notion of abortion as grounded on a privacy right. Further, the Dobbs majority United States Supreme Court discarded the view that privacy is, in any case, a constitutionally protected fundamental right. However, it should be understood that privacy is regarded as a fundamental human right under international human rights law. This is illustrated by the following selected examples including Article 12 of the *Universal Declaration of Human Rights*; the Declaration being considered by many legal scholars as *customary law*. Note that Article 17 of the *International Covenant on Civil and Political Rights*, which the United States ratified in 1992, duplicates almost exactly Article 12 of the *Universal Declaration of Human Rights*:

> **Universal Declaration of Human Rights Article 12:**
> "No one shall be subjected to arbitrary interference with his privacy, family, home or correspondence, nor to attacks upon his honour and reputation. Everyone has the right to the protection of the law against such interference or attacks."[18]

International Covenant on Civil and Political Rights Article 17

Article 17

1. No one shall be subjected to arbitrary or unlawful interference with his privacy, family, home or correspondence, nor to unlawful attacks on his honour and reputation.
2. Everyone has the right to the protection of the law against such interference or attacks.[19]

---

[17]Washington v Glucksberg 521 U. S., at 720. Cited in Thomas E. Dobbs, State Health Officer of the Mississippi Department of Health et al. v Jackson Women's Health Organization et al. 597 U. S. ____ (2022) Majority Opinion at p. 14.

[18]Universal Declaration of Human Rights Article 12 https://www.un.org/en/about-us/universal-declaration-of-human-rights (Accessed August 22, 2024).

[19]International Covenant on Civil and Political Rights https://www.ohchr.org/en/instruments-mechanisms/instruments/international-covenant-civil-and-political-rights (Accessed August 22, 2024).

Given (a) the international consensus on the privacy right as a fundamental human right and (b) the fact that government bans on pre-viable abortion indisputably interfere with the woman's and her family's privacy, it is here argued that it is misguided at best, and disingenuous at worst, for the United States Supreme Court majority in *Dobbs* to essentially maintain that abortion is *not* in itself (independent of any other consideration or constitutional analysis) a fundamental human rights matter but rather a political and policy question for the individual American States.

Since the US ratified *The International Covenant on Civil and Political Rights* (ICCPR*),* the US would generally be bound by the treaty: "Upon ratification, the ICCPR became the "supreme law of the land" under the Supremacy Clause of the U.S. Constitution, which gives ratified treaties the status of federal law."[20] This then would include also ICCPR Article 17, the right to privacy, as a fundamental human right under US federal law. However, likely the Dobbs United States Supreme Court majority would counter that the US reservations regarding the ICCPR (filed by the US upon treaty ratification) allow the Court (based on its contentious analysis/ interpretation of fundamental rights) to ignore Article 17 of the ICCPR and hold that (a) privacy is not a protected fundamental right[21] under US federal law or the US Constitution[22] and that (b) there is no implied constitutionally protected derivative right to abortion encompassed within an alleged US constitutionally based privacy right. On the view here, however, one wonders if a privacy right does not in fact

[20] American Civil Liberties Union FAQ The International Covenant on Civil and Political Rights https://www.aclu.org/other/faq-covenant-civil-political-rights-iccpr#:~:text=The%20U.S.%20ratified%20the%20ICCPR,the%20status%20of%20federal%20law (Accessed August 22, 2024).

[21] University of Minnesota Human Rights Library, U.S. Government Reservations, Declarations and Understandings: International Covenant on Civil and Political Rights: "IV Nothing in this Covenant requires or authorizes legislation, or other action, by the United States of America prohibited by the Constitution of the United States as interpreted by the United States." http://www1.umn.edu/humanrts/usdocs/civilres.html (Accessed August 22, 2024).

[22] The Dobbs majority did not rule that there is no constitutionally protected privacy right linked to personal autonomy. However, Justice Thomas in his Dobbs concurrence, essentially encourages the Court in future cases to reconsider certain United States Supreme Court precedents that *in effect* affirm a constitutionally protected broad sphere of privacy understood as autonomous decision-making (i.e. when it comes to consensual same-sex intimacy, access to contraception and a number of other situations). See Thomas E. Dobbs, State Health Officer of the Mississippi Department of Health et al. v Jackson Women's Health Organization et al. 597 U. S. ____ (2022), Justice Thomas Concurring Opinion at pp 2–3. Indeed, arguably consistent with Justice Thomas' aforementioned invitation to the Court to reconsider the privacy right, the United States Supreme Court agreed, for instance, to hear a case *Food and Drug Administration v. Alliance for Hippocratic Medicine* concerning access to an abortion pill (mifepristone); an issue that certainly implicates privacy rights (in terms of private decision-making). See *Food and Drug Administration v. Alliance for Hippocratic Medicine* (consolidated with Danco Laboratories, L.L.C. v. Alliance for Hippocratic Medicine) 598 U. S. ____ (2023). https://www.supremecourt.gov/opinions/22pdf/22a901_3d9g.pdf (Accessed August 22, 2024). The Supreme Court of the United States in the latter case agreed to review a Fifth Circuit Court of Appeals decision that reinstated pre-2016 significant restrictions on how mifepristone can be accessed by patients, but did not remove the abortion pill from the market. The USSC ruled in the Alliance for Hippocratic Medicine case that the plaintiffs had no standing to challenge the FDAs actions regarding regulation of the abortion pill.

underly the First Amendment so cherished by conservative and liberal justices alike. How can a citizen autonomously exercise freedom of religion, thought, speech and conscientious objection without freedom from interference in the private deliberation, consultation and practice of those beliefs? It may be that a right to privacy is an essential element of and precondition for the realization of the First Amendment right. If such a constitutionally based privacy right exists; it is yet another question whether it encompasses a right to abortion of the previable fetus. In this regard the majority United States Supreme Court in *Dobbs* contentiously maintains that:

> Attempts to justify abortion through appeals to a broader right to autonomy and to define one's "concept of existence" prove too much... Abortion is different because it destroys what *Roe* termed "potential life" and what the law challenged in this case calls an "unborn human being. None of the other decisions cited by *Roe* and *Casey* involved the critical moral question posed by abortion. Accordingly, those cases do not support the right to obtain an abortion."[23]

Post *Dobbs* some States have activated 'trigger laws' (preexisting or new) that allow for the implementation of draconian abortion statutes that permit for few if any exceptions. For instance, Arkansas allows abortion only when the health of the mother is at risk but not for rape or incest. Rape and incest are also not accepted exceptions allowing for abortion in Kentucky, Louisiana, Missouri, Oklahoma, South Dakota, Tennessee, and Texas.[24] It may very well be the case that certain US States post *Dobbs* implementing a statutory bar on abortion of the previable fetus in cases of incest or rape constitutes a systemic abuse of the rights of pregnant women so affected in those States. That abuse then arguably may, depending on all the facts and circumstances, rise to the level of "forced pregnancy." Note that footnote 2 (f) to the Rome Statute definition of 'forced pregnancy' specifies that the definition "shall not in any way be interpreted as affecting national laws relating to pregnancy."[25] It remains to be seen then whether a US domestic constitutional case can be brought addressing alleged *forced pregnancy* per the statutory bar post *Dobbs* in some US States on abortion of the previable fetus in cases also of rape or incest. The argument might in part be that such specific bars to rape and incest exceptions to securing an abortion of the previable fetus do in fact represent the kind

---

[23] Thomas E. Dobbs, State Health Officer of the Mississippi Department of Health et al. v Jackson Women's Health Organization et al. 597 U. S. ____ (2022) Syllabus at p. 4.

[24] Dube N, Orlando, J, Schaeffer-Helmecki, J (Office of Legislative Research, Connecticut Legislature) Research Report: *State Abortion Laws Enacted Post-Dobbs Decision* September 29, 2022, 2022-R-0227 Table 1 pp. 3–5.

[25] Crimes Against Humanity Forced Pregnancy Article 7(g) Rome Statute of the International Criminal Court https://www.ohchr.org/en/instruments-mechanisms/instruments/rome-statute-international-criminal-court (Accessed August 22, 2024).

Note that the contextual elements of the crime against humanity of forced pregnancy do *not* require that the crime occur during armed conflict. Also, the crime can be perpetrated against any civilian population or a part thereof.

of "invidiously discriminatory animus" against women"[26] that the United States Supreme Court majority discounted in *Dobbs* as being operative in the regulation of abortion as a more general matter. Note that the dissenting United States Supreme Court justices in *Dobbs* in fact predicted that some States, in the wake of *Dobbs*, would *in effect* permit 'forced pregnancy' also in cases of rape and incest:

> Most threatening of all, no language in today's decision stops the Federal Government from prohibiting abortions nationwide, once again from the moment of conception and without exceptions for rape or incest.[27]

The majority in *Dobbs* then, it is here argued, sidestepped the core issues regarding (a) whether an unborn human life ought to be considered a human person under the law which any State has a compelling interest to protect and, if so, at what gestational stage and in what range of other circumstances that should be the case[28] and (b) what, if any, factors related to the health and well-being of the mother and/or fetus should act as countervailing to any State interest in protecting the unborn and within which parameters. On the view here, the Dobbs United States Supreme Court decided a case *not* put before the Court; namely one concerning *State's rights* in the abortion space. On this author's analysis then States rights regarding the abortion matter was decided by the Dobbs United States Supreme Court majority rather than the fundamental human rights questions put to the Court that arose given the particular Mississippi statute in question. The Dissenting Justices in *Dobbs* went so far as to contend that, given the *Dobbs* majority opinion, in fact "The constitutional regime we enter today erases the woman's interest and recognizes only the State's (or the Federal Government's)."[29] This author concurs that the United States Supreme Court *Dobbs* majority in fact gave supremacy to the State interest over both that of the woman and the unborn. In effect, *Dobbs* held that the recognition and protection of any interests of the woman or the unborn is to be left to the particular political and other discretionary calculations and machinations of the individual States. Such an approach serves, on the view here, to (a) contribute to masking the actual *fundamental human rights* nature of such determinations and (b) morphing the question instead into a purported largely political one of individual State's rights.

---

[26] Bray v. Alexandria Women's Health Clinic, 506 U. S. 263, 273–274 (1993) Cited in Thomas E. Dobbs, State Health Officer of the Mississippi Department of Health et al. v Jackson Women's Health Organization et al. 597 U. S. ____ (2022) Majority Opinion at p 11.

[27] Thomas E. Dobbs, State Health Officer of the Mississippi Department of Health et al. v Jackson Women's Health Organization et al. 597 U. S. ____ (2022) Dissenting Opinion at p. 3 (Breyer, Sotomayor, and Kagan JJ., dissenting).

[28] For the most part "the state interest in protecting fetal life plays no part in the majority's analysis." To the contrary, the majority takes pride in not expressing a view "about the status of the fetus." Thomas E. Dobbs, State Health Officer of the Mississippi Department of Health et al. v Jackson Women's Health Organization et al. 597 U. S. ____ (2022) Dissenting Opinion at p. 26 (Breyer, Sotomayor, and Kagan JJ., dissenting).

[29] Thomas E. Dobbs, State Health Officer of the Mississippi Department of Health et al. v Jackson Women's Health Organization et al. 597 U. S. ____ (2022) Dissenting Opinion at p. 12 (Breyer, Sotomayor, and Kagan JJ., dissenting).

Marked societal dissention on the abortion issue (to which the Dobbs majority opinion refers multiple times) is, on the view here, *not* a just rationale for returning fundamental human rights matters such as this to the States as a supposed but policy issue as did the Dobbs United States Supreme Court. Indeed, one might argue reasonably that Justice Alito's rejection of the notion of a constitutional right to abortion (correct or not) puts the abortion question even more squarely into the category of a fundamental human rights quandary in need of a judicial resolution by the highest court. The latter then to be preferred to a hodgepodge of divergent decisions by various State legislatures with often arbitrary self-serving interpretations of the Constitution and of human personhood and its concomitant rights entitlements. It is disappointing then that Justice Alito, writing for the majority in *Dobbs*, states "our decision is not based on any view about when a State should regard prenatal life as having rights or [a] legally cognizable interest."[30] Rather the focus of the Dobbs United States Supreme Court majority (reflected in the written opinion of Justice Alito for the Court) focused on the claim that "The Court [in *Roe*] short-circuited the democratic process by closing it to the large number of Americans who disagreed with *Roe*."[31] The latter perspective, it is here contended, significantly undercuts the important and proper role in a democracy of the *independent* judiciary in (a) addressing highly divisive fundamental human rights matters and (b) seeking to formulate a resolution that best considers the *competing* basic rights at issue.[32] That is not to say, however, that such judicial resolutions always properly meet that objective, but rather it is to recognize that there is always the possibility in the next case for an improved judicial resolution.

In *Dobbs*, having shirked the core question of "when a State should regard prenatal life as having rights or [a] legally cognizable interest,"[33] it is not surprising that the United States Supreme Court declined to then hear subsequent fetal rights cases. In the fetal personhood case *Benson*[34] the plaintiffs petitioned the Supreme Court of the United States to consider whether the Rhode Island Supreme Court was, in light of the *Dobbs reversal* of *Ro*e, mistaken in holding that (a) regardless of the gestational age of the unborn; due process and equal protection constitutional guarantees do *not* apply and that (b) the unborn have *no* legal standing notwithstanding *Dobbs*. However the Supreme Court of the United States declined to weigh in on what the Benson petitioners construed as constitutional matters implicating fundamental human rights questions as pertain to the unborn. Thus, while the Rhode

---

[30] *Dobbs* Thomas E. Dobbs, State Health Officer of the Mississippi Department of Health et al. v Jackson Women's Health Organization et al. 597 U. S. ____ (2022) Majority Opinion at p. 29.

[31] Dobbs Thomas E. Dobbs, State Health Officer of the Mississippi Department of Health et al. v Jackson Women's Health Organization et al. 597 U. S. ____ (2022) Syllabus at p. 5.

[32] Assuming here then that the Court will not sidestep the fetal rights issue and fail to address the issue at all.

[33] *Dobbs* Thomas E. Dobbs, State Health Officer of the Mississippi Department of Health et al. v Jackson Women's Health Organization et al. 597 U. S. ____ (2022) Majority Opinion at p. 29.

[34] Benson et al. Next Friend of Baby Roe et al. v McKee (Governor of Rhode Island) No. 2020-66-Appeal, Supreme Court of Rhode Island Judgment May 4, 2022.

Island courts ruled in *Benson*[35] on the core issue of whether or not, in the State courts' view, the unborn are persons who enjoy constitutional rights, the United States Supreme Court resisted doing so. The same occurred with the fetal rights case *Jane Doe et al v McKee*.[36] On the view here then, the United States Supreme Court majority in *Dobbs*, as in the aforementioned fetal rights cases, by various means, shifted *their* judicial burden in this regard to the States.

Note that in *Jane Doe et al v McKee*, Petitioners in their brief presented the argument that the Fourteenth Amendment offers no definition of 'person' and thus, in Petitioner's view, provides no basis for excluding the unborn human life from the Fourteenth Amendment's protection.[37] Interestingly, the petitioners maintained that they did *not* seek that the Supreme Court of the United States adopt "any particular theory of life" in response to their petition but rather asserted that they sought the Court's clarification as to (a) whether the Plaintiffs. including the unborn petitioners (Baby Roe was 15 weeks gestational age and Baby Mary Doe was 34 weeks gestational age when Petitioners first filed their complaint in the Rhode Island courts), were entitled to protection under the Fourteenth Amendment or (b) whether all unborn, regardless of gestational age, were to be denied access to the courts through a next friend to contest abortion law.[38]

The petitioners in *Jane Doe et al v McKee* maintained that the Rhode Island Law; the *Reproductive Privacy Act* (permitting previable abortions and post viable abortions where the health or life of the mother is at risk) violated the rights of the unborn plaintiffs-Baby Doe and Baby Roe. This by stripping them of their personhood[39] recognized under the previous Rhode Island general law that affirmed personhood from conception.[40] Petitioners argued that (a) since *Roe* was overturned through the Dobbs decision and (b) there was no clarity in Rhode Island as to if and when the unborn enjoy constitutional protections (as under the Fourteenth Amendment), the

---

[35] Benson et al. Next Friend of Baby Roe et al. v McKee (Governor of Rhode Island) No. 2020-66-Appeal, Supreme Court of Rhode Island Judgment May 4, 2022.

[36] Jane Doe as parent and next friend of Baby Mary Doe, Nicole Leigh Rowley, parent and next friend of Baby Roe, and Catholics for Life, Inc. d/b/a/ Servants of Christ for Life v McKee (Governor of Rhode Island) Petitioners brief at p. i.

[37] Jane Doe as parent and next friend of Baby Mary Doe, Nicole Leigh Rowley, parent and next friend of Baby Roe, and Catholics for Life, Inc. d/b/a/ Servants of Christ for Life v McKee (Governor of Rhode Island) Petitioner brief at p. 3.

[38] Jane Doe as parent and next friend of Baby Mary Doe, Nicole Leigh Rowley, parent and next friend of Baby Roe, and Catholics for Life, Inc. d/b/a/ Servants of Christ for Life v McKee (Governor of Rhode Island) Petitioner brief at p. 3.

[39] The current author would argue that personhood is *inherent* for all human life as all human life has dignity that deserves full respect, but such personhood is not always recognized in law. At the same time, the law may create a legal fiction and recognize a nonhuman entity such as a corporation as a person though the corporation has no dignity nor capacity for suffering in the sense that a human being does.

[40] Jane Doe as parent and next friend of Baby Mary Doe, Nicole Leigh Rowley, parent and next friend of Baby Roe, and Catholics for Life, Inc. d/b/a/ Servants of Christ for Life v McKee (Governor of Rhode Island) Petitioner brief at p. 4.

United States Supreme Court should review and consider the Rhode Island *Reproductive Privacy Act*, This to determine whether the Act is constitutional or instead violates the Fourteenth Amendment due process and equality guarantee. However, as mentioned, the United States Supreme Court dodged the opportunity to consider a central issue posed here, as in *Dobbs*, that issue being when, if ever, the unborn enjoys constitutional protections. The United States Supreme Court declined to hear the case punting it to the individual States to tackle instead. This then once again amounted to sidestepping the fundamental questions posed of (a) whether the unborn at any gestational age have constitutional rights and, if so, what is their scope and (b) if such be the case, what is the proper balancing of fetal and maternal rights.

The current author contends that the United States Supreme Court majority analysis in *Dobbs* centered on a question not posed. That question was whether it is the purview of States to legislate as each State wills as the purported proper *final arbiters* on the abortion question. The abortion question then, on the latter view, ultimately being a matter of States' rights in its legal resolution. In fact, the Dobbs United States Supreme Court majority *in effect* ruled that individual State constitutional and/or statutory legislative resolutions on the abortion question should *supersede* the possibility for any United States Supreme Court constitutional interpretation and resolution of the abortion matter that would be universally applicable across all US States. This being the case notwithstanding the vehement minority dissent in *Dobbs disputing* that no federal constitutional resolution was feasible. The United States Supreme Court majority position in *Dobbs* in this regard thus arguably contributed to the Court declining to hear fetal personhood/fetal rights cases filed with the Court post *Dobbs.*

On the current author's view, regardless of one's position on abortion, it cannot be correct that (a) a right to life for Petitioners 'Baby Roe' and 'Baby Doe', whilst unborn, would be a matter of geography, namely in which State their mother happens to reside; that (b) for other unborn their right to life will be determined by whether the mother seeking an abortion can afford to travel to a State where abortion at the relevant gestational age and in the relevant circumstance is legal or that (c) whether a woman is held to have a right to abortion is also in some other way situationally dependent in regard to the State in which she seeks to exercise this right (assuming she has the economic means to access that medical procedure).[41] Fundamental rights must instead, it is here contended, be clarified in the abortion context and cannot be so capriciously denied without *unconstitutionally presupposing* an arbitrary denial of those rights.

[41] President Biden issued an Executive order post Dobbs that protects a woman's legal right to secure an abortion in a State that holds abortion legal (generally with some restrictions) even if the woman resides in a State that would not permit a lawful abortion in her particular circumstances: See Biden Executive Order on Reproductive Rights, August 3, 2022 See FACT SHEET: President Biden Issues Executive Order at the First Meeting of the Task Force on Reproductive Healthcare Access https://www.whitehouse.gov/briefing-room/statements-releases/2022/08/03/fact-sheet-president-biden-issues-executive-order-at-the-first-meeting-of-the-task-force-on-reproductive-h (Accessed August 22, 2024).

Justice Alito maintains in *Dobbs* that (a) “ordered liberty” takes account of competing interests and sets the boundaries for these competing interests but that (b) the people in the various States may have a different approach to assessing those competing interests and the positioning of those boundaries.[42] On the view here, however, with respect, such an approach cannot be justified in a democracy, This since such diversity amongst States on a fundamental human rights question does not deliver consistent protection of the inherent rights, such as may exist, of the vulnerable. Rather those rights are *in effect* arbitrarily granted or denied based on particular State discretionary policy preferences most often tied to the majoritarian view in that State. In any case, the current author is in accord with the view of the Dissenting Justices in *Dobbs* that the “Constitution … puts some issues off limits to majority rule.”[43] Abortion is one of those issues off limits to majoritarian rule it is here argued (concurring with the Dissent in *Dobbs*). This since abortion implicates fundamental human rights questions involving concerns regarding, for instance, life, liberty, bodily integrity, and the essential wellbeing of the mother and the unborn. The latter point should, on the current analysis, be self-evident no matter on what side of the abortion debate one has positioned oneself.

Since the *Dobbs* United States Supreme Court majority found *Roe* unworkable (holding that the balance in *Roe* struck between competing interests was supposedly inappropriate and the ‘viability[44] of the fetus’ as a marker[45] inadequate), the Court’s Dobbs majority, on the view here, had a responsibility to offer a legally sound alternative framework. It is here argued with respect, however, that the Dobbs majority reneged on that obligation. This by deferring to each of the States to independently develop their own individual framework addressing the abortion matter.

This author concurs with the Dissenting Justices in *Dobbs* that “the Court does not act “neutrally” when it leaves everything up to the States.”[46] Rather, on the respectful view here, returning such a fundamental rights matter to the States might

---

[42] Thomas E. Dobbs, State Health Officer of the Mississippi Department of Health et al. v Jackson Women’s Health Organization et al. 597 U. S. ____ (2022) Majority Opinion at p. 31.

[43] Thomas E. Dobbs, State Health Officer of the Mississippi Department of Health et al. v Jackson Women’s Health Organization et al. 597 U. S. ____ (2022) Dissenting Opinion at p. 7 (Breyer, Sotomayor, and Kagan JJ., dissenting).

[44] *Roe* (Roe v. Wade 410 U. S. 113 (1973)) set fetal viability as the standard for demarcating the point at which abortion is no longer constitutionally protected.

[45] The viability standard raises its own ethical quandaries. The standard seems to be related to the level of investment society has in the unborn. Once viability is reached presumably there is an expectation that, in all likelihood, the unborn will ultimately be born and survive and that there will be a societal relationship established with that born alive child. The question then is whether a human life’s inherent value (whether that human life is at the previable or viable stage) is or is not properly a function of the societal investment in that life (investment used here in the broadest sense of that term).

[46] Thomas E. Dobbs, State Health Officer of the Mississippi Department of Health et al. v Jackson Women’s Health Organization et al. 597 U. S. ____ (2022) Dissenting Opinion at p. 20 (Breyer, Sotomayor, and Kagan JJ., dissenting).

be viewed as *in effect*, whether intentionally or not, providing those States that are conservative on the abortion issue the good opportunity to work to culturally dismantle a longstanding US societal norm (that is medically performed abortion as lawful *pre-viability* of the fetus). This may, in fact, correctly or incorrectly, be in the main the public's perception of the *modus operandi* of the *Dobbs* United States Supreme Court conservative majority. This given the failure of the *Dobbs* majority to address the fundamental human rights issues in the case and their instead punting to the States to decide the matter as essentially a State political policy discretionary determination.

The Dobbs Supreme Court of the United States majority opinion held, as discussed, that there is no explicit constitutionally protected privacy right nor one implicit which is derivative of any other constitutionally accepted right that supports a right to abortion. Further, the Dobbs majority *rejects* the notion of a liberty right that undergirds a constitutional right to abortion. That is, the *Dobbs* majority dismisses also the notion that a broad personal autonomy right (as an aspect or derivative of the liberty right) encompasses a right to bodily integrity that grounds a constitutional right to abortion: "Attempts to justify abortion through appeals to a broader right to autonomy and to define one's "concept of existence" prove too much."[47] Yet, US Supreme Court case longstanding precedent (*Roe*[48] and *Casey*[49]) and US State laws following *Roe* and *Casey* but *pre-Dobbs* in fact found just such a privacy and personal autonomy right to be the grounding for a federal constitutional right to abortion, a basis the United States Supreme Court Dobbs majority rejects.

It is noteworthy that certain State legislatures perceive a need to have *private citizens* act under color of law to enforce State conservative and *highly restrictive* abortion policies/laws. This intrusion arguably creates a public perception of a significant invasion of privacy and of family life. These legislatures consider, it would appear, that the invasion of privacy might be perhaps even more unpalatable if carried out in all aspects more directly by State authorities. Thus, it seems that for the reason of immunizing the State from legal challenges, private citizens are delegated the power under statute to sue those who aid and abet abortion in specified particular factual contexts. This even if the person suing has no connection to any of the parties involved in the abortion situation. *Pre-Dobbs*, State interference with then federally constitutionally protected abortion rights (under US Supreme Court case precedent now overruled) was held to be unconstitutional if carried out by US State authorities when the unborn was still pre-viable.

This author has argued elsewhere that in fact private citizens acting under color of law to enforce highly restrictive State abortion statutes are delegates/agents of the State wielding State authority and not independent actors.[50] Empowering private

---

[47] Thomas E. Dobbs, State Health Officer of the Mississippi Department of Health et al. v Jackson Women's Health Organization et al. 597 U. S. ____ (2022). Syllabus at p. 4 point 3.

[48] Roe v. Wade 410 U. S. 113 (1973).

[49] Planned Parenthood of Southeastern Pa. v Casey 505 U.S. 833 (1992).

[50] Grover (2022), pp. 181–187.

citizens to intrude into another's private life in this way creates a 'chilling effect' for those women and girls who would wish to seek an abortion and, to some extent, even if they wish to travel out of State to do so. For example, Oklahoma, under a statute signed by the Governor May 3, 2022 (*post-Dobbs*), prohibits abortion after a fetal heartbeat is detected. The legislation delegates enforcement to private citizens as follows, it:

> *Authorizes enforcement of the act only by private civil actions and not by the state or its political subdivisions.* Allows civil action against a person that performs or induces an abortion and any person who helps someone do so. Establishes certain defenses and non-defenses for these civil actions and minimum statutory damages of $10,000 for claimants who prevail (emphasis added).[51]

On the view here then, the United States Supreme Court majority in *Dobbs* muddied the waters as to the Court's proper role in determining highly divisive fundamental human rights questions and finding nationally applicable resolutions. This by shifting the burden of deciding abortion rights from the Court to the States, arguably without a proper constitutional justification for the shift. The United States Supreme Court, furthermore, in *Whole Women's Heath* endorsed the blurring of the distinction between 'private' versus 'State' action[52] regarding interference under statute in the private family matter of abortion. *Dobbs* subsequently relegated abortion to the status of a State matter such that each State may (a) craft its abortion statute reflecting the State's particular biases as to the type and scope of abortion restrictions and (b) its preferred idiosyncratic enforcement scheme. This then, ostensibly at least, allows for a State to continue to delegate to private citizens of that State an authority under color of law to interfere with others' abortion decisions (i.e., this by way of statutorily permissible private lawsuits against abortion providers and those who assist in any way in facilitating or potentially facilitating the procurement of an abortion). This author thus respectfully argues that the United States Supreme Court majority in *Dobbs* declined its jurisdiction using, on the view here, a smokescreen to avoid its responsibility to construct a workable, constitutionally sound legal framework for addressing the abortion matter. That smokescreen took the form of a States' rights formulation of the core issue. That legal construction of the central issue in *Dobbs*, it is here argued, does not properly apply to fundamental human rights matters that in a democracy must not be left to discretionary legislative decision-making. Yet the latter was precisely the purported proper resolution that the Dobbs majority crafted as is evidenced by the majority's 'bottom line' legal analysis as articulated below:

---

[51]Dube N, Orlando, J, Schaeffer-Helmecki, J (Office of Legislative Research, Connecticut Legislature) Research Report: *State Abortion Laws Enacted Post-Dobbs Decision* September 29, 2022, (2022-R-0227) at p. 12.

[52]Whole Women's Heath et al. v Jackson (United States Supreme Court) Decided 10 December 2021 https://www.supremecourt.gov/opinions/21pdf/21-463_3ebh.pdf (Accessed August 22, 2024).

> Abortion presents a profound moral question. The Constitution does not prohibit the citizens of each State from regulating or prohibiting abortion. *Roe* and *Casey* arrogated that authority. The Court overrules those decisions and returns that authority to the people and their elected representatives.[53]

The *Dobbs* dissenting United States Supreme Court justices expressed the arguably inflammatory view that the Majority overturned *Roe*, not based on facts and the law and principles of *stare decisis*, but rather "for one reason and one reason only: because the composition of this Court has changed."[54] Indeed the dissenting Supreme Court justices in *Dobbs* allege that "The majority [*in Dobbs*] ... substitutes a rule by judges for the rule of law."[55] The current author does not here address what might be termed, at least in part, 'the politics of the Court' on the latter point. Rather suffice it to say that returning the abortion issue to the States is arguably a dereliction of the proper exercise of the Court's authority. Furthermore, this author is in accord with the dissenting United States Supreme Court justices in *Dobbs* that leaving the fundamental human rights matter of abortion to the States to decide individually as they will is *not* to inject neutrality contrary to Justice Kavanaugh's contention in *Dobbs*.[56] Rather returning the matter to the States, it is here argued, is to threaten by implication the democratic value structure underlying *all* fundamental human rights. This since (on the view here) it erroneously makes the grant of dignity, here whether to the mother, her unborn or both, a discretionary State decision. Such an approach is antithetical to the very notion of inherent fundamental human rights which are not situationally dependent (as embodied in international human rights law, and also, it is here argued, as understood under the US Constitution). Pursuant to *Dobbs*, both the woman's contested right to an abortion and the fetal right to life question could *in effect* be subordinated as concerns by a particular court's idiosyncratic assessment of what is the purported legitimate *State interest* at play.[57]

---

[53] Thomas E. Dobbs, State Health Officer of the Mississippi Department of Health et al. v Jackson Women's Health Organization et al. 597 U. S. ____ (2022). Syllabus at p. 8.

[54] Thomas E. Dobbs, State Health Officer of the Mississippi Department of Health et al. v Jackson Women's Health Organization et al. 597 U. S. ____ (2022). Dissenting Opinion at p. 6 (Breyer, Sotomayor, and Kagan JJ., dissenting) Here the Dissenters are suggesting that because the conservatives now outnumber the liberal judges on the United States Supreme Court, the Majority took the opportunity to overturn *Roe* consistent with the conservative philosophical position of the Majority and the longstanding agenda of conservatives more generally.

[55] Thomas E. Dobbs, State Health Officer of the Mississippi Department of Health et al. v Jackson Women's Health Organization et al. 597 U. S. ____ (2022). Dissenting Opinion (Breyer, Sotomayor, and Kagan JJ., dissenting) at p. 33.

[56] Thomas E. Dobbs, State Health Officer of the Mississippi Department of Health et al. v Jackson Women's Health Organization et al. 597 U. S. ____ (2022). Dissenting Opinion at (Breyer, Sotomayor, and Kagan JJ., dissenting) at p. 20.

[57] Compare Thomas E. Dobbs, State Health Officer of the Mississippi Department of Health et al. v Jackson Women's Health Organization et al. 597 U. S. ____ (2022). Dissenting Opinion (Breyer, Sotomayor, and Kagan JJ., dissenting) at p. 35: "The majority says a law regulating or banning abortion 'must be sustained if there is a rational basis on which the legislature could have thought that it would serve legitimate state interests.'"

The dissenting United States Supreme Court justices in *Dobbs* maintained that:

> Rescinding an individual right[58] in its entirety and conferring it on the State, an action the Court takes …for the first time in history [in *Dobbs*], affects all who have relied on our constitutional system of government and its structure of individual liberties protected from state oversight.[59]

We turn next to comparative law for a broader perspective on privacy rights and an inferred derivative right to abortion (albeit normally with some restrictions). The following selected comparative law cases (a) illustrate a focus on the fundamental human rights questions at the core of the abortion matter (something the Dobbs majority United States Supreme Court arguably largely assiduously avoided by deferring to the States) and (b) reveal how such a fundamental human rights focus may shape judicial decision-making in the abortion space.

4.2 Comparative Law Perspectives on the Right to Privacy and the Abortion Issue

4.2.1 Introduction

The cases on privacy and bodily integrity we begin with here were decided by the European Court of Human Rights. The Court is enabled by the *European Convention on Hunan Rights and Fundamental Freedoms.* That Convention at Article 8 sets out, as will be recalled, a privacy guarantee as follows: "Everyone has the right to respect for his private and family life, his home and his correspondence…" The Article 8 Convention privacy rights guarantee sets out certain exceptional limitations where there is a compelling public interest and consistent with democratic principles and as prescribed by law.[60] Convention Article 8 encompasses both negative State obligations (the State must refrain from undemocratic intrusions into private life) and positive State obligations (i.e. implementing measures to better ensure respect for privacy and even as between private individuals).[61] The latter is particularly noteworthy in contrast to the effort of certain US States to delegate to private citizens the authority under color of law to intrude into the private decision-making of others

---

[58] The Dobbs dissenting United States Supreme Court justices are referring here to a presumed constitutional right to abortion.

[59] Compare Thomas E. Dobbs, State Health Officer of the Mississippi Department of Health et al. v Jackson Women's Health Organization et al. 597 U. S. ____ (2022). Dissenting Opinion (Breyer, Sotomayor, and Kagan JJ., dissenting) at p. 54.

[60] European Convention on Human Rights and Fundamental Freedoms https://www.unhcr.org/4d93501a9.pdf (Accessed August 22, 2024).

[61] European Court of Human Rights: Guide on Article 8 of the European Convention on Human Right: Rights to respect for privacy and family life, home and correspondence (updated 31 August, 2022) at p. 8 https://www.echr.coe.int/documents/guide_art_8_eng.pdf (Accessed August 22, 2024).

concerning abortion. This intrusion is carried out by private citizens bringing lawsuits against those who in any way facilitate an abortion (see *Whole Women's Heath et al. v Jackson* in which the US Supreme Court upheld a Texas law that employed such a statutory scheme. The Court (a) considered that the statute created a certain novel procedural framework and that the plaintiffs had not met their burden to strike the law but (b) the Court did *not* make a finding on the constitutionality of the law).[62]

The European Court of Human Rights has "defined the scope of Article 8 [addressing privacy] broadly"[63] just as the United States Supreme Court did *pre-Dobbs* in regard to privacy legally constructed as encompassed in the liberty and due process rights according to various of the Court's then precedents (i.e., *Casey*).[64]

4.2.2 Contemporary Highly Restrictive Polish Law on Abortion

In October 2020, the Polish Constitutional Court ruled that the Family Planning Act of 1993 allowance for legal abortion in cases involving fetal abnormalities is unconstitutional. Subsequently there was imposed "an almost total ban on abortion in Poland."[65] More than a thousand women have appealed Poland's restrictive abortion laws to the European Court of Human Rights (i.e., cases include, for instance, *K.B. v. Poland and 3 other applications*; *K.C. v. Poland and 3 other applications*; and *A.L.- B. v. Poland and 3 other applications*).[66] There were several

[62]Whole Women's Heath et al. v Jackson USSC Decided 10 December 2021 https://www.supremecourt.gov/opinions/21pdf/21-463_3ebh.pdf (Accessed August 22, 2024).

[63]European Court of Human Rights: Guide on Article 8 of the European Convention on Human Rights: Rights to respect for privacy and family life, home and correspondence (updated 31 August 2022) at p. 7 https://www.echr.coe.int/documents/guide_art_8_eng.pdf (Accessed August 22, 2024).

[64]Planned Parenthood Southeastern Pennsylvania et al. v Casey et al. USSC __ 505 U.S. 833 (1992).

[65]Kapelańska-Pręgowska (2021), pp. 213–224.

[66]K.B. v. Poland and 3 other applications; K.C. v. Poland and 3 other applications; and A.L.- B. v. Poland and 3 other applications Amici written comments Amnesty International, the Center for Reproductive Rights, Human Rights Watch, the International Commission of Jurists (ICJ), the International Federation for Human Rights (FIDH), the International Planned Parenthood Federation European Network, Women Enabled International, Women's Link Worldwide and the World Organisation Against Torture (OMCT) https://reproductiverights.org/wp-content/uploads/2022/01/Written-Comments_KC-v-Poland-and-3-other-applications.pdf (Accessed August 22, 2024).

See also Intervention by UN Working Group on Discrimination Against Women and Girls, UN Rapporteur of the Right of Everyone to the Enjoyment of the Highest Attainable Standard of Physical and Mental Health, and the UN Rapporteur on Torture and Other cruel, inhuman or degrading treatment or punishment https://www.ohchr.org/sites/default/files/2021-11/AC-Poland-10Nov2021.pdf (Accessed August 22, 2024).

amicus briefs filed in these cases. The following are just a few highlights regarding a number of the key contentious points in the amicus briefs:

- Legal restrictions on abortion affect a diverse group of persons who can become pregnant including women and girls of reproductive age, non-binary persons, and transgender men.
- The European Convention on Human Rights is a living document and must be interpreted with some acknowledgement of changing knowledge and socio-cultural norms.
- Restrictive abortion laws create grave risks to the mental and physical safety of women and girls of reproductive age (see for example here RR v Poland as an example)
- The rights guarantees of the European Convention must be more than illusory and hence this factor should be considered per Article 34 when assessing individual or group complaints under the Convention.
- Women and girls of reproductive age as a class are adversely affected by restrictive abortion law whether or not they are currently pregnant or attempting to obtain an abortion. (Such a perspective of who may be categorized as a victim was affirmed by the European Court of Human Rights in for example *Open Door and Well Women v Ireland* Application 14234/88 (1992).[67] In the latter case the European Court of Human Rights ruled that all women of child bearing age (whether currently pregnant or not) could allege to be victims of the injunction imposed by the Irish Supreme Court on providers of abortion information).
- Women and girls thus are a distinct group who due to restrictive abortion laws are being denied an essential health service.
- The adverse impact of these restrictive abortion laws are disproportionately higher for marginalized groups of women and girls such as members of the LGBTQ plus community, persons of color and those who are persons with disabilities

The UN Working Group on Violence Against Women; in intervening in the same cases against Poland regarding claimed abortion rights, maintains that highly restrictive abortion law "is a form of instrumentalization and subordination of women to a patriarchal agenda."[68]

The current author concurs with the aforementioned interveners in the Polish abortion cases before the European Court of Human Rights that highly restrictive abortion laws can, in the particular circumstance, constitute an affront to the human

[67] *Open Door and Well Women v Ireland* European Court of Human Rights Application 14234/88 and 14235/88 Judgement 29 October 1992 https://hudoc.echr.coe.int/fre#{%22itemid%22:[%22002-9896%22]} (Accessed August 22, 2024).

[68] Intervention by UN Working Group on Discrimination Against Women and Girls, UN Rapporteur of the Right of Everyone to the Enjoyment of the Highest Attainable Standard of Physical and Mental Health, and the UN Rapporteur on Torture and Other cruel, inhuman or degrading treatment or punishment https://www.ohchr.org/sites/default/files/2021-11/AC-Poland-10Nov2021.pdf (Accessed August 22, 2024) at p. 2.

dignity of women and girls (i.e., See *RR v Poland* discussed below). Let us consider in that regard the example of the Human Rights Committee case of *K.L. v Peru*[69] brought to the UN Human Rights Committee under the *International Covenant on Civil and Political Rights*. K. L. was a 17-year-old pregnant girl carrying an anencephalic fetus at the time she filed her complaint to the United Nations Human Rights Committee. The fetal condition at issue is predictive of an extraordinarily brief life expectancy, if at all. Further, carrying such a fetus in KL's case put the mother's life at risk. KL's physician recommended an abortion but the girl was denied the abortion due to unclear Peruvian regulations surrounding the matter at that time. KL was forced to carry the baby to term and breast feed the baby for the 4 days the child survived. KL suffered severe depression subsequent to this trauma. The UN Human Rights Committee ruled in the case that violations of the International Covenant on Civil and Political Rights included (a) the right to be free from cruel, inhumane, and degrading treatment (Art. 7), (b) the right to privacy (Art. 17), and (c) the right to special measures of protection for minors (Art. 24) The Committee recommended compensation for KL and that Peru take measures to ensure such violations do not occur in future.[70]

While this author concurs with the decision in *KL v Peru*, it is noteworthy that it is *not*, on the view here, one that requires or justifies a finding that the anencephalic fetus is any less a member of humanity (a member of the human family) with full moral status compared to a fetus with an intact brain or a born alive healthy child.[71] Rather, it requires, from one perspective on the abortion issue at least and separate from any religious considerations, arguably a compassionate, never fully satisfactory balancing of the rights, or if not rights, a comparison of expected cognizant suffering of the fetus and the mother in the particular case (i.e. in *LC v Peru* the Committee on Ending Discrimination Against Women ruled that the State had arbitrarily, based on stereotypes and pre-existing biases, prioritized the protection of the fetus over the health and wellbeing of the mother. In *LC* the mother was denied an abortion and the spinal surgery that would have avoided paralysis precipitated during the pregnancy).[72]

In the final analysis it should always be a concern, it is here contended, that there are incalculable risks to legal decisions (by courts, UN committees or other adjudicative bodies) on abortion rights matters that rely on *post hoc* rationales or justifications for their ruling based on a denial of the humanity of the unborn human. The

---

[69] KL v Peru CCPR/C/85/D/1153/2003, Communication No. 1153/2003 UN Human Rights Committee Decided 24 October 2005 https://www.escr-net.org/caselaw/2016/kl-v-peru-ccprc85d11532003-communication-no-11532003 (Accessed August 22, 2024).

[70] KL v Peru CCPR/C/85/D/1153/2003, Communication No. 1153/2003 UN Human Rights Committee Decided 24 October 2005 https://www.escr-net.org/caselaw/2016/kl-v-peru-ccprc85d11532003-communication-no-11532003 (Accessed August 22, 2024).

[71] Camosy (2017), pp. 53–65.

[72] LC v Peru Committee on the Elimination of Discrimination against Women Judgement 17 October 2011https://reproductiverights.org/wp-content/uploads/2020/12/CEDAW-C-50-D-22-2009-English-clean-copy.pdf (Accessed August 22, 2024).

latter as opposed to formulating a ruling that, in the first instance, courageously addresses the moral quandary of abortion and seeks to balance interests of mother and unborn in the most humane way possible.

4.2.3 SFK v Russia (Application 5578/12) European Court of Human Rights Judgment 11 October 2022

SFK v Russia[73] and *GM and others v Moldova*[74] concern the issue of reproductive rights in the context of *forced abortion* inflicted upon disabled women. In these cases then the fetal interest in life and the disabled women's interest in not having a 'forced abortion' align. Cases of 'forced abortion' are arguably also a quintessential example of what the UN Committee on Violence Against Women has termed, in another pregnancy context, a form of instrumentalization and subordination of women to a patriarchal agenda"[75] that strips women of their personal autonomy, bodily integrity and dignity.

In *SFK v Russia* doctors and the women's parents forced their daughter aged twenty to have an abortion when she was 5 weeks pregnant. SFK was married and cohabited with her husband. The woman repeatedly protested to all, including the physicians, that she did *not* want to have an abortion. SFK finally relented when her mother informed her that her father would kill both her and her mother if SFK did not allow the abortion to proceed. SFK did not sign any documents in regard to the abortion and received no information about the procedure. Furthermore, she did not undergo a medical exam in proximity to the abortion nor soon after. A later examination by a medical expert determined that SFK had suffered psychological trauma as a result of the forced abortion. SFK argued that she was a mentally competent adult and that her parents had no right to make the abortion decision as her proxies. The European Court ruled that the forced abortion amounted to a violation of Article 3 of the *European Convention on Human Rights* ("No one shall be subjected to torture or to inhuman or degrading treatment or punishment").[76] The violation was the result of coercion by SFKs parents and a doctor and nurse at a public hospital. The medical staff's actions in performing a forced abortion were *not* in fact in accord with domestic law. In this case the European Court of Human Rights

---

[73] SFK v Russia, European Court of Human Rights Application 5578/12 European Court of Human Rights Judgment 11 January 2023 https://hudoc.echr.coe.int/eng#{%22itemid%22:[%22001-219642%22]} (Accessed August 22, 2024).

[74] GM and others v Moldova, European Court of Human Rights.

[75] Intervention by UN Working Group on Discrimination Against Women and Girls, UN Rapporteur of the Right of Everyone to the Enjoyment of the Highest Attainable Standard of Physical and Mental Health, and the UN Rapporteur on Torture and Other cruel, inhuman or degrading treatment or punishment https://www.ohchr.org/sites/default/files/2021-11/AC-Poland-10Nov2021.pdf at p. 2 (Accessed August 22, 2024).

[76] European Convention on Human Rights https://www.echr.coe.int/documents/convention_eng.pdf (Accessed August 22, 2024).

ruled that "...the respondent State bears no direct responsibility under the substantive limb of Article 3 of the Convention in respect of the acts of the applicant's parents, who are private individuals."[77]

Note, in contrast, cases involving the intrusion of the State into the private family sphere through *the delegation of power to private individuals* to implement Sate policy. In *Canadian Foundation*[78] (a case which has to do not with abortion but rather corporal punishment and other assaults of a child) this author argues that the State (Canada) delegated state authority to parents, delegates of parents and teachers to potentially violate the child's right to be protected from cruel and unusual punishment or treatment under the *Canadian Charter of Rights and Freedom*, Article 12.[79] This by creating a criminal defense in the Criminal Code of Canada to assault of a child (with certain constraints) available to *statutorily designated* select persons in authority. 'Persons in authority' in Canadian Supreme Court precedent is a term to be interpreted as 'agents of the State.' The Canadian Criminal Code s 43 defense to assault of a child designates parents, parental delegates and teachers as 'persons in authority' who may raise the s. 43 defense. The point being that there are instances where the State delegates State authority to private individuals in circumstances that can reasonably be foreseen to put certain vulnerable individuals at risk of serious rights violations. Similarly, in the abortion context, recall the Texas abortion law SB8. That law, as explained, *in effect* delegates to private citizens implementation of an abortion ban. This in that private citizens can, under that law, even if unconnected to anyone involved with the particular abortion situation, sue for 10,000 dollars damages anyone aiding or abetting or otherwise facilitating an abortion in Texas. The way Texas and like abortion US State law is structured (i.e., to allow such private lawsuits) serves, as explained previously, to ostensibly immunize the State from court challenges in this abortion context. This as the State authorities can claim they are not involved in the abortion ban implementation though the State has simply delegated its authority in this regard such that the intrusions into private life are arguably still State actions. The Texas State Supreme Court in fact ruled *against* abortion providers in the State and held that State licensing authorities could *not* enforce the Texas abortion law[80] under the abortion law as structured thus immunizing the government from suit.[81] The United States

[77] SFK v Russia, European Court of Human Rights Application 5578/12 European Court of Human Rights Judgment 11 January 2023 https://hudoc.echr.coe.int/eng#{%22itemid%22:[%22001-219642%22]} at p. 17 (Accessed August 22, 2024).

[78] Grover (2017).

[79] Canadian Charter of Rights and Freedom https://laws-lois.justice.gc.ca/eng/const/page-12.html (Accessed August 22, 2024).

[80] The Texas abortion law bans abortion after about 6 weeks of pregnancy when a fetal heartbeat can be detected even in cases of rape and incest but permits abortion in medical emergencies.

[81] Whole Woman's Health, et al. v Judge Austin Reeve Jackson; Penny Clarkston; Mark Lee Dickson; Stephen Brint Carlton; Katherine A. Thomas; Cecile Erwin Young; Allison Vordenbaumen Benz; Ken Paxton, Supreme Court of Texas (Justice JS Boyd delivered the opinion of the Court March 11, 2022) https://www.txcourts.gov/media/1453763/220033.pdf (Accessed August 22, 2024).

Supreme Court did *not* strike down the Texas abortion enforcement scheme[82] and the same model then was duplicated in certain other US States.

The European Court of Human Rights in *SFK v Russia*, however, (in contrast to the opposite United States Supreme Court ruling in the US Texas abortion case here discussed; albeit on some key different facts) found that *the State was in part responsible* for the violations of SFKs rights in the abortion context. The European Court of Human Rights found a *State violation* of Convention Article 3 perpetrated by the doctor and the nurse who worked for a *public hospital.* This while ruling, as mentioned, that the State was *not* responsible for the parents' acts regarding SFK's forced abortion since the parents were acting as private individuals *not* agents of the State with delegated State power.

4.2.4 RR v Poland (Application 27617/04) Judgment May 26, 2011 European Court of Human Rights: Highly Restrictive Abortion Law as an Affront to Human Dignity

In *R.R. v Poland*[83] the facts were that a woman was informed pursuant to an ultrasound at her 18th week of pregnancy that her fetus may have abnormalities. Doctors were reluctant to refer the woman for amniocentesis so that she could have the diagnosis regarding fetal abnormalities confirmed or disconfirmed, Consequently the amniocentesis was not conducted until the 23rd week of the pregnancy. At that time the woman reiterated her request for an abortion. By the time the woman received confirmation of the fetal abnormality it was too late to have the abortion. The woman was unable to have the doctors prosecuted but in domestic civil proceedings she was successful in suing for compensation relating to (a) the doctors' refusal to refer her on time for the amniocentesis and (b) for their failure to make a record of the fact that they had refused to refer her on several occasions. There was nothing in Poland's domestic law that would have barred the woman from receiving the timely genetic testing, proper genetic counselling and the information she had been denied. Polish law at the time also required that pregnant clients receive full information on their and their fetus' health thus setting out a positive State-mandated obligation on physicians in that regard.

In the opinion of the European Court of Human Rights in this case the woman had been humiliated to such an extent as to meet the minimum threshold under Article 3 of the European Convention: "Article 3 – Prohibition of torture: No one shall be

[82]Whole Women's Heath et al. v Jackson, United States Supreme Court No. 21-463. Argued November 1, 2021—Decided December 10, 2021 https://www.supremecourt.gov/opinions/21pdf/21-463_3ebh.pdf (Accessed August 22, 2024).

[83]*R.R. v. Poland* https://hudoc.echr.coe.int/fre#{%22itemid%22:[%22001-104911%22]} (Accessed August 22, 2024).

subjected to torture or to inhuman or degrading treatment or punishment."[84] Thus the dignity of the woman was a central aspect of the ruling. In addition, the European Court of Human Rights found a violation of the Convention's guarantee of respect for private life (Article 8). The latter reflected the fact that though Polish law at the time permitted lawful abortion; in the circumstances in which the woman found herself, she had no access in fact to a diagnostic service. That service would have allowed her to take a timely decision since she wished to abort if the fetal abnormalities were confirmed. In her case then the right under Polish law to access abortion in her situation was theoretical and not a reality. The complainant was awarded non-pecuniary damages for these violations. Thus, the European Court of Human Rights in this case affirmed the State's positive obligation to provide, in practice and not just theory, a right to access legal abortion as set out in Poland's domestic law and as an aspect of the Convention privacy right.

4.3 Concluding Comment

The European Court of Human Rights cases here discussed are in stark contrast to the United States Supreme Court decision in *Dobbs*.[85] This in that in these cases the European Court of Human Rights affirms both the dignity of women and their privacy rights in the abortion context; at least where there is some sort of compelling medical issue involved (i.e. the health of the mother at grave risk, fetal abnormalities etc.). In *Dobbs*, in contrast, (a) no fundamental privacy right was affirmed by the United States Supreme Court (in fact such was explicitly rejected) and (b) the abortion issue was not framed as a fundamental rights question to be addressed by the United Sates Supreme Court in order to formulate a nationally applicable resolution. Rather, in essence, the issue was morphed into a supposed discretionary policy matter for the individual US States to decide.

Materials

American Civil Liberties Union (ACLU) FAQ *The International Covenant on Civil and Political Rights* https://www.aclu.org/other/faq-covenant-civil-political-rights-iccpr#:~:text=The%20U.S.%20ratified%20the%20ICCPR,the%20status%20of%20federal%20law (Accessed August 22, 2024)

[84] European Convention for the Protection of Human Rights and Fundamental Freedoms, as amended by Protocol No. 11 https://www.unhcr.org/4d93501a9.pdf (Accessed August 22, 2024).

[85] Thomas E. Dobbs, State Health Officer of the Mississippi Department of Health et al. v Jackson Women's Health Organization et al. 597 U. S. ____ (2022).

Biden Executive Order on Reproductive Rights, August 3, 2022 FACT SHEET: President Biden Issues Executive Order at the First Meeting of the Task Force on Reproductive Healthcare Access https://www.whitehouse.gov/briefing-room/statements-releases/2022/08/03/fact-sheet-president-biden-issues-executive-order-at-the-first-meeting-of-the-task-force-on-reproductive-h (Accessed August 22, 2024)
Canadian Charter of Rights and Freedom https://laws-lois.justice.gc.ca/eng/const/page-12.html (Accessed August 22, 2024)
Dube N, Orlando, J, Schaeffer-Helmecki, J (Office of Legislative Research, Connecticut Legislature) Research Report: *State Abortion Laws Enacted Post-Dobbs Decision* September 29, 2022 (2022-R-0227) Table 1 pp. 3–5
European Convention for the Protection of Human Rights and Fundamental Freedoms, as amended by Protocol No. 11 https://www.refworld.org/legal/agreements/coe/1950/en/18688 (Accessed August 22, 2024)
European Court of Human Rights: Guide on Article 8 of the European Convention on Human Rights (Rights to respect for privacy and family life, home and correspondence (updated 31 August, 2022) https://www.echr.coe.int/documents/guide_art_8_eng.pdf (Accessed August 22, 2024)
International Covenant on Civil and Political Rights https://www.ohchr.org/en/instruments-mechanisms/instruments/international-covenant-civil-and-political-rights (Accessed August 22, 2024)
Rome Statute of the International Criminal Court, Crimes Against Humanity, Forced Pregnancy Article 7(g) https://www.ohchr.org/en/instruments-mechanisms/instruments/rome-statute-international-criminal-court (Accessed August 22, 2024)
Universal Declaration of Human Rights Article 12 https://www.un.org/en/about-us/universal-declaration-of-human-rights (Accessed August 22, 2024)
University of Minnesota Human Rights Library, U.S. Government Reservations, Declarations and Understandings: International Covenant on Civil and Political Rights, 138 Cong. Rec. S4781-01 (daily ed., April 2, 1992) http://www1.umn.edu/humanrts/usdocs/civilres.html (Accessed August 22, 2024)

United States Supreme Court Cases

Bray v. Alexandria Women's Health Clinic, 506 U. S. 263, 273–274 (1993)
Food and Drug Administration v. Alliance for Hippocratic Medicine (consolidated with Danco Laboratories, L.L.C. v. Alliance for Hippocratic Medicine) (United States Supreme Court) 598 U. S. ____ (2023) https://www.supremecourt.gov/opinions/22pdf/22a901_3d9g.pdf (Accessed August 22, 2024)
Planned Parenthood of Southeastern Pa. v Casey 505 U.S. 833 (1992)
Poe v. Ullman, 367 U. S. 497, 542 (1961)
Roe v. Wade 410 U. S. 113 (1973)
Thomas E. Dobbs, State Health Officer of the Mississippi Department of Health et al. v Jackson Women's Health Organization et al. 597 U. S. ____ (2022)

Washington v Glucksberg 521 U. S. 702 (1997)

Whole Women's Heath et al. v Jackson, United States Supreme Court No. 21-463. Argued November 1, 2021—Decided December 10, 2021 https://www.supremecourt.gov/opinions/21pdf/21-463_3ebh.pdf (Accessed August 22, 2024)

United States Lower Court Cases

Benson et al. Next Friend of Baby Roe et al. v McKee (Governor of Rhode Island) No. 2020-66 Appeal Supreme Court of Rhode Island Judgment May 4, 2022 (United States Supreme Court declined to hear the case) https://www.courts.ri.gov/Courts/SupremeCourt/SupremeOpinions/20-66.pdf (Accessed August 22, 2024)

Jane Doe as parent and next friend of Baby Mary Doe, Nicole Leigh Rowley, parent and next friend of Baby Roe, and Catholics for Life, Inc. d/b/a/ Servants of Christ for Life v McKee (Governor of Rhode Island) https://www.supremecourt.gov/DocketPDF/22/22-201/236882/20220901130349933_Petition%20Brief.pdf (Accessed August 22, 2024)

Whole Woman's Health, et al. v Judge Austin Reeve Jackson; Penny Clarkston; Mark Lee Dickson; Stephen Brint Carlton; Katherine A. Thomas; Cecile Erwin Young; Allison Vordenbaumen Benz; Ken Paxton, Supreme Court of Texas (Justice JS Boyd delivered the opinion of the Court March 11, 2022) https://www.txcourts.gov/media/1453763/220033.pdf (Accessed August 22, 2024)

European Court of Human Rights Cases

GM and others v Moldova (Application no. 44394/15) European Court of Human Rights https://hudoc.echr.coe.int/fre#{%22tabview%22:[%22document%22],%22itemid%22:[%22001-220954%22]} (Accessed August 22, 2024)

KB v Poland, KC v Poland, and AL-B v Poland, (Applications 1819/21, 3039/21, 3801/21) (European Court of Human Rights) Intervention by UN Working Group on Discrimination Against Women and Girls, UN Rapporteur of the Right of Everyone to the Enjoyment of the Highest Attainable Standard of Physical and Mental Health, and the UN Rapporteur on Torture and Other cruel, inhuman or degrading treatment or punishment https://www.ohchr.org/sites/default/files/2021-11/AC-Poland-10Nov2021.pdf (Accessed August 22, 2024)

K.C. v. Poland and 3 other applications (Application no. 3639/21) (European Court of Human Rights) Amici Commentary https://reproductiverights.org/wp-content/uploads/2022/01/Written-Comments_KC-v-Poland-and-3-other-applications.pdf (Accessed August 22, 2024)

Open Door and Well Women v Ireland, European Court of Human Rights Application 14234/88 and 14235/88 Judgement 29 October 1992 https://hudoc.echr.coe.int/fre#{%22itemid%22:[%22002-9896%22]} (Accessed August 22, 2024)
R.R. v. Poland European Court of Human Rights (Application no. 27617/04) https://hudoc.echr.coe.int/fre#{%22itemid%22:[%22001-104911%22]} (Accessed August 22, 2024)
SFK v Russia, European Court of Human Rights (Application 5578/12) Judgment 11 January 2023 https://hudoc.echr.coe.int/eng#{%22itemid%22:[%22001-219642%22]} (Accessed August 22, 2024)

UN Human Rights Committee

KL v Peru CCPR/C/85/D/1153/2003, Communication No. 1153/2003 (UN Human Rights Committee) Decided 24 October 2005 https://www.escr-net.org/caselaw/2016/kl-v-peru-ccprc85d11532003-communication-no-11532003 (Accessed August 22, 2024)

UN Committee on the Elimination of Discrimination Against Women

LC v Peru (UN Committee on the Elimination of Discrimination against Women) Judgement 17 October 2011 https://reproductiverights.org/wp-content/uploads/2020/12/CEDAW-C-50-D-22-2009-English-clean-copy.pdf (Accessed August 22, 2024)

References

Camosy CC (2017) The moral status of the anencephalic Homio Sapiens. In: Eberl JT (ed) Contemporary controversies in Catholic bioethics, Philosophy and medicine series, vol 127. Springer, pp 53–65
Grover S (2017) Rewritten judgment: dissenting opinion, Canadian Foundation for Children, Youth and the Law v. Canada (Attorney General) 2004 SCC 4. In: Hollingsworth K, Stalford H, Gilmore S (eds) Rewriting children's rights judgments: from academic vision to new practice. Hart
Grover S (2022) Chapter 7: Concluding remarks: on the role of the courts in upholding the democratic rule of law. In: The democratic rule of law on trial: first amendment cases of the Trump era. Routledge, London, pp 181–187

Kapelańska-Pręgowska J (2021) The scales of the European Court of Human Rights: abortion restriction in Poland, the European consensus, and the state's margin of appreciation. Health Hum Rights J 23(2):213–224

Ziegler, M (2018) Beyond abortion: Roe v Wade and the battle for privacy (Chapter 1). In: A history of privacy politics, pp 15–40

Chapter 5
US Education Culture Wars: The Right in a Democracy to Exposure to a Plurality of Views

Abstract This chapter considers the US culture war over the contested freedom of religion rights of child and parent as impacted by State authorities in the public education setting. A child's autonomous right to freedom of thought, conscience and religion is articulated in the *Convention on the Rights of the Child* (CRC) Article 14, Also considered is the tension between the child's right in a democracy to exposure to diversity in the student population and pluralism in viewpoints more generally versus the wish of some fundamentalist religious parents to shelter their children from such diversity. The case law reveals a lack of consistency in how that tension is resolved amongst various Western States. In addition, the notion is explored that a denial of exposure of schoolchildren to diversity is a violation of their right to education under CRC Article 29. The latter article sets out the child's right as part of the preparation to be a citizen in a free society to be educated for tolerance, peace and respect for diversity.

5.1 Kennedy v Bremerton School District (Supreme Court of the United States) No. 21-418. Argued April 25, 2022—Decided June 27, 2022

In *Kennedy* a high school football coach, Mr. Kennedy, was dismissed from his position with Bremerton School District after repeatedly quietly praying for about 30 s on the school football field after football games. The prayers consisted of giving thanks for the game and for being part of the players' lives. At times there were still members of the public in the stands when this occurred. Mr. Kennedy sued the school district alleging that his First Amendment rights had been violated in terms of his right to free speech and free exercise of his religious rights. The District Court found that Mr. Kenney had been suspended due to the School District's fear of constitutional liability due to the football coach's public display on the school football field of a particular religious practice. The School District feared the perception would be that it endorsed a particular religious faith when in fact public schools are to maintain a secular stance. The District Court granted summary judgment to the Bremerton School District and the Appeals Court affirmed that

S. C. Grover, *Litigating the Politics of Human Rights*, Ius Gentium: Comparative Perspectives on Law and Justice 121, https://doi.org/10.1007/978-3-031-82463-0_5

ruling. The request to have the case reheard by the Appeals Court *en banc* (with the full panel of appeals judges) was denied. The United States Supreme Court reversed the decision of the lower court with a vote of six to three. The majority United States Supreme Court view in the case was that the School District was *mistaken* in believing that to allow Mr. Kennedy to pray on the midfield after football games was precluded by the First Amendment. The majority United States Supreme Court held that "Both the Free Exercise and Free Speech Clauses of the First Amendment protect expressions like Mr. Kennedy's."[1] The United States Supreme Court majority classed Mr. Kennedy's conduct as "private religious speech."[2] Such expression, the Court majority found, is *not* disallowed under the First Amendment's Establishment Clause.[3]

At first Mr. Kenney had prayed alone at the midfield but over time some players on both teams came to join him on different occasions to pray with him at the conclusion of school football games. Eventually Mr. Kennedy included some motivational speech in his prayers and there were also, on occasion, pre and post-game prayers in the school locker room. Mr. Kennedy maintained that students were always free to decide for themselves whether they wished to participate in these prayer activities and that they were never pressured by him to do so.

There had been no complaints for about 7 years about the prayer practices overseen by the football coach at the school. Upon first learning of these practices after so many years, the superintendent sent a letter to Mr. Kennedy advising him that the religious practices at the conclusion of school football games at the midfield and those pre and post-game in the locker room were problematic. The District advised Mr. Kennedy that he should cease including religious speech in his motivational talks but to allow students on their own to engage in prayers if they so desired. The District also advised Mr. Kennedy that any religious activity on his part should be private and not demonstrably (outwardly) evident to the students. The School District explained that its position was that the school's duty in respect of the Establishment Clause overrode any alleged unfettered right of free religious expression by Mr. Kennedy when he was acting in his capacity as football coach and dealing with students. Initially, Mr. Kennedy complied with the School District's advisory but then in a moment of conscience returned to the school after a football game and prayed a *silent prayer* at the midfield at a point in time where everyone else had already left the stadium. Mr. Kennedy sent a letter asking the School District for permission to continue that practice when the players had left the field or were

---

[1]Kennedy v Bremerton School District No. 21-418. Argued April 25, 2022—Decided June 27, 2022 (Supreme Court of the United States) Majority Opinion at p. 1 https://www.law.cornell.edu/supct/pdf/21-418.pdf (Accessed August 22, 2024).

[2]Kennedy v Bremerton School District No. 21-418. Argued April 25, 2022—Decided June 27, 2022 (Supreme Court of the United States) Majority Opinion at p. 3 https://www.law.cornell.edu/supct/pdf/21-418.pdf (Accessed August 22, 2024).

[3]Kennedy v Bremerton School District No. 21-418. Argued April 25, 2022—Decided June 27, 2022 (Supreme Court of the United States) Syllabus at p. 1 https://www.law.cornell.edu/supct/pdf/21-418.pdf (Accessed August 22, 2024).

engaged in some other activity like heading to lockers. The District refused and held that Mr. Kennedy should *not* engage in any demonstrable activity *on school premises while serving as football coach* which activity could be interpreted by a reasonable observer as prayer. This being the case as such activity, on the School District's view, created the possibility of the District violating the Establishment Clause. Presumably a student(s) might still observe Mr. Kennedy in this activity (a private prayer of thanks involving kneeling on the field) even when the coach had not intended for the same. After the coach, Mr. Kennedy, received the admonition from the District he still engaged in a prayer at midfield after a game while the team was leading the audience in a fight song. Members of the team and of the audience joined the coach in prayer at some point. This led to media coverage of the dispute over prayer between Mr. Kennedy and the District.

In correspondence with the school superintendent about the situation, it was noted that the coach had originally led students in a prayer after games but then shifted to silent private prayer at midfield. The District thereafter instructed Mr. Kennedy that if he wished to engage in prayer after games, he would need to do so in a private location not visible to students or public. Subsequently, there was an after-game occasion where Mr. Kennedy engaged in prayer at midfield after a game while the players were engaged in other traditional after-game activities. While Mr. Kennedy was praying, other adults joined him on the field on that occasion At that point Mr. Kennedy was placed on paid administrative leave for what the District described as "public" and "demonstrative religious conduct" while still on duty as the coach. Thereafter, Mr. Kennedy received a poor performance evaluation from the District which advised not rehiring him due to his engaging in repeated public religious activity while still on duty as the football coach.

As previously mentioned, the lower courts ruled against Mr. Kennedy. However, the United State Supreme Court majority in the case held that (a) when Mr. Kennedy prayed at midfield after the school football games he was *not* involved in government speech that could be attributed to the School District of which he was a paid employee and (b) nor was Mr. Kennedy through such prayer activities espousing government policy of any sort. The United States Supreme Court majority found that it would be an overbroad interpretation of Mr. Kennedy's job description to maintain that every moment he was on duty his speech activities constituted government speech. This being the case notwithstanding the fact that as the school's football coach Mr. Kennedy was perceived to be a role model for the players. The United States Supreme Court majority held that Mr. Kennedy's *silent prayers* at midfield (when he was not leading students in prayer as he had done prior to the District's admonitions not to do so) constituted "private speech." The Majority rejected the notion that viewing Mr. Kennedy, the coach, in silent prayer at midfield was sufficient to establish that the students were under some coercive pressure to engage in prayer with him. In fact, the United States Supreme Court majority in *Kennedy* appeared to imply instead that the District was reinforcing a tacit rule that "government role models for students are those who eschew any visible religious expression;" a rule contrary to acceptance of diversity in a pluralistic society.[4]

The United States Supreme Court majority in *Kennedy* held that a concern about violation of the Establishment Clause on facts such as in this case is a concern about "phantom constitutional violations."[5] The Majority in *Kennedy* thus granted summary judgment in favor of Mr. Kennedy holding that (a) his conduct constituted "personal religious observance" and (b) to disallow the same was discriminatory. The latter since, in the Court majority's view, analogous secular speech was allowed.[6]

The Dissenting Justices in *Kennedy* (Justice Sotomayor, Breyer and Kagan) hold that the endorsement of religion test for violation of the Establishment Clause of the First Amendment is *not* reducible to a 'heckler's veto' (i.e., an objection to the religious public display raised due, for instance, to the individual observer's potential discomfort with the public religious display by the public official while that official was on duty). Rather the issue is, according to the Dissenting Justices, whether in all the particular circumstances Mr. Kennedy's public demonstrable prayer at the football midfield amounts to State endorsement of Christianity. The Dissenting Justices hold that it did violate the Establishment Clause in that Mr. Kennedy had been leading and inviting his football high school team to participate in prayer at midfield after football games for a year prior to the last three incidents in which no invitation to participate was given. The Dissenting Justices maintain that as Mr. Kennedy was the coach who could grant or withhold benefits from his players regarding football, and he had previously invited players to join him in prayer at midfield and in the locker room, there was an implicit coercive element involved. This even if Kennedy did not directly instruct players to join him in prayer postgame on the field during the last three incidents. Further, the Dissenting Justices noted that the factual record included evidence that some students on Mr. Kennedy's football team did feel coerced to participate in the prayers for fear of being excluded by (alienated from) the rest of the team and being treated as outsiders. This coercive element was particularly acute, the Dissenting Justices contend, in that here there are children involved (persons under age 18) who are allegedly impacted by Mr. Kennedy's demonstrable public prayer displays in a school setting (on the school's football field) while the coach was still on duty.

The United States Supreme Court Dissenting Justices in *Kennedy* highlight the fact that the particular context, a public school setting with students, demands (a) close adherence to the Establishment Clause prohibition on State endorsement of religion and (b) concern about the message a violation would send to the political

[4]Kennedy v Bremerton School District No. 21-418. Argued April 25, 2022—Decided June 27, 2022 (Supreme Court of the United States) Majority Opinion at pp. 4–5.

[5]Kennedy v Bremerton School District No. 21-418. Argued April 25, 2022—Decided June 27, 2022 (Supreme Court of the United States) Majority Opinion at p. 5.

[6]Kennedy v Bremerton School District No. 21-418. Argued April 25, 2022—Decided June 27, 2022 (Supreme Court of the United States) Majority Opinion at p. 5.

community at large. Schools, the Dissenting Justices in *Kennedy* remind us, are the bedrock of the democracy in teaching *the positive value of plurality* and societal harmony. The Dissenting Justices in *Kennedy* in this regard note that the County in which the School District involved is located "is home to Bahá'ís, Buddhists, Hindus, Jews, Muslims, Sikhs, Zoroastrians, and many denominations of Christians, as well as numerous residents who are religiously unaffiliated."[7] Further the Dissenters noted that one of the purposes of the Establishment Clause is to protect the parental right to raise their children in the parents' religious and philosophical traditions without intrusion by the State.

The media came to know of the dispute Mr. Kennedy had with the School District due to a Facebook post of Mr. Kennedy's and his appearance on local media. In one particular game, the media went onto the field to film the prayer circle and members of the public rushed the field. This led to security concerns that the District had to address for future school football games. The Dissenting Justices held that this created an undue burden on the District which Mr. Kennedy was responsible for creating. The latter due to his refusal to cease his demonstrable public prayer displays at the school while on duty as a football coach. The Dissenting Justices further noted that Mr. Kennedy refused to discuss or respond to the District's attempts to reach a reasonable accommodation on the matter.

In short, the Dissenting Justices agreed with the lower courts in this case that Mr. Kennedy's prayers at midfield after school football games; prayers visible to students and the public while he was still on duty as a coach, were *not* as a private citizen in the circumstances. Rather the Dissenting Justices held that the prayers were conducted by Mr. Kennedy as a public official (an agent of the State) in a public manner before students and the public. Hence the Dissenting Justices maintained that Mr. Kennedy's prayers on the school football field after games and elsewhere visible to the students and/or public violated the Establishment Clause and were not constitutionally protected by the Free Exercise Clause.

On the current author's view, public demonstrations of religious activity while on duty as a government employee, by definition, cannot constitute personal private religious speech or other private religious activity. One wonders why it was apparently necessary for Mr. Kennedy, in his view, to kneel at midfield on the school football field after each game in order to express an ostensibly personal prayer of thanks for the game and his students involvement in it. Presumably the prayer would be as meaningful as a religious exercise if conducted post-game outside of public or student view but when the coach was still on duty. One may query also what is the alleged comparable allowable secular activity (referred to by the United States Supreme Court majority in the case without any specifics) that would auger for negation of any constitutional prohibition on Mr. Kennedy's demonstrable religious Christian speech at school in full view of the students and even, at times, the general public. Arguably public speech by a government representative/employee

[7]Kennedy v Bremerton School District No. 21-418. Argued April 25, 2022—Decided June 27, 2022 (Supreme Court of the United States) Dissenting Opinion at p. 3.

advocating a particular philosophical or 'secular position' on a religious question (such as atheism or agnosticism) would in fact also (a) violate the Establishment Clause and (b) would not be saved by the First Amendment free speech clause when that speech was demonstrably observable by students to whom that government employee owed a duty of care or if visible to members of the public. Furthermore, on the analysis here, the constitutionally mandated religious neutrality of public schools *cannot* legitimately or properly be equated to either (a) an endorsement of non-religion (atheism or agnosticism) or to (b) an hostility to religion as the United States Supreme Court conservative majority in *Kennedy* seems at times explicitly and, at other times, implicitly to suggest. Not to permit public school employees to advocate for religion or a particular religion while performing their government duties in a public space does *not* speak to the issue of advocacy for non-religion (atheism or agnosticism). Rather it speaks, on the view here, to the constitutional necessity of the separation of Church and State. The latter importantly in part through neutrality on religious questions by public employees when performing their official duties.

In *Kennedy*, the United States Supreme Court appears to have found that a school may *constitutionally* permit a school official *while on duty* to engage in *repeated* public displays of a particular religious tradition (i.e., praying in the Christian tradition). The latter while knowingly or inadvertently visible to the students (and even the public) and with no effort to expose the children of that school to alternate religious perspectives and practices. That is, the Court did *not* hold that such was a violation of the Establishment Clause nor did the Court find the activity tantamount to religious indoctrination.

It should be noted that (a) student expressions of religion[8] and (b) instructors teaching about religion are both permissible under the First Amendment[9] where it is clear that the State (i.e., the school through its agents) is *not* endorsing any particular

[8]There is currently a case winding its way through the Quebec courts in Canada concerning whether *public schools*, based on a principle of institutional secularism, can still constitutionally offer 'prayer rooms' to their students. In such rooms public school students can practice their religion through prayer in *overt ways*. The Quebec government has instituted *a ban* on such prayer rooms in public schools. The Quebec government ban on prayer rooms in public schools is being challenged in court by the Canadian Civil Liberties Association and the National Council of Canadian Muslims. The legal challenge is an effort to quash the ban as an alleged violation of (a) the students' constitutional right to non-discriminatory equal treatment (This as the ban has a disproportionate alleged harmful effect on Muslim students whose prayer practices are more overt and cannot be accommodated through the permitted private prayer rule in Quebec public schools) and (b) a violation of the students' constitutional right to freedom of religion. See *Quebec Court rejects urgent relief for Muslim students in prayer room case* Global Village Space June 15, 2023 https://www.globalvillagespace.com/quebec-court-rejects-urgent-relief-for-muslim-students-in-prayer-room-case/ (Accessed August 22, 2024).

[9]US Department of Education: Guidance on Constitutionally Protected Prayer and Religious Expression in Public Elementary and Secondary Schools January 16, 2020, https://www2.ed.gov/policy/gen/guid/religionandschools/prayer_guidance.html (Accessed August 22, 2024).

religion or philosophical position on religion but rather respecting plurality as a value.

5.2 City of Ocala, Florida v Art Rojas et al. (Supreme Court of the United States) On Petition for a Writ of Certiorari to the US Court of Appeals for the Eleventh District No. 22-278. Decided March 6, 2023

In *Ocala* a group of atheists sued the City of Ocala, Florida for holding a prayer vigil after a shooting in that city that injured several children. Several police chaplains participated in the prayer vigil led by a local minister and organized by the Chief of Police. The atheists claimed that the prayer vigil violated their constitutional right to freedom of religion as the vigil purportedly infringed the Establishment Clause that bars the government from establishing any religion. The District Court (a) ruled in favor of the atheist plaintiffs on Article III standing and (b) in favor also on the merits. The District Court ruled that the Establishment Clause of the First Amendment had been violated and granted summary judgment in favor of the plaintiffs. The District Court held that the fact that the atheists attended the event knowing it was a Christian prayer service was irrelevant to their standing. That legal standing related in part to the alleged harms created by their being offended, feeling uncomfortable at the event and being unable to participate due to their atheistic stance and the Christian theme of the vigil. The Eleventh Circuit Court of Appeals held that at least one of the plaintiffs had standing but *overruled* the District Court on the merits issue given the United States Supreme Court decision in *Kennedy* discussed above. The Appeals Court vacated the District Court decision on the merits and remanded the case back to the lower court to reconsider in light of the United States Supreme Court decision in *Kennedy v Bremerton School District*.[10] The Respondents (the City of Ocala) petitioned the Supreme Court of the United States to intervene arguing that the plaintiff atheists did *not* have standing. The majority of the United States Supreme Court, however, was of the opinion that the Court should *not* intervene to quash the suit. This though Justice Thomas dissented from that view. Hence the Ocala case was allowed to continue for the lower courts to decide the merits taking *Kennedy v Bremerton School District* into consideration. We will consider next then Supreme Court Justice Gorsuch's opinion in *Ocala* (Gorsuch J. writing for the Majority) and that of Justice Thomas who dissented from the majority United States Supreme Court decision not to intervene.

Justice Gorsuch maintains that the District Court should be reconsidering not only the merits but also standing. Justice Gorsuch argues that the United States Supreme Court has never held that a violation of the Establishment Clause suit can be brought

[10] Kennedy v Bremerton School District No. 21-418. Argued April 25, 2022—Decided June 27, 2022 (Supreme Court of the United States).

where the plaintiff's claim to standing is based solely on having been exposed to a religious ceremony, or practice or belief/doctrine that the plaintiff finds offensive (the 'offended observer' alleged standard for legal standing). Such harm (if it is harm), Gorsuch explains, in his view, does *not* meet the required standard for standing of 'a concrete and particularized harm or injury to the plaintiff(s)'. Indeed, one could argue that being exposed to a Christian prayer service, as in this case, *in and of itself* should not create discomfort for the viewer in a democratic pluralistic society (In the comparative cases to be discussed here the European Court of Human Rights stressed the right and even advisability of school boards in a democracy offering pluralistic religious courses and events wherein no singular religious faith or practice is favored and hence proselytized. This to teach democratic values of tolerance for diversity in various domains and to encourage open critical thinking, inquiry and discussion).[11] In any case, Justice Gorsuch is of the view that "…[i]n a large and diverse country, offense can be easily found. Really, most every governmental action probably offends somebody…. But recourse for disagreement and offense does not lie in federal litigation. Instead, in a society that holds among its most cherished ambitions mutual respect, tolerance, self-rule, and democratic responsibility, an 'offended viewer' may 'avert his eyes' or pursue a political solution."[12]

The key legal questions in *City of Ocala, Florida v Art Rojas et al.*[13] would seem to be (a) whether the City's involvement in organizing the prayer vigil was an endorsement of a particular religion and (b) whether this then constitutes an infringement of the Establishment Clause that created concrete and particularized harm or injury to the plaintiffs. Justice Gorsuch, however, maintained that as the Eleventh Circuit had remanded the case for reconsideration in light of the United Sates Supreme Court decision in *Kennedy v Bremerton School District No.* 21-418,[14] it was premature for the United States Supreme Court to intervene, This was his view though Justice Gorsuch agreed with the City that standing was a central issue in the case along with the merits. Let us now turn to Justice Thomas' dissent in *Ocala.*

Justice Thomas held in *Ocala* that the United States Supreme Court should have granted certiorari in this case in order to examine the question of standing. Justice Thomas found that the courts below had operated beyond their jurisdiction if in fact the plaintiffs had no standing. He thus maintained that the fact that the Appeals Court

---

[11] Perovy v Russia Application 47429/09 European Court of Human Rights Judgment 19 April 2021 at para. 7 https://hudoc.echr.coe.int/eng#{%22itemid%22:[%22001-205133%22]} (Accessed August 22, 2024).

[12] City of Ocala, Florida v Art Rojas et al. (Supreme Court of the United States) Justice Gorsuch Majority Opinion at p. 3 https://www.supremecourt.gov/opinions/22pdf/22-278_869d.pdf (Accessed August 22, 2024).

[13] City of Ocala, Florida v Art Rojas et al. (Supreme Court of the United States) https://www.supremecourt.gov/opinions/22pdf/22-278_869d.pdf (Accessed August 22, 2024).

[14] Kennedy v Bremerton School District No. 21-418. Argued April 25, 2022—Decided June 27, 2022 (Supreme Court of the United States).

remanded the case to be decided on the merits (taking into account *Kennedy Bremerton School District No. 21-418I*)[15] was irrelevant to whether the United States Supreme Court should have weighed in on the standing issue to ensure it was properly decided. Justice Thomas in this regard opined that "Because standing based on mere offense is in significant tension with Article III and our precedents, I would have granted certiorari to determine whether the courts below lacked jurisdiction."[16] Justice Thomas, as did Justice Gorsuch in this case (*Ocala*), emphasized that the "offended observer" standard for legal standing has "no basis in law."[17] Justice Thomas argues, based on United States Supreme Court precedent, that plaintiffs who share a *generalized grievance* with a certain class of others may not have the particularized concrete injury necessary to demonstrate a specific harm to themselves flowing from a violation of the Establishment Clause ("…offended observer standing "established[s] . . . a class of 'eggshell' plaintiffs of a delicacy never before known to the law."[18]

Justice Thomas, on the respectful view here, appears to minimize the controversy in the Ocala case as to whether the city government overstepped its jurisdiction in organizing the prayer vigil and having several of its police chaplains participate in the vigil on stage. On the view here, those potential violations of the Establishment Clause *in effect* are set aside and reduced, on Thomas's analysis, to an issue of whether there can be standing based on an alleged 'offended observer standard.'[19] However here there is not just the reference by government to God at the vigil. Rather the facts in *Ocala* are that of (a) a prayer vigil based on Christian religious text and practice; (b) a vigil organized by government and (c*) an absence of a plurality of religious observance at the vigil and an absence of any secular non-religious form of paying respect to the shooting victims*. The latter facts do, on the view here, raise an issue of whether or not such a prayer vigil *based on a singular religious tradition* (Christianity) violates the Establishment Clause It seems especially ironic that Justice Gorsuch and Justice Thomas should bemoan the 'offended observer' standard for legal standing in *Ocala.*[20] This while, at the same

---

[15]Kennedy v Bremerton School District No. 21-418. Argued April 25, 2022—Decided June 27, 2022 (Supreme Court of the United States).

[16]City of Ocala, Florida v Art Rojas et al. (Supreme Court of the United States) Justice Thomas Dissent at p 2 https://www.supremecourt.gov/opinions/22pdf/22-278_869d.pdf (Accessed August 22, 2024).

[17]City of Ocala, Florida v Art Rojas et al. Supreme Court of the United States Justice Thomas Dissent at p 2 https://www.supremecourt.gov/opinions/22pdf/22-278_869d.pdf (Accessed August 22, 2024).

[18]Washegesic v. Bloomingdale Public Schools, 33 F. 3d 679, 684–685 Cited in City of Ocala, Florida v Art Rojas et al. Supreme Court of the United States Justice Thomas Dissent at pp. 3–4 https://www.supremecourt.gov/opinions/22pdf/22-278_869d.pdf (Accessed August 22, 2024).

[19]City of Ocala, Florida v Art Rojas et al. Supreme Court of the United States Justice Thomas Dissent at p 3 https://www.supremecourt.gov/opinions/22pdf/22-278_869d.pdf (Accessed August 22, 2024).

[20]City of Ocala, Florida v Art Rojas et al. Supreme Court of the United States https://www.supremecourt.gov/opinions/22pdf/22-278_869d.pdf (Accessed August 22, 2024).

time, supporting the Texas abortion law here previously discussed. This in that the Texas abortion law affords private persons who are morally, religiously or otherwise offended by abortion (even those unconnected to the parties in a particular abortion situation) legal standing under statute to sue those who aid or abet an abortion in Texas after the pregnancy has advanced beyond 6 weeks.[21]

5.3 Comparative Law: The Freedom of Expression of Public Authorities and the Vulnerability of Students as Audience

5.3.1 Perovy v Russia Application 47429/09 (European Court of Human Rights) Judgment 19 April 2021

In Perovy v Russia[22] the applicants include the parents of the third applicant, a child and also a priest of the Church of the Community of Christ. The child was seven and enrolled at elementary school. On the first day of school, the school held a ceremony to celebrate new incoming students and there were no classes that day. After the ceremony there was a parent-teacher meeting but the parents of the child in question had to leave and were unable to attend. The parents at the meeting decided to invite a priest from the Russian Orthodox Church (who was also the father of one of the new pupils) to perform a blessing of the classroom. Parents not at the meeting were not informed of that decision. On the morning of the first day of regular classes, the parent of the child applicant arrived with her child to the school and then left. In the class, the Russian Orthodox priest began the blessing and when he was told one child (without the identity being revealed) was of a different faith he said that that was not an issue and the child could just stay in the class. "Fr M., who was wearing a cassock, distributed small paper icons among the children and sang prayers in Church Slavonic. Candles were lit; Fr M. used a censer to burn incense and sprinkled the classroom with holy water. Certain children and adults made the sign of the cross as per the Russian Orthodox tradition. Fr M. then invited the children to kiss a crucifix; they did so in turns. The rite of blessing lasted for some fifteen to twenty minutes. During the rite the third applicant picked up a small paper icon which the priest had put on his desk, but neither kissed the crucifix nor made the sign of the

---

[21] See Whole Woman's Health v Jackson (Supreme Court of the United States) No. 21-463. Argued November 1, 2021—Decided December 10, 2021 https://www.supremecourt.gov/opinions/21pdf/21-463_3ebh.pdf (Accessed August 22, 2024).

[22] Perovy v Russia Application 47429/09 European Court of Human Rights Judgment 19 April 2021 (Accessed August 22, 2024).

cross."[23] The parents of the child applicant submitted to the European Court of Human Rights that their child was made to feel very uncomfortable. This in that his classmates pressured him to kiss the crucifix and mocked him for not knowing how to make the sign of the cross per the manner used by the Russian Orthodox Church student attendees. The parents of the child in question alleged a violation of Article 2 of Protocol 1 to the *European Convention on Human Rights* on right to education:

> **Right to education (Article 2 of Protocol 1 to the European Convention on Human Rights)**
> No person shall be denied the right to education. In the exercise of any functions which it assumes in relation to education and to teaching, the State shall respect the right of parents to ensure such education and teaching in conformity with their own religious and philosophical convictions.[24]

The parents and priest applicant also alleged a violation of Article 9 of the Convention (Freedom of thought, conscience and religion) holding that the child in question had been forced to participate in the Russian Orthodox blessing contrary to his faith.

The European Court of Human Rights held in *Perovy v Russia* that Article 9 of the Convention, among other things, guarantees freedom of thought, conscience and religion. That freedom also includes the freedom to be agnostic and not to belong to any faith/religious community. This then in turn imposes a "duty of neutrality and impartiality" on the States Parties in the education setting.[25] The European Court interpreted this duty as essential in promoting the democratic values of public harmony and tolerance for diversity as well as inclusion.[26] The European Court of Human Rights noted that the State had investigated and took disciplinary measures against the teacher involved for not notifying all parents before such a ceremony was considered or conducted in the classroom.

The European Court of Human Rights found that the parents' religious rights under Article 2 Protocol I had *not* been violated by this one-time non-State endorsed religious school event. The European Court of Human Rights agreed that the blessing of the classroom on the first day of scheduled classes in a public school fell within the scope of Article 2 Protocol 1 but, on the specific facts of the case,

[23] Perovy v Russia Application 47429/09 European Court of Human Rights Judgment 19 April 2021 at para 11–13 https://hudoc.echr.coe.int/fre#{%22tabview%22:[%22document%22],%22itemid%22:[%22001-205133%22]} (Accessed August 22, 2024).

[24] European Convention on Human Rights, Protocol I Article 2 https://www.echr.coe.int/documents/convention_eng.pdf (Accessed August 22, 2024).

[25] Perovy v Russia Application 47429/09 European Court of Human Rights Judgment 19 April 2021 at para 55 https://hudoc.echr.coe.int/fre#{%22tabview%22:[%22document%22],%22itemid% 22:[%22001-205133%22]} (Accessed August 22, 2024).

[26] Perovy v Russia Application 47429/09 European Court of Human Rights Judgment 19 April 2021 at para 55 https://hudoc.echr.coe.int/fre#{%22tabview%22:[%22document%22],%22itemid% 22:[%22001-205133%22]} (Accessed August 22, 2024).

regarded the incident as an isolated one-off. The Court found it was *not* able to determine whether the isolated event involving the 15-to-20-minute Russian Orthodox religious ceremony had any impact on the child in question in terms of his religious world view which he was still in the process of forming given his young age. The European Court of Human Rights held therefore that this isolated event could *not* be deemed as "coercion" or "indoctrination" contrary to the parents' claims. The Court importantly found that (a) *the State had not mandated the religious ceremony, the ceremony was not part of the curriculum,* and that (b) *the State was not involved other than in the fact of the ceremony having taken place in a public school.*[27] The latter under the auspices of a State-employed teacher who had given but tacit approval of the ceremony in response to the wishes of the majority of the parents who had attended a parent-teacher meeting. The European Court of Human Rights found further that no evidence had been adduced that the child's upbringing in his faith had been adversely affected in any way by this isolated exposure to another faith nor that the child had been adversely psychologically impacted. Interestingly, the Court noted that Article 2 Protocol 1, in that it promotes tolerance and pluralism, does not confer a right not to witness other individuals or groups manifesting their faith or their lack of religious belief, convictions or faith,[28] The European Court of Human Rights concluded that the child in question in this instance was not coerced to participate in the ceremony but was simply present during it in the classroom and witnessed the event. For instance, the child was invited to kiss the crucifix but not compelled to do so and he declined doing so. Further no attempt was made to have the child acknowledge the small paper icon left on the desks and there was, in the view of the Court, no attempt to proselytize. For all of the aforementioned reasons. The European Court of Human Rights found that the child's Convention Article 9 right to freedom of thought, conscience and religion had *not* been violated.

[27] One wonders, however, whether the religious ceremony having taken place in a public school classroom, even though not organized by the State, still sends the implicit, if unintended, perceived message to parents and students of State endorsement.

[28] Perovy v Russia Application 47429/09 European Court of Human Rights Judgment 19 April 2021 https://hudoc.echr.coe.int/fre#{%22tabview%22:[%22document%22],%22itemid%22:[%22001-205133%22]} at para 73 (Accessed August 22, 2024).

5.3.2 *Konrad v. Germany, European Court of Human Rights (Fifth Section), (Application 35504/0311) September 2006*

5.3.2.1 Introduction to Konrad

In *Konrad*[29] the facts are quite different than in *Kennedy v Bremerton School District*[30] insofar as *Konrad* concerns the issue of whether parents have a right, for religious reasons, to homeschool their children at the elementary school level. However, at the same time, the underlying issue, to some degree, overlaps with that in *Kennedy*. This in that both cases concern the controversial issue of parents objecting or potentially objecting to their schoolchildren being exposed at public school to perspectives with which the complainant parents may disagree and which, in certain respects, conflict with their religious beliefs (i.e., in *Kennedy* exposure to another religious faith perspective or practice was through the demonstrable display of Christianity by way of the high school football coach praying on the football field after games such that students and even the public may observe him doing so). In *Konrad*, fundamentalist Christian parents objected to sex education in the public school[31] and their children's exposure also to other information and perspectives with which the parents disagree based on their religious faith. As a result, the parents wished to homeschool their children. However, in Germany, primary education is compulsory either at a State public school or in a private school which may be a religious denominational school. Exemptions are provided only for practical reasons as where a child's disabilities prevent attendance at public or private school or parents must constantly relocate for professional reasons. The parent complainants in *Konrad*[32] filed their complaints with the European Court of Human Rights on some articles on their own behalf and on others also on their children's behalf.

[29] Konrad v. Germany (European Court of Human Rights) Application 35504/03 https://hudoc.echr.coe.int/eng#{%22itemid%22:[%22001-76925%22]} (Accessed August 22, 2024).

[30] Kennedy v Bremerton School District No. 21-418. Argued April 25, 2022—Decided June 27, 2022 (Supreme Court of the United States).

[31] The Freiburg Administrative Court that dismissed the parents' complaint and their request to homeschool their children held that (a) the sex education concerns were likely overstated considering an elementary school curriculum and that (b) the Konrad parents in any case could have sent their children to a private religious school where the sex education, if included in the curriculum, may have been more compatible with the parents' religious perspective.

[32] Konrad v. Germany (European Court of Human Rights) Application 35504/03 https://hudoc.echr.coe.int/eng#{%22itemid%22:[%22001-76925%22]} (Accessed August 22, 2024).

5.3.2.2 Procedural History of Konrad in the German Domestic Courts

The German domestic courts ruled in *Konrad*[33] that the child's right to an education, and the State's interest therein, meant that the parents' freedom of religion could *not* restrict the implementation of compulsory schooling in elementary school. The domestic courts further found that even if the homeschooling provided an adequate education (in terms of content and quality of curriculum and teaching), home schooling could not provide the child with the contact with a population of diverse other children necessary for the development of democratic values. To develop democratic values, the domestic courts held, requires exposure of children to other children from varied backgrounds with a plurality of views. In other words, developing democratic values requires schooling in a democratic inclusive context. In this respect then it is noteworthy that the facts in *Konrad* include the parents wishing their children to avoid contact with other children outside their fundamentalist Christian community. The domestic courts in this case found that such sheltering of the Konrad children away from a diverse group of other children was contrary to the personal and educational interests and rights (per Article 2 of Protocol I to the *European Convention on Human Rights*: Right to Education)[34] of the complainants' children.

The domestic courts found further that fundamentalist parents could still educate their children in their religious tradition in the evenings and weekends. Hence the courts found that the parents' freedom to raise their children according to their own religious convictions and traditions was not undermined by compulsory elementary school attendance. Furthermore, the State school at issue was dedicated to religious neutrality hence there was no question of religious indoctrination in this instance. The German Federal Constitutional Court "stressed that the State's obligation to provide education did not only concern the acquisition of knowledge, but also the education of responsible citizens to participate in a democratic and pluralistic society."[35]

The Constitutional Court further found that the State's requirement for compulsory elementary education of schoolchildren was a proportionate interference with the parents' freedom of religion given (a) "the general interest of society in avoiding the emergence of parallel societies based on separate philosophical convictions" and

[33] Konrad v. Germany (European Court of Human Rights) Application 35504/03 https://hudoc.echr.coe.int/eng#{%22itemid%22:[%22001-76925%22]} (Accessed August 22, 2024).

[34] Guide to Article 2 protocol I Right to Education, European Convention on Human Rights (European Court of Human Rights) https://www.right-to-education.org/sites/right-to-education.org/files/resource-attachments/ECHR_Guide_Art_2_Protocol_1_ENG_0.pdf (Accessed August 22, 2024).

[35] Konrad v. Germany (European Court of Human Rights) Application 35504/03 https://hudoc.echr.coe.int/eng#{%22itemid%22:[%22001-76925%22]} at p. 3 (Accessed August 22, 2024).

(b) the State's interest in "integrating minorities."[36] Indeed one might reasonably suggest that currently in the United States the so-called 'culture wars' are, to some degree, a reflection of such 'parallel societies based on separate philosophical convictions.' Such a state of affairs is ultimately highly divisive and corrosive for democratic values and institutions. It is a situation exacerbated by restrictions on legitimate pluralistic viewpoints in curriculum and the elimination or reduction in the diversity of the student body.

5.3.2.3 The European Court of Human Rights Ruling in Konrad

The European Court of Human Rights found in *Konrad*[37] that the domestic courts had well-reasoned the position that right to education under the European Convention encompasses integration of school-aged children into the school system through compulsory elementary schooling (at State or private schools) as their first significant experience with the larger society. The European Court of Human Rights held that the German State was operating within the 'margin of appreciation' to consider that the democratic objective of exposure of children to a plurality of diverse other children could not be met through homeschooling. The European Court of Human Rights also found that the complainant parents were free to educate their children in their own religious traditions outside of school hours. For the aforementioned reasons, the European Court of Human Rights ruled the complaint to be manifestly ill-founded as to Article 2 of Protocol I on right to education. The Court also rejected the claim of a violation of the right to respect for private and family life and of the parents' right to freedom of thought, conscience and religion (Convention articles 8 and 9 respectively) and of infringement of the non-discrimination guarantee Article 14 of the European Convention in connection with Articles 8 and 9. The latter complaints were also rejected by the European Court of Human Rights as manifestly ill-founded. This since the interference with the parents' rights was held to (a) serve a legitimate societal interest and (b) to be proportionate and to be within the State's scope of discretion in administering the relevant law for a legitimate democratic purpose. For all of these reasons, the complaint in its totality was ruled inadmissible.

It is to be recalled, at the same time, that not all European States approach the right to education in the same way. This in that many European States permit parents to opt out of compulsory schooling in favor of homeschooling that may include a strong and very particular religious orientation. In some instances, the

---

[36] Konrad v. Germany (European Court of Human Rights) Application No. 35504/03 https://www.lawpluralism.unimib.it/en/oggetti/163-konrad-v-germany-dec-no-35504-03-e-ct-hr-fifth-section-11-september-2006 at p. 3 (Accessed August 22, 2024).

[37] Konrad v. Germany (European Court of Human Rights) Application No. 35504/03 https://www.lawpluralism.unimib.it/en/oggetti/163-konrad-v-germany-dec-no-35504-03-e-ct-hr-fifth-section-11-september-2006 at p. 3 (Accessed August 22, 2024).

homeschooling may potentially be inconsistent with promoting tolerance and respect for other religious traditions and beliefs.

5.4 The Scope of Children's Right to Education: A Contrasting Landmark US Supreme Court Case: Yoder v Wisconsin 406 U.S. 205 (1972)

The Constitutional Court of Germany and the European Court of Human Rights perspective in *Konrad* was that (a) children have an autonomous right to be exposed to a diverse student population at school (as part of the right to education) and that (b) it is important in a democracy and is in the societal interest to expose schoolchildren to a plurality of views. Contrast that perspective with that in the United State Supreme Court's approach in *Yoder v Wisconsin*.[38] In *Yoder*, the United States Supreme Court majority ruled in favor of the parents and the case is still 'good law' precedent in the US. In the Yoder case, Amish parents were successful in asserting a purported *religious right* to terminate their children's attendance for compulsory schooling at public (State) school or a private school[39] by grade eight (when the children are about age 14). This on the basis that (a) the parents did not want their children exposed to non-Amish views and values at that young vulnerable age (presumably, in part, as they feared the children at that age might be more easily enticed to abandon their Amish traditions and community) and that (b) school attendance beyond grade eight is not the Amish tradition. The United States Supreme Court majority in *Yoder* found it constitutional for Amish parents to opt for vocational training of their children in the Amish religious communal lifestyle as opposed to having their children attend at least the first couple of years of high school.[40]

Justice Douglas, the Dissenting Justice in *Yoder*, held that (a) the children's freedom of religion and religious views were also implicated in this case and not just those of the parents and that (b) where the children were old enough to express their position on attending school outside the Amish community beyond grade eight, they should have all been allowed to testify at trial (which did not occur as to each and every child in question). Justice Douglas stated "It is the future of the student, not the future of the parents, that is imperiled by today's decision. If a parent keeps his child out of school beyond the grade school, then the child will be forever barred

---

[38] Yoder v Wisconsin 406 U.S. 205 (1972).

[39] The Amish community does not itself offer formal schooling at the high school level.

[40] See Yoder v Wisconsin 406 U.S. 205 (1972) https://supreme.justia.com/cases/federal/us/406/205/#tab-opinion-1949690 (See also Justice Douglas' partial dissent in *Yoder* (Accessed August 22, 2024).

from entry into the new and amazing world of diversity that we have today."[41] The latter, on the view here, is a central issue in such cases, namely the autonomous right of children in a democratic society to be exposed, through schooling, to a diversity of children and pluralistic viewpoints.

Through (a) exclusion of certain groups of children from potential student diverse populations (exclusion through i.e., homeschooling or discrimination etc. and/or by removing a plurality of views from the educational curriculum in State and/or private schools); children are potentially deprived of their right to be educated for tolerance and other democratic values. The latter is contrary to the right to education, for example, in *the Convention on the Rights of the Child* as articulated at Article 29 (d).[42] It is to be noted, however, that a homeschool curriculum could be designed to include pluralistic views and the child given opportunities also through community clubs and other resources to interact with a diversity of children their age. The latter, however, is not always the agenda for parents who opt for homeschooling as *Konrad* for instance illustrates.

5.5 Lautsi and Others v Italy

5.5.1 Lautsi and Others v Italy: Procedural History in the Domestic Courts and the Chamber of the European Court of Human Rights

In *Lautsi*[43] the applicant parents and their children were the complainants. The parents' complaints concerned the fact that a crucifix was attached to the classroom wall of their children's classroom in a State school. One of the parents asked at a meeting whether the crucifixes could be removed. At a subsequent meeting of the school's governors, it was decided by the school governors *not* to remove the crucifixes. The parents appealed to an administrative court complaining of an infringement of their right to equality, freedom of religion and their right to impartial public authorities under the Italian Constitution and of a violation of Article 9 of the Convention regarding freedom of thought, conscience and religion. In addition, the parent complainants claimed a violation of the Protocol I to the Convention Article 2 right to education in regard to their right as parents to educate their children

[41] See Yoder v Wisconsin 406 U.S. 205 (1972) https://supreme.justia.com/cases/federal/us/406/205/#tab-opinion-1949690 (Accessed August 22, 2024).

[42] Convention on the Rights of the Child Article 29(d): "States Parties agree that the education of the child shall be directed to…The preparation of the child for responsible life in a free society, in the spirit of understanding, peace, tolerance, equality of sexes, and friendship among all peoples, ethnic, national and religious groups and persons of indigenous origin." https://www.ohchr.org/en/instruments-mechanisms/instruments/convention-rights-child (Accessed August 22, 2024).

[43] Lautsi and Others v Italy (European Court of Human Rights) Grand Chamber (Application no. 30814/06) Judgment 18 March 2011 (Accessed 29 December 2023).

according to the parents' religious and philosophical convictions. The Minister of Education in reply to the complainant parents and child argued that the crucifixes in public school classrooms was based on various historic royal decrees. The Administrative Court referred the matter to the Constitutional Court.

The Constitutional Court ruled the reference to be *inadmissible* since what was being challenged was the text of various royal decrees which do *not* have the status of law. Thereafter, the Administrative Court dismissed the complaint. The Administrative Court held that (a) the secular nature of the public school classrooms was well understood given the secular nature of Italy and Europe and that (b) therefore the presence of the crucifixes in the State-run school classrooms did *not* offend any of the rights claimed by the plaintiffs to have been infringed. The Administrative Court emphasized that in its view (a) the crucifix is a symbol of Christianity and not Catholicism in particular and (b) the crucifix is a cultural symbol linked to the development of Italian and European society and reflects the values of the Italian people as expressed in Italy's Constitution. The parents appealed to the Supreme Administrative Court which upheld the Lower Administrative Court's ruling that the crucifixes in public school classrooms did *not* offend the principle of secularism nor religious plurality but rather simply denoted the religious basis for the societal values of Italy. The latter perspective seems to echo the majority perspective in the United States Supreme Court case *Kennedy v Bremerton School District No. 21-418*[44] that does *not* view the celebration and practice of Christian traditions in public institutions (such as public schools) as offensive to secularism through the *exclusion* of pluralistic religious and non-religious symbols and practices. The Courts in fact in such cases, in expressing this view, seem to have morphed Christianity, its symbols and practices, into an indicium of the particular society itself and its "civil values." This notwithstanding the issue of, the appearance at least to many, of the State promoting a certain religious belief system and tradition.[45]

In *Lautsi*, the European Court of Human Rights Chamber found a violation of Article 2 Protocol 1 (right to education) and of Convention Article 9 (freedom of thought, conscience and religion) and found it unnecessary to examine the case under Convention Article 14 (non-discrimination). The European Court of Human Rights Chamber focused in part on the vulnerability of young children to religious and other forms of indoctrination, particularly in a school setting where attendance is compulsory. The crucifix, the Chamber held, had a predominantly religious meaning and thus its "compulsory and visible" presence every day in the public school classroom could be upsetting to students of non-Christian faiths or those students with no professed religious faith. The European Court of Human Rights Chamber further found that the State schools' religious neutrality required not simply

---

[44] Kennedy v Bremerton School District (Supreme Court of the United States) No. 21-418. Argued April 25, 2022—Decided June 27, 2022 https://www.law.cornell.edu/supct/pdf/21-418.pdf (Accessed August 22, 2024).

[45] Not all European Member States forbid religious symbols in State schools and only a few prescribe it. Lautsi and Others v Italy European Court of Human Rights Grand Chamber (Application no. 30814/06) Judgment 18 March 2011 at p. 13.

refraining from promulgating and endorsing religious teaching and services but also from displaying religious symbols or symbols of atheism in the school generally including in the classrooms. The Chamber, in addition, highlighted the State's duty, for the sake of religious harmony and tolerance in a democratic society, and for the development of student critical thought to (a) maintain a stance of impartiality with respect to religion and to (b) allow for religious and other plurality. Thus, it appears that the European Court of Human Rights Chamber found a violation of the child's autonomous right to education in these regards. The Chamber also found a violation of Article 2 with respect to the parent's right to educate their child in conformity with their personal religious or non-religious views. This in that the State school had not maintained a position of religious neutrality in the Chamber's view. The case was subsequently referred to the European Court of Human Rights Grand Chamber.

5.5.2 *Lautsi and Others v Italy: European Court of Human Rights, Grand Chamber Judgement*

The European Court of Human Rights Grand Chamber held that since there was considerable variety in how the European member Sates dealt with the issue of religious practice and symbology in State schools; they were owed a large 'margin of appreciation' on that issue. The Grand Chamber further opined that it was up to the European member States to set the educational curriculum and school environment, including any possible religious instruction, and not the Court nor the parents. However, the Grand Chamber held that such religious curriculum must be delivered in a pluralistic and impartial manner so as to avoid indoctrination and instead develop students' critical thinking. The Grand Chamber also affirmed that deeply held secular philosophical views are to be considered convictions within the meaning of Article 9 of the Convention and Article 2 Protocol I to the Convention.

In reviewing the facts of the case, the European Court of Human Rights Grand Chamber held that the display of crucifixes in State-run schools was a cultural tradition linked to Italy's historical development and hence that it fell, in the Court's majority view, under the State 'margin of appreciation' as the government had argued. The Grand Chamber further held that the fact that there was no consensus among the European member States as to how to set up the school environment and organize the curriculum as to religious teaching (if such were included) supported the Court's allowing a broad 'margin of appreciation' on such matters. At the same time, the Grand Chamber majority conceded that allowing crucifixes to be hung on the walls of State-run schools gave Christianity a heightened acknowledgement and visibility in the State schools. However, the Court majority did *not* find the latter to be sufficient to constitute a violation of Article 2 Protocol I (right to education). This display of the crucifix in public school classrooms was acceptable, the Grand Chamber majority held, essentially due to the overarching role that Christianity had played in European history and in Italy's history specifically. The Grand

Chamber majority on this issue referred also to what it considered its own relevant case precedent where it ruled that there was no violation of Article 2 Protocol I where Christianity was assigned more lessons than other religions in a comparative religion course. However, note that in the latter cases (concerning the share of the religious curriculum devoted to Christianity) at least other religions were represented. In *Lautsi*, in contrast, this is not the case as there were no non-Christian religious (or non-religious) symbols affixed to the public school classroom wall alongside the crucifix.

In the current author's view, however, giving Christianity a high visibility in a State-run school (or any other particular religion or non-religious conviction for that matter) through whatever vehicle (the football coach while on duty praying while kneeling on the school football field in view of students with student players after games at times joining him in prayer, crucifixes attached to the public school classroom wall etc.) is *ipso facto* inconsistent with the secular objective to instill in public school students the valuing of diversity and respect for plurality (including religious plurality). The prominence given to particular religious symbols and/or practices, it is here argued, is (a) an unjustified violation of European Convention Article 2 Protocol I (the right to education), and of Convention Article 9 (freedom of thought, religion and conscience), Article 10 (freedom of expression) and Article 14 (the prohibition on discrimination) in the European context that properly should be considered *outside* the 'margin of appreciation' and (b) in analogous cases; an unjustified infringement of, for instance, the First Amendment freedom of religion guarantee in the US context. To consider such as within the margin of appreciation as occurred in the European Court of Human Rights Grand Chamber decision in *Lautsi*, it is here argued, is to tear at the value of respect for plurality which is one central in sustaining a democracy.

The Lautsi Grand Chamber, it is perhaps telling, declined to consider whether the crucifixes on display attached to the walls of Italian State-run schools had an impact on children's developing minds in terms of their religious or non-religious views. This was the ruling though the Grand Chamber conceded that the crucifix is at least in large part a religious symbol. The majority Grand Chamber *declined* to do that analysis providing the rationale that there was no evidence presented to the Court on that issue one way or another (that is on the issue of the extent of impact, if any, on children's thinking regarding religious or philosophical conviction of seeing every school day the crucifixes affixed to their school classroom wall). Hence the Grand Chamber majority found that the complainant parents' perception that the State had not accorded them due respect in regard to their children's education as required under Article 2 Protocol I was allegedly just that-perception and not necessarily factual.

Furthermore, the Grand Chamber majority found that a crucifix affixed to the classroom wall of a State-run school is what the majority termed a 'passive symbol.' That is, the crucifix, in the view of the Grand Chamber majority, can be differentiated from active teaching or forced participation in certain religious activities. Hence the presence of crucifixes affixed to classroom walls of Italian State-run schools, the Grand Chamber majority opined, does *not* constitute indoctrination in violation of

Article 2 Protocol I. As regards to the latter point, the current author would argue, with respect, in opposition that a so-called 'passive symbol' (such as the crucifix affixed to the school classroom wall) that is present each day in the State-run school classroom is a powerful vehicle potentially for religious and cultural indoctrination. This is the case, on the view here, even where there is no compulsory overt teaching of Christianity or explicit forced religious participation in specific ceremonies or practices. Indeed, one could argue that the children's forced presence in the public-school classroom (due to compulsory schooling) where a crucifix is attached to the classroom wall is itself forced participation in a religious practice; one involving giving obligatory acceptance and tacit reverence to the crucifix as a Christian religious symbol.

The daily presence of the religious/cultural symbol in the school classroom (here a crucifix) and hence of what it symbolizes (Christianity) is thereby normalized as a taken-for-granted compelling majority social norm. The crucifix thus is potentially understood by the public school students as an expression of the dominant religious view and may further be perceived by students as a symbol of a religious norm that must be adhered to. This potential student perceived pressure to conform in their religious views to the majority culture is likely reinforced where there is no discussion or debate in the classroom on the matter of religious plurality and its role and place in a democratic secular society. The presence of a crucifix in State-run school classrooms in Italy thus runs the considerable risk of reinforcing the notion of Christianity as an uncontested State national religion though, in fact, the Italian State is officially secular and pluralistic.[46]

In summary then the Grand Chamber held that there had been *no violation* of (a) the right to education Article 2 Protocol I to the European Convention on Human Rights regarding the right of parents to ensure education and teaching of their child consistent with their religious and philosophical beliefs nor of (b) Article 9 of the European Convention on Human Rights regarding the freedom of thought, religion and conscience. Further the Grand Chamber found that there was no basis to examine whether any violation had occurred regarding Article 14 of the Convention respecting the prohibition against discrimination in affording any of the rights and freedoms of the Convention.

The Dissenting Judge in *Lautsi*, Judge Kalaydjeva, noted that few member States regulate the use of religious symbols in State schools. That judge therefore maintained that it was difficult therefore to reach any conclusion about the extent of consensus on the issue amongst the members and what margin of appreciation would be appropriate in this circumstance on the continuum of narrow to broad. Judge Kalaydjeva also noted that the royal decrees (upon which the practice of crucifixes in State-run Italian schools is based) are non-democratic dictates as they are not law enacted by Parliament.

[46]It should be noted that Italy allows students to wear headscarves and various symbols of religion, including those pertaining to faiths other than Christianity, and schools often also celebrate non-Christian holidays.

On the view here, the Grand Chamber majority in *Lautsi* engaged in a kind of de-judicialization of the fundamental rights issues surrounding religious freedom. This in that the Grand Chamber majority arguably (a) creates a large 'margin of appreciation' in *Lautsi* without solid factual basis (as Judge Kalaydjeva points out) while (b) at the same time conceding that the crucifix is inexorably viewed as a religious symbol referencing Christianity in particular and not just as a cultural/traditional symbol in some abstract sense. Hence this increases the risk that basic rights to freedom of religion and right to education are being undermined by the State and in this case without compelling reason. On this point Judge Kalaydjeva perhaps puts the aforementioned central problem with the ruling more delicately when he says that the Grand Chamber in *Lautsi*, as in all cases, must ensure that the member States meet their obligations including positive obligations under Article 19 of the Convention:

European Court of Human Rights
ARTICLE 19

Establishment of the Court

"*To ensure the observance of the engagements undertaken by the High Contracting Parties in the Convention and the Protocols thereto,* there shall be set up a European Court of Human Rights, hereinafter referred to as "the Court". It shall function on a permanent basis (emphasis added)."[47]

In the Lautsi case these positive obligations, the Dissenting Judge held, include fostering a school climate of tolerance and mutual respect for the diversity (including religious diversity) in the school population and in the Italian society at large and more generally. Judge Kalaydjeva maintained that the positive obligations encompassed by Article 2 Protocol I and Article 9 of the Convention suggest that a narrower margin of appreciation in such cases as *Lautsi* is appropriate. However, the majority Grand Chamber in *Lautsi* opted for a broad margin of appreciation. Judge Kalaydjeva further noted that the Grand Chamber's finding in *Lautsi* was that there was no violation of Article 2 Protocol I. This even though the Grand Chamber conceded that the Italian State was giving priority to Christianity, the majority religion in that State, through the presence of crucifixes (a primarily religious symbol) on the classroom walls of State-run schools. This Judge Kalaydjeva found is *not* consistent with meeting the Court's obligation to ensure that the margin of appreciation is not overstepped in the manner in which member States organize their educational curricula and settings (educational settings including thus also incorporation of religious and other symbols in public schools and classrooms).

The Dissenting Judge further argued that the need for promoting tolerance in a democratic and pluralistic secular society requires that a strict narrow margin of

[47] European Convention on Human Rights and Freedoms Article 19 https://www.echr.coe.int/documents/convention_eng.pdf (Accessed August 22, 2024).

appreciation be applied in cases such as *Lautsi*. This also in order to avoid discrimination and ensure equality under the law for the minority religious faiths (and non-religious minority) as well as the majority. Exposing a child in public (State) school to a religious/cultural symbol representative of the dominant/majority religion on a daily basis without fail and without possibility of avoiding viewing the symbol, the Dissenting Judge held, is *not* consistent with the State's obligation under the Convention of maintaining denominational/religious neutrality. In addition, Judge Kalaydjeva concluded that (in his view) the European Court of Human Rights Grand Chamber in *Lautsi* undermines (contrary to its protestations to the converse) the notion of a secular society and pluralism inconsistent with the rulings of most European Member States constitutional courts in such cases.

5.6 Grzelak v Poland European Court of Human Rights (Application 7710/02) Judgment 15 June 2010

In *Grzelak v Poland*[48] the parents of a third applicant were agnostics. Given the parents lack of religious orientation as agnostics, and at their request, their child was exempted from religious instruction during his entire schooling. As a substitute the parents had repeatedly requested that the school provide instruction for their child in ethics instead of the religious instruction. The school, however, did not provide the child the ethics class at any level of his schooling, primary or secondary. This the school justified by maintaining that there were not enough students at the particular school involved who were interested in taking an ethics class to make it feasible. As a consequence, the child never did receive a grade for a course listed as religion/ethics on his report cards.

The Court ruled the case inadmissible *ratione personae* as far as the parents were concerned in that it concerned the absence of a grade in ethics or religion on their child's report card. The Court agreed with the government that this impacted only the child as a victim.[49] However, the Court held that the denial of a grade for religion/ethics on all of the child's report cards adversely affected/interfered with the child's Article 9 right under the European Convention on Human Rights to freedom of thought, conscience and religion. The Court found a violation of Article 14 (the prohibition against discrimination) in conjunction with Article 9 of the Convention. The Court held that the absence of a grade for the 'religion/ethics course' on the child complainant's report card (unlike the situation for most other students since they had completed a religion course) (a) might be interpreted as indicating the complainant student's lack of religious affiliation and (b) hence

[48] Grzelak v Poland https://hudoc.echr.coe.int/fre?i=002-926 (Accessed August 22, 2024).

[49] One could argue that the parents were also victims in that they were unable under Article 2 Protocol I to the Convention to secure the education in ethics that they desired for their child consistent with their own convictions.

amounted to discrimination and what might be considered 'outing' the student: "The third applicant had complained of the discriminatory nature of the non-provision of courses in ethics and resultant absence of a mark for "religion/ethics" in his school reports"[50] The Court found that a grade for religion/ethics listed on a report card would *not* constitute discrimination with respect to the student's right to freedom of thought, conscience and religion as long as the report card indicated that the student had completed one or the other route *but not which one*. The Court found that "The absence of a mark for "religion/ethics" would be understood by any reasonable person as an indication that the third applicant had not followed religious education classes, which were widely available, and that he was thus likely to be regarded as a person without religious beliefs."[51] Under the European Convention, however, Article 9 rights include the right not to be compelled directly or indirectly to reveal one's religious orientation or lack thereof. The fact that the child was "outed" as a non-believer was particularly onerous and stigmatizing, the Court maintained, in that Poland is a majority religious society where one particular religious faith predominates. The Court also found a discriminatory element was established in that, from a certain date, marks for the religion/ethics course were calculated in a student's overall average. Hence the child in this case (the third applicant) was disadvantaged in his overall average by not having a grade for a course in religion/ethics (referring to either a religion or an ethics course). The Court concluded on this point that "Such pupils would either find it more difficult to increase their average mark or might feel pressurized – against their conscience – to attend a religious-education class in order to improve their average mark."[52] The Court found that there had been unjustified disproportionate differential treatment accorded students who wished to pursue a religious course versus those who wished to take an ethics course as an alternative. The Court concluded also that the State's discretion or margin of appreciation had been exceeded on these facts. The latter as the child's right under Article 9 of the Convention not to reveal his religion or convictions had been violated. In somewhat (on the view here) contradictory fashion, no violation was found in the fact that Poland required a certain minimum number of students be willing to take the ethics course before the school would offer the course[53] and the complaint in that narrow connection was deemed inadmissible only insofar as that element.

[50] Grzelak v. Poland—7710/02 Judgment 15.6.2010 Information Note on the Court's case-law No. 131 (June 2010) at p. 1.

[51] Grzelak v. Poland—7710/02 Judgment 15.6.2010 Information Note on the Court's case-law No. 131 (June 2010) at p. 1.

[52] Grzelak v. Poland—7710/02 Judgment 15.6.2010 Information Note on the Court's case-law No. 131 (June 2010) at p. 2.

[53] There was no report card mark for a 'religion/ethics course' for the child complainant as no ethics course had ever been offered at the school and the child did not take any available school religious course due to his convictions of conscience. Hence the child could not receive a grade for a religion/ ethics course on the report card (where the report card would not indicate which course he had completed; religion or ethics).

If one compares *Grzelak v Poland* to the US case *Kennedy v Bremerton School District* one arguable similarity, though the facts are largely very disparate in each case on other points, is perhaps present. This in that the students in both cases were arguably being implicitly pressured, directly or indirectly, to make a show of religious faith publicly. The latter such that a failure to do so might be interpreted as a display of lack of dedication to the dominant or any religious faith. In *Grzelak v Poland* this show of religious faith was to be by way of pursuing a religious course at school (the only option as an ethics course was not available) and in *Kennedy v Bremerton School District* this was related to joining the coach and other teammates after school football games to kneel and pray on the field consistent with the Christian faith.

5.7 Concluding Comment

On the view here, the legal and logical case can reasonably be made that preventing exposure of public school students to diversity in religious and philosophical, including secular perspectives, is antithetical to the democratic State's agenda in fostering harmony and respect for plurality. This undemocratic approach is particularly insidious when it occurs in schools. This is the case since the schools are tasked in a democracy with fostering tolerance and mutual respect amongst the people of that State. Such is therefore, on the view here, a violation of (a) the child's/student's right to education under Article 29 of the *Convention on the Rights of the Child* (CRC)[54] which articulates also the child's right to be educated for tolerance and peace and respect for diverse distinct groups, (b) Article 14 of the CRC on the child's right to freedom of thought, conscience and religion and (c) Article 13 of the CRC regarding the child's right to freedom of expression. It is here argued further that highlighting, through whatever means, by public authorities in public schools a particular religious faith violates (a) the State's obligation to secular neutrality of State schools, and (b) the people's right to freedom of thought and religion in a democracy. Those latter rights are set out in relevant international human rights law and democratic State Constitutions and/or in their State Bill of Rights. So-called 'culture wars' relating to religion and public schools are arguably thus a microcosm of an aspect of the struggle between democratic and undemocratic forces in the larger society. It is essential, on the view here, that the courts, domestic and international (i.e., international human rights courts) not defer to the State government on such matters but rather intervene to protect the fundamental democratic values relating to respect for pluralism.

[54] Convention on the Rights of the Child https://www.ohchr.org/sites/default/files/crc.pdf (Accessed August 22, 2024).

References

Materials

Convention on the Rights of the Child https://www.ohchr.org/en/instruments-mechanisms/instruments/convention-rights-child (Accessed August 22, 2024)

European Convention on Human Rights, Protocol I Article 2 https://www.echr.coe.int/documents/convention_eng.pdf (Accessed August 22, 2024)

European Court of Human Rights: Guide to Article 2 Protocol I Right to Education, European Convention on Human Rights https://www.right-to-education.org/sites/right-to-education.org/files/resource-attachments/ECHR_Guide_Art_2_Protocol_1_ENG_0.pdf (Accessed August 22, 2024)

News Desk Global Village Space (2023) Quebec Court rejects urgent relief for Muslim students in prayer room case: Quebec Court denies suspension of prayer room ban in public schools, reigniting debate on religious freedom and secularism. June 15, 2023 https://www.globalvillagespace.com/quebec-court-rejects-urgent-relief-for-muslim-students-in-prayer-room-case/ (Accessed August 22, 2024)

US Department of Education Guidance on Constitutionally Protected Prayer and Religious Expression in Public Elementary and Secondary Schools January 16, 2020, https://www2.ed.gov/policy/gen/guid/religionandschools/prayer_guidance.html (Accessed August 22, 2024)

United States Supreme Court Cases

City of Ocala, Florida v Art Rojas et al. (Supreme Court of the United States) No. 22-278. Decided March 6, 2023 (Justice Gorsuch and Justice Thomas Opinions) https://www.supremecourt.gov/opinions/22pdf/22-278_869d.pdf (Accessed August 22, 2024)

Kennedy v Bremerton School District (Supreme Court of the United States) No. 21-418. Argued April 25, 2022—Decided June 27, 2022 https://www.law.cornell.edu/supct/pdf/21-418.pdf (Accessed August 22, 2024)

Whole Woman's Health v Jackson (Supreme Court of the United States) No. 21-463. Argued November 1, 2021—Decided December 10, 2021 https://www.supremecourt.gov/opinions/21pdf/21-463_3ebh.pdf (Accessed August 22, 2024)

Yoder v Wisconsin 406 U.S. 205 (1972) https://supreme.justia.com/cases/federal/us/406/205/#tab-opinion-1949690 (Accessed August 22, 2024)

US Lower Court Cases

Washegesic v. Bloomingdale Public Schools, 33 F. 3d 679 (United States Court of Appeals, Sixth Circuit)

European Court of Human Rights Cases

Grzelak v. Poland (European Court of Human Rights) Application 7710/02 Judgment June 15, 2010 Information Note on the Court's case-law No. 131 (June 2010) Discrimination (Article 14 in conjunction with Article 9) at p. 16 https://www.echr.coe.int/documents/d/echr/CLIN_2010_06_131_ENG_878693 (Accessed August 22, 2024)

Konrad v. Germany (European Court of Human Rights) Application No. 35504/03, ECtHR (Fifth Section), 11 September 2006 https://www.lawpluralism.unimib.it/en/oggetti/163-konrad-v-germany-dec-no-35504-03-e-ct-hr-fifth-section-11-september-2006 (Accessed August 22, 2024)

Lautsi and Others v Italy (European Court of Human Rights) Grand Chamber (Application no. 30814/06) Judgment 18 March 2011

Perovy v Russia (European Court of Human Rights) Application no. 47429/09 Judgment 19 April 2021

Chapter 6
Selected US Culture Wars Involving the Scope of Authorities of Competing Sovereign Powers: The Court's Role

Abstract This chapter further examines the challenge to the US courts in so-called 'culture war' cases to straightforwardly reaffirm certain basic human rights through constitutional interpretation. The argument is made here that judicial reticence in this regard is a form of 'de-judicialization' undermining the role and sanctity of the courts in a democracy. The U.S. indigenous child welfare case discussed highlights the US Supreme Court's missed opportunity there to frame the core issues in the case as *not* just involving (a) the scope of competing authorities of various US sovereigns (the federal government, State government and indigenous tribal government) in the indigenous child welfare space but rather as (b) issues implicating also the need for judicial shielding of democratically based fundamental human rights. The 'Independent Legislature Theory' cases (discussed in the latter part of the chapter) raise the question of whether US States, through their legislatures, should be permitted to draw up extremely gerrymandered districting maps for federal voting purposes (i.e., thereby unfairly advantaging the candidates of the legislature's preferred party) without being fettered by State courts or the United State Supreme Court.

6.1 Introduction

For each of the cases discussed in this work, whether US cases or comparative law cases, cultural issues were central to the litigation for both sides of the contest. The 'culture war' issues involved arguably, in the final analysis, concern basic human rights. In the context of a court case, these so-called 'culture wars' raise the question as to whether (a) the courts are willing to step in and reaffirm basic human rights through constitutional interpretation or in contrast (b) select another option i.e., such as greatly narrowing the scope of the basic right at issue, negating the existence of that fundamental right, or deferring the matter to State legislatures etc. The reticence in such cases (where such occurs) of the courts to affirm basic human rights, it is here argued, is a form of 'de-judicialization' of the courts themselves that undermines democratic principles, values, and institutions.

Chapter 1 examined US Supreme Court Justice Thomas' view that personal autonomy in decision-making in a host of contexts could be constitutionally subject

S. C. Grover, *Litigating the Politics of Human Rights*, Ius Gentium: Comparative Perspectives on Law and Justice 121, https://doi.org/10.1007/978-3-031-82463-0_6

to State interference. Justice Thomas held in *Dobbs*[1] that private decision-making in the abortion context is not protected by any allegedly wrongly constitutionally inferred privacy right nor is such a privacy right, in his view, encompassed by the due process liberty guarantee. Chapter 2 examined a case in which the United States Supreme Court was asked to consider whether mandatory compliance with a State anti-discrimination public accommodation law constituted ‘compelled service’ or instead ‘compelled speech.’ This by requiring a custom wedding web designer to serve also same-sex couples and design their wedding websites notwithstanding the web designer’s religious belief that same-sex marriages are supposedly not true marriages. Chapter 3 addressed selected culture war litigation relating to the education setting. These latter cases concern the State banning of certain contested topics in classroom instruction at the school and university level and the State-ordered termination of diversity, equity, and inclusion initiatives at the university level. Also addressed in Chap. 3 was the United States Supreme Court’s analysis regarding challenges to affirmative action in admissions to US universities and its interpretation of the notion of ‘meritocracy’ in the US cultural ethos. The cases in sum implicate free expression rights, and the democratic value of plurality (in viewpoint and student population) and raise the specter of the State attempting to implement revisionist history. In Chap. 4 we revisited *Dobbs*,[2] this time to consider further the implications of the majority United States Supreme Court view in that case that rejected the notion of a constitutionally based right to abortion. This the majority did while simultaneously punting the practical implications of its decision to the States to sort out. However, no *Dobbs* United States Supreme Court guidelines were provided in that regard. Hence there is no assurance of any modicum of consistency between the various US States in their attempted resolution of the abortion issue nor in how the US States will address the potential broader rights implications of *Dobbs*[3] (i.e., for access to contraception, access to medication abortions, and for the right to US interstate travel to secure an abortion etc.). In Chap. 5 we examined the United States Supreme Court’s elevation of the supposed right of a school official to public displays of Christianity visible to the students at his/her/their public school arguably above that of (a) the students’(and parents’) right to freedom from State interference with their personal form of religious expression and belief or non-religious conviction and (b) above the need for protection at public school of religious plurality (including for agnostics and atheists) free from State interference.

---

[1]Dobbs, State Health Officer of the Mississippi Department of Health et al. v. Jackson Women’s Health Organization et. (United States Supreme Court) No. 19-1392. Argued December 1, 2021—Decided June 24, 2022.

[2]Dobbs, State Health Officer of the Mississippi Department of Health et al. v. Jackson Women’s Health Organization et. (United States Supreme Court) No. 19-1392. Argued December 1, 2021—Decided June 24, 2022.

[3]Dobbs, State Health Officer of the Mississippi Department of Health et al. v. Jackson Women’s Health Organization et. (United States Supreme Court) No. 19-1392. Argued December 1, 2021—Decided June 24, 2022.

Many would consider at least certain of the aforementioned so-called 'culture war' litigation examples to be premised on theatrics motivated by political agendas; and hence 'faux' or contrived culture wars in a sense. Others may view these and additional examples of US culture war litigation as premised on exaggerated and unfounded fears. This as manifest perhaps, for instance, by the Conservative leaning US Supreme Court majority holding in *Kennedy*.[4] That decision appears, at least in significant part, to be premised on a speculative need to protect religious expression (for instance of Christianity) even if by public officials while on duty and in a public manner. This need, according to the United States Supreme Court Kennedy majority, arises due to the already existing protection for secular views and practices in many public spaces. Hence, it would appear, the presumed underlying fear arises for some that such secular views may come, therefore, to dominate if there is no countervailing protection for public expression of religious perspectives even in supposedly neutral forums such as public school settings.

The cases discussed in this concluding chapter, however, cannot reasonably be characterized as involving 'faux' culture wars or exaggerated fears of loss of identity. *Haaland v Brackeen*,[5] for example, involves the placement in adoptive or foster homes of "Indian children" (to use the language of the US federal *Indian Child Welfare Act* (ICWA) of 1978 which language refers to children of indigenous North American ethnicity/ancestry). 'Indian child' under the ICWA federal law is defined as:

> Any unmarried person under the age of 18 who is either:
>
> 1. A member of a federally recognized Indian Tribe; or,
> 2. The biological child of a member of a federally recognized Indian Tribe and is eligible for membership in a federally recognized Indian Tribe.[6]

Note that the Tribe can enroll an eligible child in the Tribe even over parental objection or other lack of parental consent circumstance.[7]

The Haaland case is properly to be considered in the larger historical context of (a) the separation of significant numbers of North American indigenous children from their biological family and indigenous communities in the US through the residential school system in pre-ICWA times and (b) the contested historical and ongoing disproportionately high rate of removal of North American indigenous children in the US from their families of origin for placement in US non-indigenous foster and adoptive settings outside their indigenous communities. *Haaland* then involves, in large part, the risk to North American indigenous culture,

---

[4] Kennedy v Bremerton School District (Supreme Court of the United States) No. 21-418. Argued April 25, 2022—Decided June 27, 2022.

[5] Haaland v Brackeen 599 U. S. ____ (2023) https://www.scotusblog.com/case-files/cases/brackeen-v-haaland/ (Accessed August 22, 2024).

[6] US Department of the Interior: Indian Affairs ICWA https://www.bia.gov/bia/ois/dhs/icwa/icwa-notice (Accessed August 22, 2024).

[7] Haaland v Brackeen 599 U. S. ____ (2023) In the Supreme Court of the United States Dissent (Justice Thomas) at p. 4.

community and Tribal survival should there no longer be any mitigation measures imposed on the aforementioned patterns through the ICWA. *Haaland v Brackeen* thus is, in every sense, a genuine 'culture war' of unique and historical significance implicating the fundamental human rights of North American indigenous children[8] and their indigenous communities and Tribes in the US.

In *Moore v Harper*[9] (also to be discussed in this chapter) the lower court found that the North Carolina State legislature had unlawfully and unfairly gerrymandered its redistricting voting map in extreme fashion to greatly favor the Republican Party in federal elections. The North Carolina State legislature petitioned the United States Supreme Court to *eliminate* the constraints on their gerrymandering (constraints effected through the State courts relying on the State Constitution).[10] The Republican proponents of the extreme gerrymandering relied on 'The Independent State Legislature Theory/Doctrine' (to be here discussed) to argue that there is a purported constitutional basis for undercutting State court authority directed to ensuring a fair redistricting voting map for federal elections. The Moore case then involves, in part, the US 'culture war' regarding the scope of "State rights', here in the context of the voting rights issue. More fundamentally, however, *Moore* involves the voting right in federal elections and whether the US State and Federal courts are prepared to protect this fundamental human right through constitutional interpretation. A parallel 'Independent State Legislature Theory' Alabama case is also discussed.

Note that both the Haaland and the Moore cases involve, in part, the issue of the proper scope of authorities of various sovereign powers and, as well, the court's obligation to shield and uphold certain fundamental human rights. In *Haaland* the legal contest is in part between North American indigenous federal tribes in the United States (the Tribes being themselves sovereign entities) versus outside political entities and individuals seeking to override the hierarchy of adoptive and foster placement preferences under the ICWA. The latter issue then implicates a) the individual and collective fundamental human rights of North American indigenous children caught up in the US child welfare system as well as b) the collective rights of North American indigenous communities and Tribes in the United States. In *Moore* there is a contest between a) a certain Republican State legislature seeking to gerrymander a voting map in order to secure an inevitable victory in a federal

---

[8]While the term "Indian" is considered offensive by some North American persons of indigenous ancestry, it is used here only since the US *Indigenous Child Welfare Act* (ICWA) uses the term and the term is used in the Haaland v Brackeen case. 'Indian' under the ICWA refers to a person who is a member of an Indian tribe while an Indian child under the ICWA is a child who is member of an Indian tribe" or both "eligible for membership in an Indian tribe" *and* "the biological child of a member of an Indian tribe." Haaland v Brackeen 599 U. S. ____ (2023) In the Supreme Court of the United States See Brief in Opposition of Respondents, Cherokee Nation, Oneida Nation, Quinault Indian Nation, and Morongo Band of Mission Indians at p 6 citing ICWA.

[9]Moore v Harper https://www.supremecourt.gov/docket/docketfiles/html/public/21-1271.html (Accessed August 22, 2024).

[10]The North Carolina Supreme Court in *Moore* reversed itself and ruled it had no jurisdiction over partisan voting map gerrymandering cases but that ruling was reversed by the United States Supreme Court.

election without the possibility of State judicial interference and b) political opponents who seek, through the courts, a fair redistricting map for voting in federal elections in the State (that is, a map which would give fair representation in the voting process to all, including African Americans in various districts in the State in question).

It is argued in this chapter that the term 'culture wars' in describing the litigation discussed in this book ought not to be used, as is commonly the case, to obfuscate the fundamental human rights matters at issue nor reduce them to purported mere policy/political disputes. *Haaland* and *Moore* are useful in highlighting the latter point as will be discussed in what follows.

6.2 Competing Sovereign Powers in the US Indigenous Child Welfare Context: Brackeen v. Haaland 994 F.3d 249 (*en banc* Fifth Circuit Court of Appeals) Decided Apr 6, 2021

The Plaintiffs in this case brought suit in Federal court and are "several couples who seek to adopt or foster Indian children, a woman who wishes for her Indian biological child to be adopted by non Indians, and the States of Texas, Louisiana, and Indiana. Defendants are the United States, federal agencies and officials charged with administering the ICWA [the Indian Child Welfare Act] …as well as several Indian tribes that intervened in support of ICWA."[11] The *en banc* Appeal Court noted that in *Brackeen* (a) the State plaintiffs challenging the ICWA are States with a very small percentage of Indian Tribes residing there and that (b) the remaining US States (which are non-plaintiffs) had no objections to the ICWA and its implications for child welfare proceedings concerning Indian children in their respective States. The Appeal Court *en banc* majority decision on standing is complex with divided opinion on which plaintiff had standing for which issue (i.e., challenging Congress' authority to enact the ICWA, anti-commandeering challenges, the equal protection challenge etc.), In the final analysis, the *en banc* majority did *not* dismiss the case for lack of standing and instead ruled on the merits. The *en banc* majority Appeals Court held that (a) Congress had the authority, (i) under the Constitution and (ii) given its historical and enduring obligations to Indian Tribes, to enact the ICWA and that (b) the "Indian child" classification does *not* violate the equal protection rights of prospective non-indigenous adoptive or foster parents seeking to adopt or foster an Indian child.

The *en banc* Court of Appeals decision regarding the equal protection issue on the ICWA hierarchy of placement preferences was complex. The ICWA articulates certain hierarchical placement preferences for "Indian children." The State court

[11] Brackeen v. Haaland 994 F.3d 249 (5th Cir. 2021) Decided Apr 6, 2021.

considering any such Indian child welfare placement case must (a) follow the ICWA placement hierarchical preference ranking or (b) an alternate hierarchy of placement preference ranking if such exists as determined by Tribal resolution. This with the proviso that the placement decided on is 'the least restrictive' of those available. As we will discuss, on the view here, these ICWA placement priorities must be considered with regard to the child's best interests, and the child's individual and collective fundamental human rights. Furthermore, such placement decisions, it is here argued, per international child human rights law, must be also guided by the fact that "considering the collective cultural rights of the child is part of determining the child's best interests."[12]

The Petitioners (Plaintiffs) argue that the ICWA hierarchy of placement preferences violates the Equal Protection Clause and places non-Indian prospective foster and adoptive parents at an unfair disadvantage respecting their foster or adoption applications. By implication, it seems fair to suggest that the Petitioners contend that allegedly too often the ICWA places Indigenous Tribal group interests above the individual rights and interests of the Indian child. This, the Petitioners hold, is possible by the ICWA's granting the child's Tribe the authority to challenge a state-ordered placement of an Indian child to a non-indigenous setting and to permit such (a) even after the child may have been in that non-indigenous setting for some time and (b) as against the wishes of one or both of the child's biological parents (where such biological parental objections exist). (However, at the same time, under the ICWA the wishes of the biological parent(s) are to be considered where feasible and appropriate).

The Defendants appear to essentially have argued that the ICWA hierarchy of placement preferences are (a) in the children's and simultaneously the Tribe's best interest and (b) are essential for the preservation of the Tribe and for the children's right to cultural continuity i.e., connection of the child to their indigenous community. In the latter regard it is relevant to note that international child human rights law recognizes the indigenous child's right to cultural continuity (note that the US signed but did not ratify the *Convention on the Rights of the Child*).[13] International humanitarian law also acknowledges the child's right to cultural continuity.[14] This as the 'best interests of the child' are (the international consensus seems to be), in

[12] See Committee on the Rights of the Child, General Comment No. 11 (2009) *Indigenous children and their rights under the Convention* CRC/C/GC/11 Best Interests of the Child para 32 https://www2.ohchr.org/english/bodies/crc/docs/gc.11_indigenous_new.pdf (Accessed August 22, 2024).

[13] See Committee on the Rights of the Child General Comment No. 11 (2009) Indigenous children and their rights under the Convention CRC/C/GC/11 Best Interests of the Child para 30–33 https://www2.ohchr.org/english/bodies/crc/docs/gc.11_indigenous_new.pdf (Accessed August 22, 2024).

[14] Protocol Additional to the Geneva Conventions of 12 August 1949, and relating to the Protection of Victims of International Armed Conflicts (Protocol I), 8 June 1977. Article 78(2) providing for continuity in the child's education including religious when a child is evacuated for safety by an occupying power https://ihl-databases.icrc.org/en/ihl-treaties/api-1977/article-78 (Accessed August 22, 2024).

part at least, importantly intricately connected to the child's right to cultural and familial continuity insofar as feasible.

The ICWA hierarchy of placement preferences upheld as constitutional by the *en banc* Appeals Court were "adoptive placements with a member of the child's extended family"[15] or "other members of the Indian child's tribe" but *not* held constitutional was the adoptive placement preference with "other Indian families."[16] Also rejected as unconstitutional was a preference for licensed Indian foster homes over non-Indian foster homes.[17] The Fifth Circuit *en banc* Court of Appeals was divided on (a) whether the adoptive placement preference for "other Indian families" and (b) whether the preference for licensed Indian foster homes over non-Indian foster homes discriminated on the basis of race. The Appeals Court *en banc* thus affirmed the District Court ruling that these latter two provisions are unconstitutional (that is they violate the Equal Protection Clause). The Fifth Circuit *en banc* majority Appeals Court decision on anti-commandeering (unconstitutional usurping through the ICWA federal statute of State authority by the federal government) is complex with the opinion varying depending on the specific ICWA provision at issue.

The parties in opposition to the plaintiffs' challenge to the ICWA hierarchy of placement preferences (that is the parties supporting the constitutionality of the ICWA) contend that the ICWA definition of "Indian child" is a *political status designation* relating to Indian tribal membership or eligibility for tribal membership and *not* a racial classification. A racial classification would no doubt, based on United State Supreme Court precedent, violate the Constitution's Equal Protection Clause. The Cherokee Nation, Oneida Nation, Quinault Indian Nation, and Morongo Band of Mission Indians argued that evidence that 'Indian child' under the ICWA is *not* a racial classification includes the fact that even *nonindigenous* extended family may receive the highest preference for foster or adoptive placement of an Indian child precisely because they are extended family. At the same time, persons who are ethnically Indian (of Indigenous North American heritage) may receive no preference for placement of the Indian child if they are not tribal members and/or not eligible for the same. The latter group would be in the same position then in terms of placement preference order of priority as were the non-indigenous individual petitioners in *Brackeen* seeking to adopt Indian children. Also, children who are not of

---

[15]National Indian Library, ICWA Guide online: Placement (16.2) "The definition of extended family member under the ICWA includes both Indian and non-Indian relatives. Some tribal laws express a preference for extended family members who are members of the tribe" https://narf.org/nill/documents/icwa/faq/placement.html#Q2 (Accessed August 22, 2024).

[16]Brackeen v. Haaland 994 F.3d 249 (5th Cir. 2021) Decided Apr 6, 2021.

[17]For foster placement and pre-adoptive placement, the ICWA first preference is given to the child's extended family, then a foster home licensed and approved by the child's Indian tribe followed in order of preference by "an Indian foster home licensed or approved by an authorized non-Indian licensing authority," and an "institution for children approved by an Indian tribe or operated by an Indian organization which has a program suitable to meet the Indian child's needs." See US Department of the Interior: Indian Affairs ICWA https://www.bia.gov/bia/ois/dhs/icwa/icwa-notice (Accessed August 22, 2024).

Indian heritage may be Indian under the ICWA if they are the child of a Tribal member (Note that the Tribes determine eligibility for membership).

In sum the Brackeen *en banc* Court of Appeals agreed that the first two ICWA placement preferences relied on *political status* and therefore did *not* offend the Constitution's Equal Protection Clause. More specifically, the Court of Appeals agreed with the indigenous Tribes that the ICWA first preference for placement with the extended family operates *independent* of 'race' and the second preference of placement with a member of the child's tribal nation refers directly to a political status.

Another question, as mentioned previously, is whether the hierarchy of placement preferences under the 1978 ICWA (federal law) exceeds Congress' constitutional authority relating to Indian affairs. That is, the question arises as to whether the ICWA's hierarchy of placement preferences constitutes 'commandeering' of State authority such that State law is preempted in State court by the requirements of federal law; here the ICWA. The Cherokee Nation, Oneida Nation, Quinault Indian Nation, and Morongo Band of Mission Indians argued that the placement preferences reflected in the 1978 ICWA represents an attempt to redress the "existential crisis" that North American indigenous peoples in the US face in large part in light of past US colonial practices and their legacy. These adverse practices include (a) the residential school system and (b) the longstanding overrepresentation of Indian children in the US child welfare system and their placement often in non-indigenous US homes (the latter due in large part to systemic negative biases in US social policy/social work attitude and practice affecting North American indigenous children). The Cherokee Nation, Oneida Nation, Quinault Indian Nation, and Morongo Band of Mission Indians emphasized that the ICWA seeks to ensure through its hierarchy of placement preferences (applied when all else is equal) that (a) the individual indigenous child's best interests are served and that (b) the stability and longevity of Indian families and Tribes is safeguarded. Indeed, there would appear to be *no rational nonbiased basis* for suggesting that the two latter ICWA objectives are generally *ipso facto* mutually exclusive.

The aforementioned Indigenous Nation parties in *Brackeen*[18] (arguing *in support* of the constitutionality and value of the ICWA) also maintained that the Petitioners had no standing in the federal court. This as US child welfare matters are decided in US State courts. The Indigenous Nations Respondents here argued further that (a) a US federal lower court judgment could *not* bind a US State court in a child welfare matter concerning an 'Indian child' and that (b) the State- specific child welfare cases at issue in *Brackeen* had, in any case, in fact ended and the cases were therefore moot. The Brackeen *en banc* Appeals Court held that while their federal ruling was not binding on the State Court, a favorable ruling for the remaining State Plaintiff (Texas) challenging the ICWA "would remedy the alleged injury to states by making

[18] Brackeen v. Haaland 994 F.3d 249 (5th Cir. 2021) Decided Apr 6, 2021 https://casetext.com/case/brackeen-v-haaland (Accessed August 22, 2024).

their compliance with ICWA and the Final Rule[19] optional rather than compulsory."[20] The *en banc* Appeals Court did *not* concur, as mentioned, that the individual and State Plaintiff claims in *Brackeen* were entirely moot and rendered a complex decision on the merits of various claims as discussed.

6.2.1 Haaland v Brackeen 599 U. S. ____ (2023) (Supreme Court of the United States)

The Supreme Court of the United States in *Haaland* held that (a) the (federal) power of Congress to regulate matters involving and impacting North American Indian persons in the United States ('Indian' as defined by federal statute) is unqualified and exclusive and that (b) the federal power *overrides* both State and tribal authority in this domain but is *not* an unlimited power.[21] The *Haaland* Supreme Court also referred to previous United States Supreme Court case precedent in which the powers of Congress overrode State authority in child welfare matters such as adoption proceedings concerning 'Indian' children.[22] Let us consider then the Court's reference to a "trust relationship" between the United States and the Indian people [that] informs the exercise of legislative power."[23] While a "trust relationship" is to inform the exercise of federal legislative powers regarding so-called 'Indian affairs' in the US; one can reasonably challenge to what degree the US Congress has exercised properly and fully its duty from that perspective. Arguably had such a "trust relationship" been the case, there would have been no need for federal legislation such as the ICWA. The latter, afterall, is designed to attempt to eliminate longstanding systemic injustices impacting especially vulnerable North American indigenous children in the US. On the respectful view here, the rather *pro forma* discussion of the Majority in *Haaland* regarding a "trust relationship" between the US federal government and North American indigenous peoples in

[19]The Final rule issued by the US Bureau of Indian Affairs is intended to "clarify the minimum Federal standards governing implementation of [ICWA]" and to ensure that it "is applied in all States consistent with the Act's express language." See Brackeen v. Haaland 994 F.3d 249 (5th Cir. 2021) Decided Apr 6, 2021 https://casetext.com/case/brackeen-v-haaland at p. 27 (Accessed August 22, 2024).

[20]Brackeen v. Haaland 994 F.3d 249 (5th Cir. 2021) Decided Apr 6, 2021 https://casetext.com/case/brackeen-v-haaland at p. 37 (Accessed August 22, 2024).

[21]The United States Supreme Court Haaland majority thus (a) *rejected* the 'anti-commandeering' arguments of the Petitioners and (b) held that the ICWA fits within the scope of US Congressional powers and was intended to protect the longevity and integrity of North American Indian tribes in the United States. The Federal government, the Haaland US Supreme Court's majority held, conceived of ICWA as in the best interests of Indian children.

[22]The Term 'Indian' is used here as it is used in the case and refers to indigenous children in the US in this context.

[23]Haaland v Brackeen 599 U. S. ____ (2023) In the Supreme Court of the United States Syllabus at p. 3.

the United States does *not* equate to the necessary deep consideration by the Haaland US Supreme Court majority of (a) the *fundamental human rights issues* at play in the case for North American indigenous children individually and collectively and (b) for their tribal communities and Tribes.

The issues in *Haaland*, on the analysis here, were in important part framed by the US Supreme Court majority strictly in terms of the tension between Congressional (federal) authority on the one hand and the Petitioner (Plaintiff) State authority on the other. As a result, for instance, the Court found that the 'Commerce Clause' also entails Congress' alleged power to regulate the requirements for foster and pre-adoption placement and adoption involving North American indigenous children in the US. This notwithstanding Petitioners' argument that "children are not commodities that can be traded."[24] The Court's majority did *not* address the fact that, in the final analysis, contested federal indigenous child welfare authority (i.e., as supposedly derived from the 'Commerce Clause' etc.) itself triggers fundamental human rights questions. Instead, the Court (on the respectful view here) simply derides that fundamental human rights frame and offers an alternate context for analysis; one that essentially evades the human rights core question. This as when it states, "This point [referring to Petitioners' point that children are not commodities to be traded] while rhetorically powerful, ignores the Court's precedent interpreting the Indian Commerce Clause to encompass not only trade but *also other Indian affairs* (emphasis added)."[25] Thus, the human rights interests of the Tribes and of indigenous children (in dispute between the parties in regards to whether these are being served well and good by the ICWA) are, on the view here, surgically and without much verbiage by the Court, essentially removed from the analysis. Such concerns are replaced by an antiseptic, formalistic consideration of the alleged 'origin story' of US Congressional (federal) powers over so-called "Indian affairs" held by the Haaland United States Supreme Court majority to (a) include the power to regulate indigenous family law matters and (b) to supersede State law in the proper case where there is a conflict with federal law.

Another example of the Haaland US Supreme Court majority sidestepping the fundamental human rights issues in this case involves, on the view here, the Court's consideration of the Petitioners' claims regarding the "active efforts" clause of the ICWA. The ICWA requires that in involuntary proceedings (those involving termination of parental rights or a foster placement), the Petitioner (private or public) be able to demonstrate that "active efforts" were made to keep the indigenous (Indian) family together. The Haaland United States Supreme Court majority found the provision to be constitutional but did *not* do so using, in whole or in part, a child

---

[24]Haaland v Brackeen 599 U. S. ____ (2023) In the Supreme Court of the United States Syllabus at pp. 3–4.

[25]Haaland v Brackeen 599 U. S. ____ (2023) In the Supreme Court of the United States Syllabus at p. 4.

rights analysis/interpretation.[26] Nor did the majority, in particular, rely on a 'best interest of the child' consideration. Rather the Court reaches this conclusion on the basis that the "active efforts" ICWA provision does not allegedly involve 'commandeering' of State powers. This, according to the Haaland majority, in that the ICWA 'active efforts' provision applies to both State (public) and private petitioners and a "demand that either public or private actors can satisfy is unlikely to require the use of sovereign power."[27] The Haaland US Supreme Court majority thus arguably does *not* address whether the ICWA "active efforts" provision, applied in all Indian child welfare cases (to keep the Indian family together and the child in his or her (their) tribal community where feasible), is always in the individual child's best interest and consistent with respect for the individual child's autonomous human rights.

Justice Barrett, writing for the US Supreme Court majority in *Haaland*, noted that the State courts are, under the ICWA, required to place the Indian child with an Indian family "if one is available. That is so even if the child is already living with a non-Indian family and the state court thinks it in the child's best interest to stay there."[28] The latter statement by Justice Barrett must, it is here argued, be properly considered, however, in the larger context. That context involves in part the child's individual and collective basic human right to cultural community and continuity. It is to be noted that in one Indian child welfare case that underlies *Haaland*, the Tribal authority ultimately withdrew its objections to the adoption by a non-indigenous applicant couple of an Indian child tribal member. The latter suggests that there was an ongoing assessment and re-assessment by that Tribal authority of the facts in the particular case. In another case, the Indian family withdrew from consideration as a potential placement for the Indian child in question.

On the view here, a central rights issue, largely if not completely ignored in *Haaland*, is that Congress, in enacting the ICWA foster and adoption placement preferences, did *not* in any significant measure speak to the matter of the Indian child's *autonomous fundamental human rights*. Rather the core issue, as framed by the ICWA, and as interpreted by the US Supreme Court majority in *Haaland*, is one of indigenous children being a vital "resource" for the indigenous Tribe as are the

---

[26] Note that the right of persons, including the child, not to have his or her family relations arbitrarily interfered with or broken are incorporated in the *International Covenant on Civil and Political Rights* (ICCPR) (which the US ratified in 1992) at Article 17:"No one shall be subjected to arbitrary or unlawful interference with his privacy, family, home or correspondence, nor to unlawful attacks on his honour and reputation. 2. Everyone has the right to the protection of the law against such interference or attacks." https://treaties.un.org/doc/treaties/1976/03/19760323%2006-17%20am/ch_iv_04.pdf (Accessed August 22, 2024).

[27] Haaland v Brackeen v. 599 U. S. ____ (2023) In the Supreme Court of the United States Syllabus at p. 4.

[28] Haaland v Brackeen v. 599 U. S. ____ (2023) In the Supreme Court of the United States Majority Opinion (Justice Barrett) at p. 2. The ICWA has been a safeguard against, for instance, North American Indian children being removed from their biological or extended family due to familial impoverished circumstances when there are alternatives which would allow for the child to stay connected to family and Tribe.

children of any sovereign State: "there is no *resource* that is more vital to the continued existence and integrity of Indian tribes than their children (emphasis added)."[29] It seems relevant to note also that for prospective foster and adoptive parents, indigenous children may seem a "resource" for fulfilling their parenting dreams. Certain of the Petitioners in this case had plans to foster and then adopt more Indian children than only those who were the subjects of the current suit. One can then appreciate that such a trend on a larger scale, if without ICWA safeguards (mitigation measures) in place, could have serious detrimental consequences for the biological and cultural longevity of the North American Indigenous Tribes in the United States. However, the central question also arises as to what is in the best interests of the indigenous child on the facts of the particular case considering the full range of their autonomous individual and collective fundamental human rights.

It will be recalled, as here previously discussed, that international child human rights law (the *Convention on the Rights of the Child*),[30] amongst other international law instruments, considers the child's right to familial and cultural continuity to be a vital aspect in determining their 'best interest.' With that in mind then, respectfully, Justice Alito arguably oversimplifies in his Dissent in the United States Supreme Court decision in *Haaland* in terms of his analysis pertaining to the equal protection and 'best interest of the child' issues. This is reflected, on the view here, in his arguably potentially incendiary statements such as: "… in many cases, provisions of the Indian Child Welfare Act (ICWA) compel actions that conflict with …fundamental state policy subordinating what family-court judges—and often biological parents—determine to be in the best interest of a child to what Congress believed is in the best interest of a tribe."[31] Rather, it is here argued, in contrast to Justice Alito's latter characterization, that Congress, through the ICWA, sought to mitigate the historically disproportionately high separation of North American Indian children from their families and Tribal communities (that separation effectuated through State child welfare activities and State court proceedings). This in that separation of any child (indigenous or non-indigenous) from their family and community for less than highly compelling non-discriminatory reasons and consistent with the child's rights and interests is unconstitutional and contrary to democratic values. Those values include respect for individual and collective human rights, for individual and collective human dignity and for the child's autonomous personhood.

The *Haaland* United States Supreme Court also held that the ICWA requirement for a "diligent search" for placements that are ICWA compliant (in terms of the statutorily articulated placement priority preferences) is lawful and constitutional.

---

[29] Congressional statement on the ICWA Cited in Haaland v Brackeen 599 U. S. ____ (2023) In the Supreme Court of the United States Majority Opinion (Justice Barrett) at p. 2.

[30] Committee on the Rights of the Child General Comment No. 11 (2009) Indigenous children and their rights under the Convention CRC/C/GC/11 Best Interests of the Child https://www2.ohchr.org/english/bodies/crc/docs/gc.11_indigenous_new.pdf (Accessed August 22, 2024).

[31] Haaland v Brackeen 599 U. S. ____ (2023) In the Supreme Court of the United States Dissenting Opinion (Justice Alito) at p. 2.

This in that it is the Tribe or other petitioning party *not* the State agencies that must demonstrate such a diligent effort[32] (thus there is no commandeering of the State's authority by federal power under the ICWA in this regard). However, the *Haaland* United States Supreme Court majority held that the *State courts* must comply with the ICWA articulated placement preferences and other requirements and that "... Congress can require state courts, unlike state executives and legislatures, to enforce federal law"[33] consistent with the Constitution's Supremacy Clause (i.e., enforce ICWA placement preferences).

6.2.2 Indigenous Tribal Status as a 'Political Status'

Recall that the Brackeen Appeal Court[34] had ruled that Indigenous tribal status is a 'political' not a 'racial' classification. Hence the Appeal Court held that the ICWA (a) concerns federal powers as applied to a *political* group and (b) therefore does *not* violate the Equal Protection constitutional guarantee regarding the prohibition against racial discrimination, at least for (i) the ICWA top two adoption placement preferences (namely extended family and, where extended family is not available, then another family of the child's Tribe) and (ii) the Tribes' power under the statute to alter ICWA ordering of placement preferences in the particular case.[35]

Complicating the situation is arguably the fact that 'racial' classification itself is inherently a political and socio-cultural construction rather than a scientifically fact-based categorization.[36] In any case, at the very least, *perceived* 'race' intersects with the political and the socio-cultural (the cultural, language, religious distinctions etc. that identify a community of people as a distinct separable group or community). This is evident also in the matter here in that "Tribal enrollment requirements preserve the unique character and traditions of each tribe. The tribes establish membership criteria based on shared customs, traditions, language and tribal blood."[37] (Tribal blood refers to lineal descendancy from someone on the Tribal membership original base list; arguably the original Tribal political entity at issue).

---

[32] Haaland v Brackeen 599 U. S. ____ (2023) In the Supreme Court of the United States Syllabus at p. 5.

[33] Haaland v Brackeen 599 U. S. ____ (2023) In the Supreme Court of the United States Syllabus at p. 6.

[34] Brackeen v. Haaland 994 F.3d 249 (5th Cir. 2021) Decided Apr 6, 2021 https://casetext.com/case/brackeen-v-haaland (Accessed August 22, 2024).

[35] US Equal Employment Opportunity Commission Employment Discrimination based on Religion, Ethnicity, or Country of Origin https://www.eeoc.gov/laws/guidance/employment-discrimination-based-religion-ethnicity-or-country-origin (Accessed August 22, 2024).

[36] Gannon (2016).

[37] Tribal Enrollment Process US Department of Labor https://www.doi.gov/tribes/enrollment (Accessed August 22, 2024).

In *Haaland*, the Tribal Respondents and the Federal government and others supporting the ICWA held Tribal status to be politically and not racially based. In *Haaland* the Petitioners, however, claimed that Indian families were given preference based on 'race'; essentially arguing then that indigenous tribal membership acted as a proxy for what the Petitioners perceived as race. It is to be recalled however that the first ICWA foster or adoptive placement preference for an Indian child under the ICWA is with extended family *whether or not they be nonindigenous extended family*. The latter particular instance then would seem *ipso facto* not to trigger Equal Protection concerns and to contradict, in part at least, the Petitioners' characterization of the ICWA's alleged overall racial discriminatory objective and implications.

6.2.3 Sidestepping the Foundational Equal Protection Rights Issue in Haaland

On the view here, the United States Supreme Court sidestepped the foundational equal protection rights issue in *Haaland*. This even though arguably it is core to the case. It is to be stressed here that the equal protection issue in this case is compelling not only with regard to the Petitioners but also the Indian children involved. For instance, the Indian child's equal protection rights are arguably being well served by the ICWA first two placement preferences at least. Those particular placement preferences serve to maintain the Indian child's connection to family and/or to the particular Indian Tribe to which they belong or are eligible to belong. The latter through placement (unless good cause can be shown to the contrary of these placement preferences) with extended family or another family of the same Tribe as the child's where extended family is not available for whatever reason.[38]

The Haaland US Supreme Court majority states "*The Court does not reach the merits of Petitioners' two additional claims—an equal protection challenge to ICWA's placement preferences and a nondelegation*[39] *challenge to …the provision allowing tribes to alter the placement preferences*."[40] The equal protection issue re ICWA placement preferences was not addressed by the US Supreme Court and all the ICWA placement preferences were left intact on the alleged basis that none of the

[38]National Indian Library 25 U.S.C. § 1915. Placement of Indian children http://www.narf.org/nill/documents/icwa/faq/placement.html#:~:text=In%20any%20adoptive%20placement%20of,(3)%20other%20Indian%20families (Accessed August 22, 2024).

[39]The delegation issue involves considering whether Tribes as sovereigns have the independent right to determine the proper placement for the Indian child enrolled in or eligible for enrollment in the Tribe such that the Tribe's view on the appropriate placement in the normal course should take precedence. Those challenging the ICWA in *Brackeen* and *Haaland* argue that the ICWA delegates legislative powers to the Tribes and that this violates the US Constitution.

[40]Haaland v Brackeen v 599 U. S. ____ (2023) In the Supreme Court of the United States Syllabus at p. 6.

individual Petitioners nor Texas had standing to bring the equal protection claims. Thus, the ICWA placement preference regarding "other Indian families" (not members of the child's Tribe) for adoption and foster homes was retained. This despite the lower court's finding that this latter placement priority is unconstitutional.[41] This was the outcome as the lower court was found by the United States Supreme Court Haaland majority to *not* have had jurisdiction to address the equal protection claims relating to the ICWA placement preferences. This being the case due to the alleged lack of standing of the Petitioners regarding advancing such claims. The end result was then regarding placement preferences, as mentioned, that the ICWA placement priorities in their entirety remain unchanged.

The individual non-State parties (the non-indigenous couples) in *Haaland* argued that they were disadvantaged in the foster and adoption proceedings regarding an Indian child compared to Indian family applicants. The Haaland US Supreme Court majority found, however, that those individual parties would *not* (on the Court's view) actually be obtaining a remedy through judicial relief if the Court granted their application for (a) an injunction on federal authorities upholding ICWA placement preferences and (b) a declaratory judgment designating the challenged ICWA placement provisions as unconstitutionally discriminatory against non-Indian families. This in that the state agencies that implement the ICWA were *not* named parties to the suit and would *not*, according to the Haaland majority, be bound by an injunction or a declaratory judgment stipulating the legal rights of the parties in this case. The Haaland US Supreme Court majority maintained on that foregoing rationale that neither (a) the individual non-indigenous couples as parties nor (b) the individual Indian biological mother as a party had standing to raise the equal protection issue.

Furthermore, Texas (the remaining State party) was held by the majority in *Haaland* (a) to have no rights of its own under the Equal Protection Act and (b) no *parens patriae* jurisdiction against the Federal Defendants here that would have conferred standing. The majority also found that the State allegedly would not be injured by the ICWA placement preferences or the ability of tribal authorities to alter placement preferences for an Indian child. It is yet an open question, it is here argued, as to whether (a) Texas had *parens patriae* jurisdiction in this case with respect to the particular Indian children at issue here and (b) whether Texas has *parens patriae* jurisdiction more generally with respect to all Indian children caught up in the child welfare system in Texas. This in that the Texas State Court is complying with a federal mandate in its placement orders (the ICWA federal law) with respect to Indian children in child welfare matters (adoption and foster placement). This then creates a unique situation in that normally the Federal government is not involved with State child welfare matters. Here, however, the State courts are

---

[41] See Haaland v Brackeen 599 U. S. ____ (2023) In the Supreme Court of the United States majority opinion (Justice Barrett) at p. 34 "On the equal protection and nondelegation claims, we vacate the judgment of the Court of Appeals and remand with instructions to dismiss for lack of jurisdiction."

intricately intertwined with a Federal jurisdictional matter (the enforcement of the ICWA) as are the State child welfare agencies that enforce the State court order. This then arguably confers standing relating to *parens patriae* on the State involved, here the State of Texas.

As to injury to the State resulting from the ICWA, the Haaland majority rejected Texas' argument that it, as a State, was injured by the ICWA placement preferences. This as the State argued the need to be "colour-blind" in regard to custody proceedings involving its citizens (the child welfare cases at issue originated in Texas). The Haaland majority found that such injury was *not* the concrete particularized injury required for standing and that the cost implications of various provisions of the ICWA also did not meet the test for conferring standing on the State. The majority also found that the State allegedly would not in fact be injured by the ICWA's placement preferences or the ability of tribal authorities to alter placement preferences for an Indian child.[42]

It would seem on the current analysis, however, that an injury to the State would result in a concrete particularized way should (a) the State not be able to exercise *parens patriae* jurisdiction over this distinct specific vulnerable child group (Indian children in the child welfare system in Texas caught up in State judicial proceedings that admittedly are informed by a controlling federal law) and (b) the State be unable to ensure that these children received equal treatment under the law and equal benefit of the law with respect to prioritizing the child's best interest and his/her (their) fundamental human rights. Note that the State courts normally are obligated to transfer such cases to tribal authorities but need not do so where there is just cause not to. Thus, the State courts still retain jurisdiction to consider each case individually.

Where the State retains jurisdiction; the Tribal authority has the right under the ICWA to intervene in the State court proceedings.[43] State courts need *not* follow a Tribal authorized reordering of the ICWA placement priorities where the placement would not result in the 'least restrictive setting.' Thus, State courts are considering ICWA placement preferences and any Tribal authorized re-ordering in concert with considerations of the child's best interests. The State then, as a sovereign, surely (on the view here) has *parens patriae* interests and jurisdiction as do the Indian Tribes; each as distinct sovereign entities. The State not being able to exercise State *parens patriae* jurisdiction over this group, Indian children in the child welfare system in Texas, would (it is here argued) seem to undermine the integrity, credibility and ultimately the authority of the State as a distinct sovereign thereby creating a concrete particularized injury to the State.

---

[42] Haaland v Brackeen 599 U. S. ____ (2023) In the Supreme Court of the United States Majority Opinion (Justice Barrett) at pp. 32–33.

[43] Ablavsky, G (Q and A with S Driscoll) (June 30, 2023) Stanford's Greg Ablavsky on the Brackeen Indian Child Welfare Act Decision https://law.stanford.edu/2023/06/30/stanfords-greg-ablavsky-on-the-brackeen-indian-child-welfare-act-decision/ (Accessed August 22, 2024).

The ICWA is grounded on the notion that its provisions (including the hierarchy of placement priorities that serve to connect the child to his/her/their Indian community to the greatest extent feasible and proper in the circumstance) do in parallel serve (a) the best interests of the child and (b) the collective interests of the indigenous Tribes. Yet the 'best interest of the child' standard applied by the State Court or Tribal Authority in the individual case with complex facts is a vague one further complicating the equal protection matter. Whether *parens patriae* concerns by the State, based on the ICWA hierarchy of placement preferences as applied in an individual case, are justified is a separate question. However, on the view here, every State has *parens patriae* jurisdiction and such jurisdiction confers standing on the State to weigh in on State judicial proceedings implicating the welfare of its citizens. The contested question is whether there are circumstances in which the State has *parens patriae* jurisdiction even where a federal law is controlling in the State court proceedings as here with the ICWA.[44] Another question then is whether stripping the State of its professed *parens patriae* interests and standing in respect of challenges to the ICWA *in effect* means that the State's sovereignty has been, to some degree, undercut. In *Haaland* the *parens patriae* matter intersects with the equal protection issues as they affect Indian children. Though the ICWA legal challenges here were undertaken in Federal Court, the implications of the Federal Court decisions or declination to decide (i.e., on the ICWA placement hierarchy's constitutionality or the Equal Protection issue etc.) ultimately play out in State Courts and through State child welfare agencies.

The Haaland Supreme Court maintained, however, that "enjoining the federal parties would not remedy the alleged injury, because state courts apply the ICWA placement preferences, and state agencies carry out the court-ordered placements."[45] And, furthermore, the state officials responsible for implementing the ICWA, including wherever possible the placement preferences therein stipulated, are not a party to the suit and thus, according to the US Supreme Court in Haaland majority, "there is no reason they should be obliged to honor an incidental legal determination the suit produced."[46] On the basis then of alleged non-redressability, the Haaland US Supreme Court did not reach the equal protection arguments of the individual non-State parties. Put differently, even *if* the individual prospective non-indigenous adoptive or foster parents had suffered racial discrimination due to the ICWA hierarchy of placement preferences; the majority in *Haaland* held that that was not enough to confer standing given the purported redressability problem.

It is here argued that the Haaland US Supreme Court majority's specific reasoning as to the purported futility of ruling on the merits of the equal protection claims

---

[44]Under the ICWA, adoption and foster placement decisions for Indian children living off the reservation involve State judicial proceedings for these child citizens of the State and also involve the relevant Indian Tribal nation as a party.

[45]Haaland v Brackeen 599 U. S. ____ (2023) In the Supreme Court of the United States Syllabus at p. 7.

[46]Haaland v Brackeen 599 U. S. ____ (2023) In the Supreme Court of the United States Syllabus at p. 7.

unfairly eviscerates much of the substance of this constitutional challenge case, one that is at its core about fundamental rights issues. That is; the case is at its base about (a) the fundamental individual and collective rights of all North American indigenous children in the United States to family and to cultural continuity and (b) the collective basic rights of North American indigenous tribal peoples in the United States to cultural and biological continuity.[47] Let us put aside for a moment whether in law and fact the non-State parties' equal protection constitutional challenge of the ICWA has merit or not. Regardless of the answer to the merit question, a US Supreme Court declaratory judgment, had it been issued, regarding (a) the constitutionality of the ICWA placement priorities and of (b) the Tribe's authority to re-order the ICWA hierarchy of placement preferences in a particular case could *not* ethically, professionally or practicably have been ignored by State child welfare officials. The latter given that indigenous children's best interests are at stake and State child welfare officials owe the children a high fiduciary duty of care. More specifically, had the ICWA placement priority provisions or the Tribal authority to re-order the preferences in a case been held by the Haaland majority to violate the equal protection and non-delegation clauses,[48] the State child welfare officials (on the view here) would have had to take this into account in exercising their authority. Thus, even if State officials had no standing in the case, that lack of standing does *not* (on the respectful view here in contrast to that of the majority in *Haaland*) speak in any way to the professional responsibilities of State child welfare officials. For that reason, the Haaland majority view is here disputed that (a) an injunction in part or in full (on the ICWA placement preferences being enforced) and/or (b) a declaratory judgment (on the constitutionality of the ICWA placement priorities and of the powers of the Tribal Authority to re-order those placement preferences), if issued by the US Supreme Court, would in practice simply be an advisory opinion with no actual real-life import.

The Haaland case is unlike the situation in other cases. This in that in *Haaland* the child welfare State authorities' *parens patriae* and general fiduciary authority and duties were *discounted* by the Court. The latter on the basis that the State was not a party as it allegedly had no standing. The question arises, however, whether State *parens patriae* standing can be constitutionally eliminated by judicial fiat as arguably for all intents and purposes occurred in *Haaland.* The question is posed in part in that Indian children are dual citizens; citizens of their Indian nation and of the US State in which they reside, and the State too has a trust relationship with those children. At the same time, there is the central matter of the implicated Indian nation's sovereignty, Indian self-government, and respect for the Tribal authority's competency to exercise its authority in the best interests of the Indian child (that is to

[47]Both the indigenous collectives' right to cultural continuity and to biological longevity is at risk through the separation of their children from their indigenous communities/Tribes.

[48]The non-State parties had raised the issue in *Haaland* of whether the Tribal authority under the ICWA to rearrange the ICWA (federal law stipulated) hierarchy of placement preferences in a particular Indian child welfare case is a violation of non-delegation of federal authorities.

function in a *parens patriae* mode with respect to the child, the Tribe and the larger indigenous community to guarantee the protection of their individual and collective fundamental human rights).

Without arguing here that an injunction and declaratory statement were or were not justified in *Haaland*, this author argues, on the analysis here, that redressability for the non-indigenous couples and State of Texas (both challenging the ICWA regarding various provisions) was feasible. This through (a) State officials' actions being informed by a US Supreme Court injunction and declaratory judgement (had they been issued) and (b) given the impact such judgements should ultimately properly have had on State child welfare officials given their fiduciary duties to Indian children. It is here contended then that there would have been compelling reasons professionally and ethically for State child welfare officials to have honored a declaratory judgment and an injunction if such were properly grounded on respect for human rights and consistent with the officials' fiduciary duties.[49] To maintain instead, as the Haaland majority did, that these rulings would have been irrelevant as a judicial remedy, it is here respectfully argued, is misguided. It was, on the view here, part of the unfortunate analytical strategy in *Haaland* to essentially excise fundamental human rights questions (such as the equal protection matter) from consideration in this ICWA constitutional challenge.

The purpose of the ICWA is inextricably tied to the right of the 'Indian child' to a healthy and supportive family life and connection to his or her (their) indigenous community; the latter being inseparable from issues of who has the right to parent the child. The latter question requires considering the best interests of the child as well as contextual issues given (a) the historical colonial injustice inflicted on North American Indian communities in the United States relating to the separation of Indian children from their families and (b) the legacy of that practice that has echoes in current day child welfare practice with Indian children. It is here argued that the fundamental human rights issues in this case cannot properly be sidestepped by essentially focusing, as arguably did the Haaland US Supreme Court majority, largely if not exclusively on competing sovereign authority matters (involving the authorities of Federal, State and Indigenous Tribal separate sovereigns). Afterall, as the Haaland Court itself at points notes, there is an overriding fiduciary constitutionally-based responsibility, ultimately both for US State and federal branches, to protect the fundamental human rights of Indian children on an individual and collective level as well as that of their Tribes/communities: "As we have explained, the Federal Government has "'charged itself with moral obligations of the highest responsibility and trust'" toward Indian tribes." ... "[T]his Court has recognized the distinctive obligation of trust incumbent upon the Government in its dealings with these dependent and sometimes exploited people". The contours of

[49] Such a declaratory judgment about the constitutionality or lack thereof of the ICWA placement preferences would arguably not then, *in practice*, be but an advisory opinion. Rather it would be a statement as to the legal rights of the parties with practical and professional implications for the state officials who carry out state court ICWA placement orders.

this "special relationship" are undefined."[50] Importantly, the Court acknowledged that the fiduciary and plenary power of Congress over so-called 'Indian affairs' is "*subject to limitations inhering in such a guardianship and to pertinent constitutional restrictions*"[51] This is as it should be in a democracy where no legislative or executive powers can be reasonably considered absolute; unconstrained by the fundamental rights of citizens considerations.

On this author's respectful view, in *Haaland* the US Supreme Court punted on its responsibility to define the constitutionally based contours of that aforementioned 'trust relationship' in the Indian child welfare context. This given its failure to focus on constitutionally based human rights matters implicated in the case i.e., the child's right to protection from arbitrary or unjustified seizure of his/her (their) person as well as from overreach by authorities and arbitrary interference in their family and community relations. The forgoing all relates to the right of the Indian child to security of the person and equal protection under the law among other additional constitutional guarantees. The latter include arguably also the right to tribal intervention to ensure the child's connection to his/her (their) indigenous tribe and community where consistent with the child's best interests.[52] In *Haaland,* it is here contended, the majority instead considered federal powers over "Indian affairs" largely divorced from the fundamental human rights issues involved. The latter approach, it is here argued, is contrary to what is required when considering federal government authorities in the context of a trust relationship with the people affected by the exercise of that federal authority. This is especially the case where vulnerable Indian children caught up in the US child welfare system are the contested subjects of the cause of action. The Haaland majority approach then, on the respectful view here, makes it impossible to adequately and fully consider whether the ICWA (reflecting Congress' regulation of Indian child and family law matters) (a) unconstitutionally oversteps Congressional legitimate powers in whole or in part or, alternatively, (b) fully complies, as the Haaland majority concluded, with Article 1 of the Constitution (vesting federal legislative powers over "Indian affairs", *including matters concerning Indian child welfare,* with Congress), In particular, unanswered is the key fundamental human rights matter of whether the ICWA hierarchy of placement preferences in part or in whole comports with the equal protection under law constitutional guarantee or violates the guarantee in some way.

Justice Gorsuch in his concurrence with the majority view in *Haaland* expresses the opinion that (a) the ICWA simply reflects the US Constitution's stipulation that Indian Tribes are independent sovereigns and as such (b) that they have the right to regulate their own internal affairs including child welfare matters and hence to

[50] Haaland v Brackeen 599 U. S. ____ (2023) In the Supreme Court of the United States Majority Opinion (Justice Barrett) at p. 12.

[51] Haaland v Brackeen 599 U. S. ____ (2023) In the Supreme Court of the United States Majority Opinion (Justice Barrett) at p. 13.

[52] Under the ICWA the child's Tribe can intervene in State court to object to the placement with a non-indigenous family and contest the child best interest analysis of the non-indigenous applicants.

ensure cultural and biological longevity of the Tribe.[53] Justice Gorsuch in his concurrence with the majority in *Haaland* characterizes Congress' adoption of the ICWA as follows:

> In adopting the Indian Child Welfare Act, Congress exercised that lawful authority to secure the right of Indian parents to raise their families as they please; the right of Indian children to grow in their culture; and the right of Indian communities to resist fading into the twilight of history. All of that is in keeping with the Constitution's original design.[54]

The foregoing Justice Gorsuch perspective places the case in the proper historical context. Yet the merit question regarding the equal protection issue was *not* reached by the *Haaland* majority nor was the fact addressed of Indian nation sovereignty and its implications in the Indian child welfare space, One might reasonably argue, it is here contended, that in fact the particular ICWA placement preferences that were upheld as constitutional in *Haaland* reflect what is necessary under the Equal Protection Clause to achieve equity in State courts insofar as child welfare matters involving Indian children are concerned. This since the ICWA stipulates arguably (a) necessary *safeguards* regarding placement of the Indian child (in terms of placement preferences or priorities) and (b) the possibility for Tribal intervention to raise proper concerns in the particular State Indian child welfare case where warranted.[55] Such safeguards then are intended to protect these vulnerable children who historically have been at a disproportionately higher risk of being removed in child welfare cases not simply from the immediate family (often unjustifiably) but also from their larger familial group, Tribe and cultural context. This (a) without due consideration of the child's autonomous individual and collective rights or best interests and the collective interests of their Tribe and indigenous peoples more generally and (b) also without consideration of how the biological family often could be supported and the family unit kept intact in many instances especially where the issue was not in fact, for instance, intentional neglect but abject poverty. Yet how the ICWA intersects with the Equal Protection Clause for the Indian child in terms of (a) the child's full panoply of individual autonomous and collective fundamental human rights and with best interests of the child; (b) the rights of their prospective non-Indian foster or adoptive parents as well as with (c) the rights of the child's biological parents, extended family and Tribe was not in fact addressed in this case.

[53] Haaland v Brackeen 599 U.S. ____ (2023) In the Supreme Court of the United States Concurring Opinion (Justice Gorsuch) at pp. 36–37.

[54] Haaland v Brackeen 599 U. S. ____ (2023) In the Supreme Court of the United States Concurring Opinion (Justice Gorsuch) at p. 38.

[55] Justice Barrett explains that (a) tribal courts have exclusive jurisdiction over child welfare matters concerning Indian children living on the reservation (ICWA does not apply in these cases) while (b) State courts and tribal courts have concurrent jurisdiction where the Indian child lives off the reservation. However under the ICWA, the State court is required to transfer the matter to the tribal court absent any compelling lawful reason not do so. If the State court is deciding the matter the ICWA controls whether the proceedings are voluntary or involuntary. Haaland v Brackeen 599 U. S. ____ (2023) In the Supreme Court of the United States Majority Opinion (Justice Barrett) at p. 3.

It is noteworthy further that unfortunately the Indian children at issue in *Haaland* were not named as parties nor amici *independently represented* and hence had no autonomous voice. There is no bar, however, to the children themselves, through independent litigation guardian counsel, bringing a constitutional case (perhaps a class action case) asking the State courts for clarity on the equal protection issue in relation to the ICWA. Afterall it is the children's best interests as considered from a human rights perspective that, on the view here, must be the first priority.

In the view of Justice Kavanaugh in his Haaland concurrence with the Majority (a) the equal protection question in this ICWA context remains *post-Haaland* a pressing *unanswered* one and (b) can be dealt with by the courts only when "… it is properly raised by a plaintiff with standing—for example, by a prospective foster or adoptive parent or child in a case arising out of a state-court foster care or adoption proceeding.[56]

Justice Alito in his dissent in *Haaland* contends that the Constitution does not confer upon Congress the power to determine the "creation, dissolution or modification" of family relations; the latter being rather State matters.[57] That is the State is normally charged with safeguarding the welfare of its citizens in family matters. Justice Alito does state he is sympathetic to "the challenges that tribes face in maintaining membership and preserving their cultures" and recognizes that "the best interests of children may *in some circumstances* take into account a desire to enable children to maintain a connection with the culture of their ancestors (emphasis added)."[58] However, it is here argued, that the ICWA was established precisely since the US States were *not* fulfilling their child welfare function properly in regard to North American Indian children. Instead, US State child welfare practices, policies and court decisions concerning Indian children were commonly highly detrimental to Indian families and Tribes *pre* ICWA. This furthermore continued against the historical backdrop of the residential school system that arguably could be considered a form of *genocide* causing extreme mental and often physical harm to the children and severe suffering to their families.[59] Justice Alito, on the respectful view here, unjustifiably downplays this point by way of his particular phrasing when he states that "the best interests of children may *in some circumstances* take into

[56] See Haaland v Brackeen 599 U. S. ____ (2023) In the Supreme Court of the United States Concurring Opinion (Justice Kavanaugh) at p. 2.

[57] See Haaland v Brackeen 599 U. S. ____ (2023) In the Supreme Court of the United States Justice Alito Dissent at p. 8.

[58] Haaland v Brackeen 599 U. S. ____ (2023) In the Supreme Court of the United States Dissenting Opinion (Justice Alito) at p. 11.

[59] The residential school system involved forcible removal of Indian children to another group (European settler group) causing severe mental and physical injury to the individual children and their Tribe and threatening the biological and cultural survival of the Tribe. This arguably fits the definition of genocide *per se* under the *Genocide Convention* and not cultural genocide as the latter term does *not* appear in the international law lexicon. See *Convention on the Prevention and Punishment of the Crime of Genocide,* entry into force January 12, 1951, Article II (Accessed 2 January 2024).

account a desire to enable children to maintain a connection with the culture of their ancestors." In fact, as discussed here previously, international human rights law such as the *Convention on the Rights of the Child* recognizes the right to cultural continuity as a fundamental right for all children.[60] While US Courts are not bound by the *Convention*, it can well inform their judicial reasoning.

Under the US Constitution and given the US Federal government's trust relationship with Indians, arguably Congress had a duty to step in and attempt to better protect the *individual and collective rights* of Indian children *and* their Tribes. The degree to which the ICWA accomplishes that objective remains controversial and vigorously contested, however. This in large part in that the equal protection issue was not decided in *Haaland.* As the equal protection question was *not* reached by the US Supreme Court in *Haaland*, even the ICWA preference for adoptive placement with Indian families outside the child's Tribe (as a possible option in some circumstances) was left undisturbed. This is part of the outcome of the Haaland majority decision opting for the default *status quo* regarding the ICWA hierarchy of placement preferences. On this author's view then, it is essential that in the next ICWA constitutional challenge, through State court, the amici should include independent legal counsel with expertise in children's human rights. The latter acting as representatives of 'Indian children' caught up in US State child welfare proceedings currently or in the past and impacted in diverse ways by the ICWA. This in order that these children's voices can be heard and properly considered.

The US State courts are duty bound under federal law to honor the ICWA hierarchy of placement preferences in child welfare cases involving Indian children living off reservation. At the same time, as discussed, the Majority in *Haaland rejects* the notion of *parens patriae* third party standing for US States in Indian child welfare cases. There is a quandary then arguably in that "...*Congress's* primacy over Indian tribes and *States'* "full and complete jurisdiction over all persons ...within [their] limits" are "fundamental principles . . .of equal dignity, and *neither must be so enforced as to nullify or substantially impair the other* (emphasis added)."[61] If a US individual State should retain *parens patriae* standing in Indian child welfare cases, even given the ICWA framework, the further issue arises as to whether that State should properly carry the burden in court to rebut (in the proper case) (a) an ICWA placement preference or (b) a Tribal Authority re-ordering of the ICWA priority placement preference. In the final analysis, on the respectful view here, the State courts in child welfare matters concerning Indian children must be guided by the principle that while both the State and the Tribal authority are separate sovereigns; the child yet has independent fundamental human rights and dignity. Therefore, the Indian child is not to be reduced through a judicial analytical approach to being *in*

[60] See Committee on the Rights of the Child General Comment No. 11 (2009) *Indigenous children and their rights under the Convention* CRC/C/GC/11 Best Interests of the Child para 30–33 https://www2.ohchr.org/english/bodies/crc/docs/gc.11_indigenous_new.pdf (Accessed August 22, 2024).

[61] Haaland v Brackeen 599 U. S. ____ (2023) In the Supreme Court of the United States Dissenting Opinion (Justice Alito) at p. 7.

effect considered but a mere "resource" for Tribes, States or prospective adoptive and foster parents. At the same time, inherent Indian Tribal sovereignty and the fundamental human right of any ethnic/cultural group to raise their children must be respected. Any placement outside the Tribal community then ought, in the normal course,[62] on the view here, be agreed to by the Tribal authority (a) acting in good faith with the best interests of the particular child and the child's specific and extenuating circumstances in mind and (b) with, insofar as possible, the biological parents' input and concurrence.

The ICWA hierarchy of placement preference framework was born of the need to counter (a) the systemic inequity perpetrated against Indian children through the residential and child welfare system in the US and (b) the continued risk to these children, without the ICWA protections, to preserving connections to their family and Tribal community. The challenge is then how to ensure that the *Indian children's* best interests, their independent *collective* right to cultural continuity as well as their *individual* human rights are prioritized over any incompatible sovereign interests wherever the latter (if they exist) may lie in a particular case (at the Tribal, State or Federal level). On the analysis here, only then will the Indian child's best interests be well served in fact and not just theory in each case.

6.3 Comparative Law: Commentary on Attorney General of Québec, et al. v. Attorney General of Canada, et al., Quebec Court of Appeal Advisory Opinion

Attorney General of Québec, et al. v. Attorney General of Canada, et al. (Supreme Court of Canada)[63] concerns a Reference to the courts by the Province of Quebec asking for an opinion on the constitutionality of An Act respecting First Nations, Inuit and Métis children, youth and families, S.C. 2019, c. 24. The Act grants indigenous communities exclusive control over the creation and management of child welfare services concerning indigenous children and families under the jurisdiction of their respective indigenous governing bodies. To date, five indigenous governing bodies have assumed such control over their community child and family social services which includes also child foster and adoption placement matters. The Attorney General of the province of Quebec has *challenged* the constitutionality of the Act which came into effect January 1, 2020. Quebec argues that the province of Quebec, not indigenous governing bodies, holds the exclusive jurisdiction to

[62] That is to say that placement outside the Tribal community ought, it would seem reasonable, to be agreed to by the Tribal authority unless the court has significant 'just cause' not to require such agreement given the facts of the particular case and the surrounding circumstances.

[63] Attorney General of Québec, et al. v. Attorney General of Canada, et al., (Supreme Court of Canada) https://www.scc-csc.ca/case-dossier/info/dock-regi-eng.aspx?cas=40061 (Accessed August 22, 2024).

exercise control over child and family social services in the province also in respect of indigenous children and families. Quebec through a Reference process seeks an advisory opinion from the Supreme Court of Canada on the constitutionality of the Act in question:

> A reference question is a submission by either the federal or provincial government that asks the courts for advice on a major legal issue. A court does not rule on a reference question. Rather, the question results in an "advisory opinion" that guides the government in determining a law's meaning or the constitutionality of a proposed course of action. A court's answer to a reference question is not binding.[64]

.

This case, as with the US Haaland case, raises the issue of the larger context that reveals the urgent and compelling need for safeguards to protect North American indigenous children and their communities from a repeat of past harmful child welfare practice. That larger context in Canada involves (a) past colonial and discriminatory practices adversely affecting indigenous children and communities and (b) the contemporary practical implications of that legacy still playing out to some extent (i.e., in terms of biases that have had a substantive impact on creating an ongoing overrepresentation of indigenous children in child welfare placements separated from their families and indigenous communities as confirmed by several recent commissions of inquiry).[65] What precise safeguards are needed in current child welfare services and policy as these affect North American indigenous children and communities in Canada then is a central matter in this case.

The case was previously submitted at a lower court level as a Reference to the Quebec Court of Appeal asking for an advisory opinion on the following question:

> Is An Act respecting First Nations, Inuit and Métis children, youth and families, S.C. 2019, c. 24, *ultra vires* the Parliament of Canada under the Constitution of Canada?[66]

The Quebec Court of Appeal held that the Act in question is constitutional except for s 21 and 22(3)[67] This in that it is intended to ensure the wellbeing of indigenous children by enacting culturally sensitive child welfare practices intended to end

[64]Centre for Constitutional Studies Reference Question https://www.constitutionalstudies.ca/2019/07/reference-question/#:~:text=A%20reference%20question%20is%20a,rule%20on%20a%20reference%20question (Accessed August 22, 2024).

[65]Blackstock, C Denouncing the continued overrepresentation of First Nations children in Canadian child welfare. https://cwrp.ca/sites/default/files/publications/FNCIS-2019%20-%20Denouncing%20the%20Continued%20Overrepresentation%20of%20First%20Nations%20Children%20in%20Canadian%20Child%20Welfare%20%2D%2D%20Final.pdf (Accessed August 22, 2024).

[66]Attorney General of Québec, et al. v. Attorney General of Canada, et al. Reference to the Court of Appeal of Quebec in relation with the Act respecting First Nations, Inuit and Métis children, youth and families. Summary https://www.scc-csc.ca/case-dossier/info/sum-som-eng.aspx?cas=40061 (Accessed August 22, 2024).

[67]Attorney General of Québec, et al. v. Attorney General of Canada, et al. Reference to the Court of Appeal of Quebec in relation with the Act respecting First Nations, Inuit and Métis children, youth and families. https://www.canlii.org/en/qc/qcca/doc/2022/2022qcca185/2022qcca185.pdf Court of Appeal of Quebec, Judgment February 10, 2022 at para 571 (Accessed August 22, 2024).

biases that lead to an overrepresentation of North American indigenous children in the child welfare system. This the Court opined is within the jurisdiction of Parliament per the Constitution Act of 1867. Importantly, the Court also maintained that indigenous self-government is included in s 35 of the Canadian Constitution Act of 1982 which would then include also jurisdiction over indigenous child welfare matters. The Quebec Appeal Court affirmed that Indigenous self-government is a long-recognized right[68] that is grounded on the fact that "Aboriginal peoples have always maintained a form of self-government that flows from their original sovereignty over the territory. This Aboriginal right is now enshrined in s. 35 [of the 1982 Constitution]."[69] However, the Court of Appeal was, at the same time, of the view that in instances where indigenous law is inconsistent with federal or provincial legislation, it would be *ultra vires* to hold that Parliament had the authority to grant indigenous law supremacy. In the opinion of the Quebec Court of Appeal, s 21 and 22(3) of the Act are both unconstitutional given the structure of the Canadian Constitution (s. 21 and s. 22(3) of the Act both grant indigenous law supremacy in instances where indigenous law is inconsistent with provincial legislation). The *Canadian Charter of Rights and Freedoms*, the Quebec Appeal Court further held, applies to indigenous self-government.[70]

The Act in question set out national standards in Canada for child welfare regulations and practice regarding North American indigenous children in Canada and s 18 affirms indigenous self-government as a right. The latter "includes legislative authority in relation to child and family services, which must be exercised in accordance with the *Canadian Charter of Rights and Freedoms* (the "Canadian Charter)."[71] The Act specifically addresses the best interests of indigenous children

---

[68] The Quebec Appeal Court in *Attorney General of Québec, et al. v. Attorney General of Canada, et al.* Reference to the Court of Appeal of Quebec in relation with the Act respecting First Nations, Inuit and Métis children, youth and families. February 10, 2022 https://www.canlii.org/en/qc/qcca/doc/2022/2022qcca185/2022qcca185.pdf (Accessed August 22, 2024). Note that recognition of Indigenous Peoples' right to self-government is consistent with the rights articulated in the *UN Declaration on the Rights of Indigenous Peoples* (at Articles 3 and 4) https://www.un.org/development/desa/indigenouspeoples/wp-content/uploads/sites/19/2018/11/UNDRIP_E_web.pdf (Accessed August 22, 2024).

[69] Attorney General of Québec, et al. v. Attorney General of Canada, et al. Reference to the Court of Appeal of Quebec in relation with the Act respecting First Nations, Inuit and Métis children, youth and families. February 10, 2022, paras. 49–50 https://www.canlii.org/en/qc/qcca/doc/2022/2022qcca185/2022qcca185.pdf (Accessed August 22, 2024).

[70] Attorney General of Québec, et al. v. Attorney General of Canada, et al.

Reference to the Court of Appeal of Quebec in relation with the Act respecting First Nations, Inuit and Métis children, youth and families. https://www.canlii.org/en/qc/qcca/doc/2022/2022qcca185/2022qcca185.pdf Court of Appeal of Quebec Judgment February 10, 2022 (Accessed August 22, 2024).

[71] Attorney General of Québec, et al. v. Attorney General of Canada, et al.

Reference to the Court of Appeal of Quebec in relation with the Act respecting First Nations, Inuit and Métis children, youth and families. https://www.canlii.org/en/qc/qcca/doc/2022/2022qcca185/2022qcca185.pdf para 32 Court of Appeal of Quebec Judgment February 10, 2022 (Accessed August 22, 2024).

and considers "inapplicable" any law that undermines or conflicts with the child's best interests.[72] Most of the constraints in the Act then are intended to protect the child's best interests which must be considered on a case-by-case basis.

The Act lists under key considerations for assessing the child's best interests the following: the "Aboriginal child's upbringing, the child's relationship with his or her family members, preservation of the child's cultural identity, and the child's own preferences. To the extent possible, these factors are to be construed in a manner consistent with applicable Aboriginal laws."[73] Further "The Act prioritizes preventive care, favours having a child continue to reside with a family member and specifies that the child's socio-economic condition alone cannot justify the child's apprehension."[74] The latter point is particularly salient as poverty has often been the legacy of colonial oppression in regards to indigenous peoples and then weaponized against that community in the child welfare arena. The latter to allegedly justify a child's removal in lieu of economic and other supports to the biological and/or extended family directed to keeping the family intact or to reunification of the indigenous family with their child at the earliest possible time. In addition, the Act (An Act respecting First Nations, Inuit and Métis children, youth and families, S.C. 2019, c. 24) stresses the importance of the parents and the child's indigenous community having a say in the ultimate placement decision by the tribal child welfare authority.

Of significance further is, of course, the fact that the Quebec Appeal Court opinion rendered in *Attorney General of Québec, et al. v. Attorney General of Canada, et al.*, is (a) a non-binding advisory opinion that (b) sets out the rights and obligations of the parties in the case (the Provincial, Federal and Tribal sovereigns). That is, the Advisory Opinion of the Quebec Court of Appeal sets out the rights and obligations of the various sovereigns (a) under the 'Act respecting First Nations, Inuit and Métis children, youth and families' and (b) purportedly does so in a manner consistent with the *Canadian Constitution*. Note that the Quebec Appeal Court Advisory Opinion was appealed to the Supreme Court of Canada by both the Attorney General of Quebec (who argued that the entire Act is unconstitutional as it allegedly usurps provincial powers) and the Attorney General of Canada (who argued in opposition that the entire Act *is* constitutional). The Supreme Court of

[72] Attorney General of Québec, et al. v. Attorney General of Canada, et al. Reference to the Court of Appeal of Quebec in relation with the Act respecting First Nations, Inuit and Métis children, youth and families. https://www.canlii.org/en/qc/qcca/doc/2022/2022qcca185/2022qcca185.pdf para 33 Court of Appeal of Quebec Judgment February 10, 2022 (Accessed August 22, 2024).

[73] Attorney General of Québec, et al. v. Attorney General of Canada, et al. Reference to the Court of Appeal of Quebec in relation with the Act respecting First Nations, Inuit and Métis children, youth and families. https://www.canlii.org/en/qc/qcca/doc/2022/2022qcca185/2022qcca185.pdf Judgment February 10, 2022 at para 30 (Accessed August 22, 2024).

[74] Attorney General of Québec, et al. v. Attorney General of Canada, et al. Reference to the Court of Appeal of Quebec in relation with the Act respecting First Nations, Inuit and Métis children, youth and families. https://www.canlii.org/en/qc/qcca/doc/2022/2022qcca185/2022qcca185.pdf Judgment February 10, 2022 at para 30 (Accessed August 22, 2024).

Canada upheld the Act, *An Act respecting First Nations, Inuit and Métis children, youth and families* as constitutional *in its entirety*.[75]

In the United States Supreme Court Haaland case, it will be recalled that the Majority held that none of the parties challenging the US Indigenous Child Welfare Act (including the State of Texas) had standing to ask for a ruling from the Court on (a) the equal protection issue or (b) the delegation of federal authority to Tribal authority matter. This since, as the Court's Majority argument went, only the State courts and State officials (both *not* parties to the case) could potentially provide redress. Without the possibility for redress there was no standing conferred to the individual petitioners (the prospective adoptive or foster non-indigenous couples). Further, Texas was held by the Haaland Majority not to have standing as in their judgment (a) the State had no *parens patriae* jurisdiction that would support an action against the federal government and (b) the State had no equal protection rights of its own. (Whether the State might have *parens patriae* standing against the Federal government in certain unique circumstances (i.e., such as in this case where *State* child welfare proceedings involving Indian children and federal law are at issue) is perhaps still an open question[76] and not as settled as Justice Barrett would have it in *Haaland*). A ruling from the Court in this case on (a) the equal protection and (b) delegation matters under these circumstances (alleged non-redressibility), the Haaland majority held, would amount to an *impermissible advisory* opinion.

This author previously here argued that a United States Supreme Court ruling on the ICWA placement priority hierarchy as it impacts equal protection and delegation of authority issues would have had a potential remedial impact and hence would have been an avenue to redressability (that is from the individual petitioner's perspective; one on which the current author does not opine as it relates to the facts of their particular indigenous child welfare cases). This (on the view here) in that the Court's judgement on the equal protection and delegation issues (had it been issued) could *not* (contrary to Justice Barrett's contention) properly have been ignored by State child welfare authorities given their fiduciary obligations to Indian children and their families.

The Majority in *Haaland* noted that the Court could *not* offer an advisory opinion in this case. This since advisory opinions, per the US Constitution, are *ultra vires* for federal courts, including the United States Supreme Court.[77] Since, according to the Majority in *Haaland,* the Court could not offer redress in this situation; their opinion, in their view, would have been but an *impermissible advisory opinion*. The ultimate

[75] In the Matter of a Reference re an *Act respecting First Nations, Inuit and Métis children, youth and families*, S.C. 2019, c. 24, Supreme Court of Canada Judgement February 9, 2024 SCC 5 https://decisions.scc-csc.ca/scc-csc/scc-csc/en/item/20264/index.do (Accessed August 22, 2024).

[76] See Cornell Law School Legal Institute *Representational Standing: States and Parens Patriae*, https://www.law.cornell.edu/constitution-conan/article-3/section-2/clause-1/representational-standing-states-and-parens-patraie (Accessed August 22, 2024).

[77] US State Courts can issue advisory opinions unless there is a bar to the same in the State Constitution.

result was then that the merits of the equal protection issue was not reached by the Court and, by default, the *status quo*, including the ICWA placement priority hierarchy, was maintained. Haaland highlights an instance where fundamental human rights questions put before the Court are, on the respectful analysis here, unjustifiably left unsettled. The latter includes the implications of the ICWA placement priories for the equal protection guarantee *also as this impacts the indigenous children caught up in the US child welfare system.*[78] In the latter regard, *Haaland* can be distinguished from the next two cases where the fundamental human rights question was addressed, and a constitutional right affirmed by the Court.

6.4 Competing US Sovereign Powers and 'The Independent State Legislature Theory'

6.4.1 Moore v Harper (North Carolina's Independent State Legislature Challenge)

The Moore case raises the issue of the alleged unfettered authority of State legislatures to set rules for federal elections without having to comply with State law or risk intervention through State court proceedings. The case reflects the 'culture war' concerning States' rights. The foregoing misapprehension is based on the fringe debunked 'Independent State Legislature Theory' that claims that since the Federal Constitution grants State legislatures the right to run federal elections, they may do so unconstrained by State courts. The United States Supreme Court in *Moore* held, in contrast, that State legislature rules for federal elections are still subject to judicial review by State courts scrutinizing whether the rules are consistent with the State and Federal Constitutions: "when a state legislature carries out its federal constitutional power to prescribe rules regulating federal elections, it acts both as a lawmaking body created and bound by its state constitution, and as the entity assigned particular authority by the Federal Constitution. Both constitutions restrain the state legislature's exercise of power."[79] In addition, the United States Supreme Court in *Moore* affirmed its duty to address the constitutional challenge so as to clarify the issue here which has profound voting rights/human rights implications. In the latter regard the Court states: "*This Court has an obligation to ensure that state court interpretations of state law do not evade federal law.*"[80] In *Moore* then the US Supreme Court

[78] In both the Haaland case and the Canadian case the Indigenous children were not independently represented as a party or an amicus group thus preventing their autonomous voices being heard.

[79] Moore in His Official Capacity as Speaker of the North Carolina House of Representatives et al. v Harper et al. No. 21-1271 (Supreme Court of the United States) Argued December 7, 2022—Decided June 27, 2023 Syllabus at p. 4.

[80] Moore in His Official Capacity as Speaker of the North Carolina House of Representatives et al. v Harper et al. No. 21-1271 (Supreme Court of the United States) Argued December 7, 2022—Decided June 27, 2023 Syllabus at p. 5.

stepped in to (a) affirm the State and Federal constitutional constraints on State legislatures in setting rules for Federal elections and also then (b) the bar against state legislatures gerrymandering[81] districting voting maps so as to essentially disenfranchise certain ethnic and other groups.

6.4.2 *Singleton et al., v. Allen et al. and Milligan et al., v Allen et al., and Allen v. Milligan et al. (Alabama's Independent State Legislature Challenge)*

There is, as has here been discussed in the context of the various cases selected for this work, a growing risk that Courts may too often inappropriately rule as non-judiciable or improperly framed various key fundamental human rights questions. This not uncommonly so as to sidestep these questions and thus unfortunately leaving vulnerable groups unprotected and certain basic constitutional rights on seeming tenuous ground. Add to that the additional potential peril of State legislatures (as in *Moore*) attempting to seize unconstrained power and neutralize the courts. While *Moore* addresses the latter risk, it is in no more stark relief than in the case Bobby Singleton et al., (Plaintiffs) v. Wes Allen, in his official capacity as Alabama Secretary of State, et al., (Defendants) and Evan Milligan et al., (Plaintiffs) v Wes Allen in his official capacity as Alabama Secretary of State, et al.(-Defendants).[82] The latter case concerns gerrymandered voting redistricting maps for federal elections that were alleged to undermine the right to vote of Black Alabamians. This by affording Black Alabamians less opportunity to select a candidate of their choice than was the case for non-minority Alabamians; something that likely is in contravention of the federal Voting Rights Act.

In a previous decision addressing the same complaint; the *District Court* had ruled that "the appropriate remedy is a congressional redistricting plan that includes either an additional majority-Black congressional district, or an additional district in which Black voters otherwise have an opportunity to elect a representative of their choice."[83] The Defendants in that previous case ultimately appealed to the United

---

[81] The North Carolina Supreme Court held that the issue of gerrymandering by the North Carolina legislature *was judiciable* in North Carolina State Courts.

[82] Bobby Singleton et al., Plaintiffs, v. Wes Allen, in his official capacity as Alabama Secretary of State, et al., Defendants and Evan Milligan et al., Plaintiffs, v Wes Allen in his official capacity as Alabama Secretary of State, et al., United States District Court (Northern District of Alabama, Southern Division) Before Marcus, Circuit Judge, Manasco and Moorer, District Judges. Injunction Opinion and Order September 5, 2023.

[83] Cited in Bobby Singleton et al., Plaintiffs, v. Wes Allen, in his official capacity as Alabama Secretary of State, et al., Defendants and Evan Milligan et al., Plaintiffs, v Wes Allen in his official capacity as Alabama Secretary of State, et al., United States District Court (Northern District of Alabama, Southern Division) Before Marcus, Circuit Judge, Manasco and Moorer, District Judges. Injunction Opinion and Order September 5, 2023, at p. 3.

States Supreme Court which upheld the lower court ruling that the map as drawn violated the Voting Rights Act and abridged or denied minority voters the genuine equal opportunity to select their representatives.[84] On the necessary remedial action the State conceded that it had *not* implemented the *ordered remedy* in its 2023 redistricting plan contrary to the previous District Court ruling that had been upheld by the Supreme Court. The congressional map without the remedy ordered incorporated arguably violates the Voting Rights Act. The District Court for various reasons thus ordered that a special master rather than the Alabama legislature would draw up the new map consistent with the Court's remedial court order. The District Court comment as follows is illuminating:

> …we are deeply troubled that the State enacted a map that the State readily admits does not provide the remedy we said federal law requires. We are disturbed by the evidence that the State delayed remedial proceedings but ultimately did not even nurture the ambition to provide the required remedy… We are not aware of any other case in which a state legislature — faced with a federal court order declaring that its electoral plan unlawfully dilutes minority votes and requiring a plan that provides an additional opportunity district — responded with a plan that the state concedes does not provide that district. The law requires the creation of an additional district that affords Black Alabamians, like everyone else, a fair and reasonable opportunity to elect candidates of their choice.[85]

6.5 Concluding Comment

What has been argued in this book through an examination of relevant case law is that so-called 'culture war' litigation most often undemocratically attempts to use the courts to legitimize the erosion of basic human rights. That effort, it is here contended, must be exposed and resisted and hopefully this book has made a small contribution in that regard. To ensure that the Courts in all instances uphold democratic principles and values will require an informed, conscientious and engaged citizenry that demands no less.

This work has highlighted the risk to a democracy of the courts *in effect* recasting fundamental human rights litigation as essentially nothing more than the sorting out of political quagmires and cultural conflicts best left to the discretion of government rather than the courts. The major risk is then that key constitutional controversies will increasingly not be decided by the courts (those matters being held non-judiciable for various reasons) but rather by self-interested politicians. This as

[84] Allen, Alabama Secretary of State et al. v. Milligan et al., US Supreme Court No. 21-1086. Argued October 4, 2022—Decided June 8, 2023 https://www.supremecourt.gov/opinions/22pdf/21-1086_1co6.pdf (Accessed August 22, 2024).

[85] Bobby Singleton et al., Plaintiffs, v. Wes Allen, in his official capacity as Alabama Secretary of State, et al., Defendants and Evan Milligan et al., Plaintiffs, v Wes Allen in his official capacity as Alabama Secretary of State, et al., United States District Court (Northern District of Alabama, Southern Division) Before Marcus, Circuit Judge, Manasco and Moorer, District Judges. Injunction Opinion and Order September 5, 2023 at pp. 8–9.

the courts increasingly decline to weigh in on highly sensitive fundamental human rights controversies and, at times, reframe the controversy so as to negate or minimize the harm being done to the vulnerable group at issue (i.e., as in *Creative*[86] *and Kennedy*[87]). A further, perhaps even more insidious risk of judicial complacency in the 'culture war' litigation space, is that such cases are decided through a judicial majoritarian political lens rather than a largely apolitical consensus judicial opinion (constructed by both philosophically left leaning and right leaning jurists). It behooves the public to demand of the courts that they impartially weigh in on and directly address the fundamental human rights questions that are implicated in constitutional challenges. This is essential to the courts remaining as a cornerstone in the preservation of democracy.

Materials

Ablavsky, G (Q and A with S Driscoll) (June 30, 2023) Stanford's Greg Ablavsky on the Brackeen Indian Child Welfare Act Decision https://law.stanford.edu/2023/06/30/stanfords-greg-ablavsky-on-the-brackeen-indian-child-welfare-act-decision/ (Accessed August 22, 2024)

Blackstock, C Denouncing the continued overrepresentation of First Nations children in Canadian child welfare: Findings from the First Nations/Canadian Incidence Study of Reported Child Abuse and Neglect-2019https://cwrp.ca/sites/default/files/publications/FNCIS-2019%20-%20Denouncing%20the%20Continued%20Overrepresentation%20of%20First%20Nations%20Children%20in%20Canadian%20Child%20Welfare%20%2D%2D%20Final.pdf (Accessed August 22, 2024)

Centre for Constitutional Studies Reference Question https://www.constitutionalstudies.ca/2019/07/reference-question/#:~:text=A%20reference%20question%20is%20a,rule%20on%20a%20reference%20question (Accessed August 22, 2024)

Committee on the Rights of the Child General Comment No. 11 (2009) Indigenous children and their rights under the Convention CRC/C/GC/11 Best Interests of the Child https://www2.ohchr.org/english/bodies/crc/docs/gc.11_indigenous_new.pdf (Accessed August 22, 2024

Convention on the Prevention and Punishment of the Crime of Genocide, entry into force January 12, 1951, Article II https://ihl-databases.icrc.org/en/ihl-treaties/genocide-conv-1948 (Accessed August 22, 2024)

---

[86] 303 Creative, Lori Smith v Aubrey Elenis, Charles Garcia, Ajay Menon, Miguel Rene Elias, Richard Lewis, Kendra Anderson, Sergio Cordova, Jessica Pocock, Phil Weiser United States Supreme Court No. 21-476. Argued December 5, 2022—Decided June 30, 2023.

[87] Kennedy v Bremerton School District (Supreme Court of the United States) No. 21-418. Argued April 25, 2022—Decided June 27, 2022.

Cornell Law School Legal Institute *Representational Standing: States and Parens Patriae,* https://www.law.cornell.edu/constitution-conan/article-3/section-2/clause-1/representational-standing-states-and-parens-patraie (Accessed August 22, 2024)

International Covenant on Civil and Political Rights (ICCPR) https://www.ohchr.org/en/instruments-mechanisms/instruments/international-covenant-civil-and-political-rights (Accessed August 22, 2024)

International Humanitarian Law Databases Protocol Additional to the Geneva Conventions of 12 August 1949, and relating to the Protection of Victims of International Armed Conflicts (Protocol I) Article 78 Evacuation of Children, 8 June 1977 https://ihl-databases.icrc.org/en/ihl-treaties/api-1977/article-78 (Accessed August 22, 2024)

National Indian Library, ICWA Guide online: Placement (16.2) "The definition of extended family member under the ICWA includes both Indian and non-Indian relatives. Some tribal laws express a preference for extended family members who are members of the tribe" https://narf.org/nill/documents/icwa/faq/placement.html#Q2 (Accessed August 22, 2024)

UN Declaration of the Rights of Indigenous Peoples (at Articles 3 and 4) https://www.un.org/development/desa/indigenouspeoples/wp-content/uploads/sites/19/2018/11/UNDRIP_E_web.pdf (Accessed August 22, 2024)

US Department of the Interior: Indian Affairs ICWA https://www.bia.gov/bia/ois/dhs/icwa/icwa-notice (Accessed August 22, 2024)

US Department of the Interior: Tribal Enrollment Process https://www.doi.gov/tribes/enrollment (Accessed August 22, 2024)

US Equal Employment Opportunity Commission, Employment Discrimination based on Religion, Ethnicity, or Country of Origin https://www.eeoc.gov/laws/guidance/employment-discrimination-based-religion-ethnicity-or-country-origin (Accessed August 22, 2024)

United States Supreme Court Cases

Allen, Alabama Secretary of State et al., *v.* Milligan et al. (Supreme Court of the United States) No. 21-1086. Argued October 4, 2022—Decided June 8, 2023 https://www.supremecourt.gov/opinions/22pdf/21-1086_1co6.pdf (Accessed August 22, 2024)

303 Creative, Lori Smith v Aubrey Elenis, Charles Garcia, Ajay Menon, Miguel Rene Elias, Richard Lewis, Kendra Anderson, Sergio Cordova, Jessica Pocock, Phil Weiser (Supreme Court of the United States) No. 21-476. Argued December 5, 2022—Decided June 30, 2023

Dobbs, State Health Officer of the Mississippi Department of Health et al. v. Jackson Women's Health Organization et. (United States Supreme Court) No. 19-1392. Argued December 1, 2021—Decided June 24, 2022

Haaland v Brackeen Weiser (Supreme Court of the United States) No. 21-376., 599 U.S. ____ (2023) Argued November 9, 2022 Decided June 15, 2023 https://www.supremecourt.gov/opinions/22pdf/21-376_7l48.pdf (Accessed August 22, 2024)

Kennedy v Bremerton School District (Supreme Court of the United States) No. 21-418. Argued April 25, 2022—Decided June 27, 2022

Moore in His Official Capacity as Speaker of the North Carolina House of Representatives et al. v Harper et al. (Supreme Court of the United States) No. 21-1271 Argued December 7, 2022—Decided June 27, 2023

United States Lower Court Cases

Bobby Singleton et al., Plaintiffs, v. Wes Allen, in his official capacity as Alabama Secretary of State, et al., Defendants and Evan Milligan et al., Plaintiffs, v Wes Allen in his official capacity as Alabama Secretary of State, et al., United States District Court (Northern District of Alabama, Southern Division) Before Marcus, Circuit Judge, Manasco and Moorer, District Judges. Injunction Opinion and Order September 5, 2023

Brackeen v. Haaland 994 F.3d 249 (5th Cir. 2021) Decided Apr 6, 2021 https://casetext.com/case/brackeen-v-haaland (Accessed August 22, 2024)

Canadian Case Law

Attorney General of Québec, et al. v. Attorney General of Canada, et al. Reference to the Court of Appeal of Quebec in relation with the Act respecting First Nations, Inuit and Métis children, youth and families, Judgment of the Quebec Court of Appeals, February 10, 2022 https://www.canlii.org/en/qc/qcca/doc/2022/2022qcca185/2022qcca185.pdf (Accessed August 22, 2024)

In the Matter of a Reference re an *Act respecting First Nations, Inuit and Métis children, youth and families*, S.C. 2019, c. 24, Supreme Court of Canada Judgement February 9, 2024 SCC 5 https://decisions.scc-csc.ca/scc-csc/scc-csc/en/item/20264/index.do (Accessed August 22, 2024)

Reference

Gannon M (2016) Scientific American, LiveScience on February 5, 2016 Race is a social construct, scientists argue racial categories are weak proxies for genetic diversity and need to be phased out. https://www.scientificamerican.com/article/race-is-a-social-construct-scientists-argue/. Accessed 22 Aug 2024